SSSP

Springer
Series in
Social
Psychology

SSSP

Alan Radley

The Body and
Social Psychology

Springer-Verlag

New York Berlin Heidelberg London Paris
Tokyo Hong Kong Barcelona Budapest

Alan Radley
Loughborough University
Loughborough LE11 3TU
United Kingdom

Library of Congress Cataloging-in-Publication Data
Radley, Alan, 1946–
The body and social psychology/Alan Radley.
    p.   cm. — (Springer series in social psychology)
    Includes bibliographical references and index.
    ISBN 0–387–97584–5
    1. Social psychology.   2. Body, Human—Social aspects.   I. Title.
    II. Series.
    HM291.R312   1991
    302—dc20   91–4196

Printed on acid-free paper.

Typeset by Best-set Typesetter Ltd., Hong Kong.
Printed and bound by Edwards Brothers, Inc., Ann Arbor, MI.
Printed in the United States of America.

9 8 7 6 5 4 3 2 1

ISBN 0-387-97584-5 Springer-Verlag New York Berlin Heidelberg
ISBN 3-540-97584-5 Springer-Verlag Berlin Heidelberg New York

For Marg

Preface

This book is about the relationship between social psychology and the body. It starts from the assumption that questions to do with the body are of paramount importance for an understanding of social life. At first sight, this is a noncontentious statement to make, and yet a moment's thought shows that social psychology has had very little to say about this subject to date. Why should this be? Is it because the boundaries of the discipline have been drawn very tightly, focusing exclusively upon such things as attitudes and groups? Is it, perhaps, because the body suggests a field of study best left to biologists and physicians? Or is it because social psychology is well advised to steer clear of problems that draw us back from the social toward what are seen as the biological and the prehistory of our discipline?

These were some of the questions that were in my mind when I decided to write this book. In addition, I was influenced by the experience of researching in the area of chronic illness. There is nothing quite like life-threatening disease to point up mortality and the issues that arise from having to live with the constraints of one's body. Looking for theoretical ideas to help with this work led me to read in the literature of medical sociology. In that literature, I discovered that sociology has for some time been addressing questions to do with the body, effectively recapturing it as a sociological phenomenon. The point was then raised, could such a project be envisaged for social psychology? The promise of attempting this lay in the possibilities for a reappraisal of certain assumptions of social psychological theory, assumptions that I had been implicitly calling into question for some time. To take one example, the field of nonverbal behavior has long seemed to me a body of work from which significance has slipped further away with the accumulation of findings.

As far as the text itself is concerned, the reader is cautioned not to seek in it for a review of studies that have the word *body* somewhere in the title. This is not a survey of "the social psychology of the body" because such a field of work, as an entity, does not exist. Even if it did, I would be reluctant to describe it in detail because my concern is with what social psychology makes of its subject matter. The focus of the book is social psychology's historical and current treatment of people as embodied (or more frequently as disembodied) beings. The topics that form the subject matter of the separate chapters are best thought of as comprising a series of excursions into the problem. These excursions are intended to raise issues that can then be reflected against one another in the course of making a wider critique of the field. It has not been possible (nor, I believe, necessary) to attempt a comprehensive coverage of matters relating to the body in social life. There are, however, significant omissions: child development, with all that it entails, and matters of psychopathology, to name two important areas. For these reasons, the book does not set out to provide a new theory of the body or even to say what a social psychology of the body would be. The intention, instead, is to draw attention to the way that this topic has been either ignored by social psychology or subsumed within its investigations. The aim is to show that this is the result of certain basic limitations in the social psychological approach, and to point to the implications for the discipline of recognizing the significance of physical existence.

The way that I have entered upon the separate criticisms in each chapter is through the ideas presented by what I hold to be some marginal topics in psychology—notably women, the sick, and profane groups. Each of these areas has been the focus for scholars upon whose work I draw but to whose overall approach I do not necessarily subscribe. For that reason, no attempt is made to adopt one of these positions as the basis for the book's critique. This means that those reading the book seeking throughout the endorsement of, say, a feminist or a phenomenological perspective might be disappointed. The response I would make to this is that I have put first and foremost the relationship between the body as a source of evidence and (what I term) mainstream thinking in the discipline. In this, my intention has been to set out a rough field or ground, presently crisscrossed by the tracks of a few marginal inquiries, and to argue that this meeting signifies something rather important about how we, as social psychologists, engage our subject matter.

Alan Radley

Acknowledgments

This book has benefited from a number of discussions with my colleagues in the Department of Social Sciences at Loughborough. I am especially grateful to Mike Gane for his helpful yet critical comments on the draft manuscript, as well as for his enthusiastic interest in the project from the beginning. I also express my thanks to Mick Billig for his advice and encouragement throughout.

The preparation of the manuscript was carried out skillfully and speedily by Cathie Ward, to whom I owe a debt of gratitude.

Much of the work for this book was carried out during a summer vacation when I spent less time with my family than I would have wished. But for their patience and understanding, the project could never have been completed on time.

Contents

Chapter 1

The Invisible Legacy

Although social psychology is mainly about people's attitudes, communications, and behavior, it sometimes takes as a problem those matters that are, superficially at least, to do with people's bodies. When one thinks of questions of gender, of racial difference, of aggression, of crowding, of attractiveness, or of nonverbal communication, one needs little persuasion as to the relevance of the human body to these matters. Yet, a survey of a sample of books or research papers dealing with these topics will show that the body in general, or the bodies of subjects in particular, have no place in the speculations and theories of the authors concerned. Of course, this is not to say that certain parts of the body might not be mentioned; in studies of social perception, the face is a focus of inquiry, while in nonverbal communication research, the various parts of the body might be detailed as to their capacities for either sending or receiving messages. In spite of these isolated and disparate citings of hands or faces, social psychology has not yet come to grips with the fact that the people who are its subject matter enjoy and suffer a bodily existence. An examination of virtually any textbook introducing the discipline shows that this omission goes quite unrecognized. Select one of these tomes and scan the subject index for the word *body*; likely as not, there is no entry for this term. Sometimes one finds reference to "bodily communication," to "body language," or to "body movement," but examination of the material reveals that the reader is being referred to matters that lie either in society or within the thoughts of the subjects under study. All in all, if the body has any status in social psychological inquiry it is a very shadowy one indeed: the discipline studies "social," "behavioral," and "interpersonal" phenomena instead.

This book begins from the position that a social psychology of disembodied beings is, at best, like a puzzle with missing pieces; at worst, it is a repetition of misconceived explanations of action and experience. The first position suggests that one merely needs to add on studies of the body alongside existing knowledge, in order to fill out and complete the picture of

1

people in their relationships with one another. This is far too simple, of course, because it assumes that *the body* is just another topic in psychology, like *cognition* or *conformity*. This suggestion also rests on a view of knowledge as being accumulated through empirical inquiry, a perspective to which fewer and fewer social scientists adhere. Instead, there is the realization that science is a matter of constructed meanings, of claim and of counterclaim, so that the theories that we have about social life also reflect issues in society itself.

The second position raises the question of whether a social psychology that conceives of people as disembodied beings is doomed to trying to capture issues of bodily existence within its circle of explanation. In the chapters that follow, I try to show how traditional social psychology attempts to deal with matters that it acknowledges to be important (e.g., emotion, communication), but that appear to lie either across or alongside of the boundary with other disciplines. No matter whether we try to erect a social psychology based upon language (Brown, 1965) or behavior (Homans, 1961) or cognition (Krech, Crutchfield, & Ballachey, 1962) or social processes (Allen, Guy, & Edgley, 1980), the exclusion of the body as a feature of existence means that certain aspects of human life will always be outside of what Kelly (1955) called a theory's "range of convenience." This might not matter, except that questions that arise from the use of our bodies are of central concern; here are issues of morality, of distinction, of development, and of mortality. It is noteworthy that psychoanalysis, in embracing such issues and making them integral within its explanations of human and social life, has remained always at the center of intellectual, if not psychological, inquiry. One explanation for why some academic psychologists cannot leave psychoanalysis alone, but subject it to repeated vituperative attacks, might be that it dared to illuminate matters that psychology has, so far, felt itself unable to address (Jahoda, 1977). Even when discussing topics seemingly unrelated to matters of morality and mortality, when psychology addresses what are sometimes called its "philosophical problems," these are often located by reference to the body; examples include issues of meaning versus mechanism, the problem of reductionism, movement versus action, objectivity versus subjectivity. Peculiar as it is, the more material aspect of human existence, by which I mean the body as opposed to the mind, can raise questions of ontology that are rarely addressed by a steady focus upon attitudes, cognitions, or group processes.

Taken together, these criticisms point to the following conclusion. Social psychology has largely proceeded upon the assumption that the body is a covert term, an indirect referent in its analyses. A cursory look at the discipline might lead one to think that this topic is entirely missing, except, for example, in studies that deal explicitly with matters of appearance or communication. Yet this would be to draw the wrong conclusion. As this book shows, social psychologists have invariably based their investigations upon one or another view of the body, which derives from their assumption of what people are as objects of psychological study. Typically, this involves a cleavage between the social and the individual, the cultural and the biological, and the psychological and the physiological. When introducing their subject matter, it is not unusual for writers to make distinctions that force a separation between humans and animals, pointing up the peculiar capacity for language, which only the former enjoy. This emphasizes that social psychology is about matters that have their origin beyond the individual, who partakes of social life only through the capacity to share language (Brown, 1965), significant symbols (Cardwell, 1971), and social representations (Moscovici, 1984). Once this distinction is established, matters concerning the body are marginalized, if not excluded from all further analysis. As this chapter shows, this exclusion of the body is often viewed in a different light; social psychologists think of it as a necessary relinquishing of matters to other disciplines (mainly, physiology), which are "better fitted" to investigate them. This has to do with methodology as well as with subject matter. As a result, the problems that psychologists left in the possession of their biologist colleagues remained those of a physiological, machinelike entity, precisely because they were sustained by the methods and world view of the latter approach.

Having drawn the lines firmly, if not always clearly, between the biological and the social, it might be thought that social psychologists have progressed unimpeded by matters concerning the human body. At the center of the discipline, the study of attitudes, social perceptions, political values, language, and group behavior have proceeded untouched by concerns about the physical existence of the subjects on whom attention is focused. Only at the edges of the discipline do these matters start to become apparent: in the study of nonverbal behavior, of illness and disability, of gender differences, of aging, and of the physical environment. In these topics are to be found, at least, some reference to the body and to its presence as a limiting feature in what people can do with and say to each other. It is from a growing awareness of the need for research in these areas of everyday life that tentative psychological explanations of the body have been put forward. Yet, we would be mistaken if we believed that such questions are restricted to these areas alone; this is one of the main messages of this book. The argument can be made that the most social aspects of social psychology rest upon assumptions that, once altered, invite a rethinking of our notions of what it is to be "an individual in society." The body that the discipline largely ignores actually supports, from its place in the conceptual shadows, what psychologists highlight as being most social about their subject matter.

The Subject of Study

There is something vaguely futile about any attempt to review what social psychology has discovered about the body, for the simple reason that the topic appears to be entirely peripheral to the discipline's main concerns. One manner of proceeding at the outset is, therefore, to examine some of the ways in which the body either fails to appear, or else makes a modest and incomplete appearance in the research tradition. First of all, a distinction must be made between those studies that acknowledge physical presence, passion, fatigue, or whatever, and those that pose the body merely as an idea. The latter kind of study, in which the body appears as an object of contemplation only, should not be confused with the former. We are concerned here with more than content; it is the relation of the investigators to their subject matter that is at stake. Put simply, what kind of individual, in what kind of society is the subject of study? As far as the body is concerned, we can distinguish three approaches that render it, in turn, (a) unseen, (b) opaque, and (c) categorized. The effect of these approaches has been to make it subsidiary in the discipline's research priorities.

The Unseen Body

It is the core of social psychology, as reflected in work published and cited in textbooks bearing that name, that presents us with the poorest diet of ideas about the body. The fields of attitude study, of social judgment, and of values and beliefs are predicated upon studies asking individuals to say what they *think*. It has been a long time since the word *attitude* suggested a person's posture, having become a term to describe what is generally held to be a mental event. Attitudes and beliefs may come from experiences that involve people in more than talking, listening and looking, and these experiences may be varied in the course of psychological experiments, but the object of study remains what individuals think about their world and other people within it. The problem of the relationship of attitudes to people's wider experience has traditionally been posed as one of how well they can predict behavior. Reminding oneself of the seminal study carried out by La Piere (1934), it is interesting that the follow-up communications to the restaurant and hotel owners (when attitudes were assessed) are now often interpreted as a *predictor* of their behavior toward ethnic-group customers, whom in fact they had *already* seen. The relationship of attitudes to behavior is posed as the problem of how the former can predict the latter. Primacy is accorded to ideas, to mental content, over the way in which people will dispose of themselves in action. Perhaps this is not so surprising, given that social psychology emerged within an individualistic, experimentalist tradition. One of the tasks of the newly emerged sub-discipline was to show that behavior was not just under the control of biological or environmental forces; how individuals acted needed to be explained also as a result of their relationships in social groups and in terms of their attitudes. While social psychology may be said to have begun by acknowledging the presence of others as an influence upon behavior (Le Bon, 1896; Triplett, 1897), it moved to a position where such physical presence needed only to be implied (Allport, 1968). Of course, the effect of other people's presence continued to be of central concern, but the physical nature of this presence was not held to be important for the study of attitudes. What people declared about things reflected their position "on an issue," "in relation to other groups"—that is, in terms of a space that was to be determined in a nonphysical sphere, one of judgment and meaning (Osgood, Suci & Tannenbaum, 1957). Within this space could be plotted people's ideas about the body, but only by rendering it, along with all other elements, an object of distant contemplation.

The social psychology of attitudes and of mental judgments is based upon a covert identification of these operations with the mind of the individual. These judgments are affected by context, in cause-and-effect relationships that have traditionally been held to be important. However, because of the design of experiments testing these assumed relationships, the context appears as the independent variable and the judgment as the dependent variable. This means that settings are arranged, as a part of which may be the physical presence of other people, but the data are collected in terms of what individual subjects say or do. For example, Asch's (1952) study of conformity behavior is one in which the (physical) presence of the confederates was accepted as being important, though the analysis was carried out in terms of the mental judgments made by the people concerned. (Interestingly, the power of the false feedback given to each subject was most effectively communicated through a set of pictures showing one such person in a disturbed state, as he took part in the experiment). In a refinement of the technique, Crutchfield (1955), for reasons of economy, arranged that subjects would be isolated and would receive false feedback from the experimenter. Results obtained from this modification retained Asch's findings about conformity, while removing the necessity for subjects to meet face to face. Though not drawing this conclusion, Crutchfield's work is testimony to the secondary nature of physical presence as compared with that of what subjects *believe* to be the case—or so it appears. The effect is to refine the study of conforming judgments at the expense of expanding the understanding of what happens when people are in each other's physical presence.

The preceding example is not an isolated one but is typical of the effort to locate the objects of explanation in the minds (i.e., the thinking, perceiving, judging) of individual subjects gathered together. It also occurs in the study of group decision making (Doise, 1978), of attributions (Kelley, 1967), and of the conditions for people to feel themselves part of a group (Tajfel, 1978). This approach, which surely reflects the vast majority of studies carried out by social psychologists, has nothing to say about people as embodied beings at all. This is a result of its determination to explain everything in terms of what individuals say and think, and to manage this through artificial settings in which these two activities are paramount. At this, the very center of the discipline, we do indeed find the least that is of immediate help in understanding how social psychology might study the body. Yet this should not be wholly surprising, for here its assumptions align most strongly with the accepted nature of its subject matter, so that we have a sense of things being obvious, inevitable, and according with common sense. One of the tasks of this book is to reexamine some of these assumptions as they appear in the light of the arguments put forward in the pages that follow. For the moment, it is sufficient to say that the bodies of subjects in this kind of study are, to all intents and purposes, irrelevant. They are quite outside the terms of theory—invisible, taken for granted. In practice, their physical presence or absence is supportive of the researcher's aims: ordered, extending into the real world, covert.

The Opaque Body

When speaking of the core of social psychology, I am referring to work that purports to study what is common to people, what affects us all as participants in social life. Not all of this work can by any means be called "attitude research," though some of it shares with attitude research the use of artificial settings and the focus upon mental activity (viz., the Asch studies). One of the most widely discussed experiments in social psychology in the past 20 years is Milgram's (1963, 1974) series on obedience. These studies involved variations upon a theme in which subjects were instructed to administer electric shocks to a man supposed to be failing at a learning task. The man was a role-playing confederate who received no shocks, and the feedback on his performance was controlled by the investigators. The results of Milgram's experiments are usually summarized as having shown that, when ordered, people will obey even to the point of inflicting severe physical harm upon another person. Equally prominent in descriptions of Milgram's work are references to the ethical problems raised by the studies. First, he duped subjects into behaving in ways about which they felt extremely guilty on learning what had really occurred; second, the subjects were placed in a situation of considerable stress in having to decide whether to administer the shocks that they were ordered to give (Baumrind, 1964).

This work is interesting, not only for its findings, but also for the reactions that it provoked among its critics. Unlike most research in social psychology, it does have something to say about the body, although this is incidental to Milgram's purpose. The experimental setup hinged upon the arrangement of potential and actual (as believed) bodily harm inflicted by one person on another. Part of Milgram's presentation of data involves descriptions of what subjects heard and saw of the pain of the supposed victim, which makes the session a realistic situation. Alongside this are descriptions of what the subjects said and did, revealing important differences in their relationships to the victim, to the experimenter, and to the situation as a whole. These relationships are realized in a far more extensive way than by the mere pulling or otherwise manipulating of the lever switches that supposedly controlled the shocks. They are supplemented by the observers' descriptions of what subjects did and of pictures portraying the enacted agony of the victim. As an example of the former, we are told that in the condition where the subject is urged on by a role-playing "common man," who takes over if the subject desists from giving punishment, one subject, "a large man, lifted the zealous shocker from his chair, threw him to a corner of the laboratory, and did not allow him to move until he had promised not to administer further shocks" (Milgram, 1974, p. 97). In spite of these descriptions, Milgram's study is often reported as if subjects either did or did not pull levers, so that the body of subject and victim are made into mere vehicles in the explanation. This is consistent with Milgram's own emphasis upon the general form of obedience, as revealed within what he termed the "agentic relationship," which certain kinds of social hierarchies make possible. The power of this experiment, as far as its author was concerned, was in its general applicability, unhindered by the specific features of the design that he had chosen.

By comparison, the power of the experiment for its commentators has been, I believe, its *specific* form; it speaks not only of obedience to authority, but also of physical cruelty and of bodily suffering. There is something particularly threatening about what the (65% of) subjects did to the victim, in the face of his cries of pain and pleas to be released. Indeed, the role-playing of the victim in expressing his tortured state is central to an appreciation of what was happening in the experiment. The body of the willing subject may be an "agentic tool," but that of the unwilling subject and that of the victim, taken together, provide evidence of an altogether different kind. The difficulty is that social psychology has no way of comprehending the body in pain, and particularly the structure of torture. However, as ordinary people, we know enough of it to be both frightened and revolted by it. As a result, Milgram's study has suffered two forms of change when being described, one making it digestible for students within a diet of straight experimental psychology, and the other a forced transformation into an object lesson on the ethics of research. In the first case, the only changes necessary are the omission of detail allowing a summary connecting the authority of the experimenter with the behavior of the subjects (i.e., "people obey orders"). In the second case, the study has been dealt with in a way that highlights the deception of the subjects by the experimenter, while also recognizing the stress under which it put them. This concentration upon deception has led not to any critical reassessment of what Milgram offers, but in some cases merely to a mild reappraisal of method in social psychology. As Mixon (1974) concluded after considering the possibilities of role-play for subjects as a substitute for deception, "The problem is to find out when, in the context Milgram created, subjects will obey and when they will disobey." In effect, start from the beginning as if the ethical issues teach us nothing about the substantive issue under investigation.

A different interpretation can be offered of the stir that this study created both inside and outside of psychology, based partly upon the issue of deception and partly upon the nature of what went on (or appeared to go on) within it. The strength of the objections lies in the pain that was *effectively* inflicted upon the victim, not just in the deception or in the stress placed upon the subjects. By this is meant that the underlying objection to the study lies not in duping people to be worse than they really are (a stated objection in some circles), but in the experimenter having tricked them into making tangible and real a side of humanity that we prefer to leave in the shadows. The importance of the body of the victim in this is that it specifies, concentrates, and ultimately displays for us a form of experience that we know enough about to want to repudiate. Interpreted in this way, Milgram's experiment becomes a statement about people who do not just judge, perceive, and attribute meaning, but are committed together in the pursuit of pain and suffering. To a psychology that is committed to discovering the nature of mental life, this relationship is unacceptable and shocking. We, as students of social psychology, are shocked, too—by the actions of the compliant subjects who took part. One of the effects of critiques of the experiment is to remove, or at least to cover over the pain and suffering of the victim by focusing upon its illusory nature. This does not mean that criticisms of Milgram's deceptions are unfounded, but that some are narrowed and superficial with regard to what the study makes significant. This results in a modification of the question from "Should the experiment have been done?" to "How can its findings be undone?" By keeping attention focused firmly upon issues of method and ethics, the way that the body figures in the study is obscured; nevertheless, it remains central to the question of what the subjects did to the victim when ordered to do so.

Because the victim was an actor, he actually experienced no physical pain. Yet, a consideration of pain shows it to be, at one level, an inexpressible condition, unsharable and defying verbal objectification (Scarry, 1985). To be the victim of extreme pain inflicted by another person is to be in a state where one's world is annihilated and fragmented. By comparison, the torturer's world, through the way that the victim's pain is magnified and made visible, expands, and its power is legitimated. Scarry argues that the distance between torturer and victim is unbridgeable, because the pain is hugely present to the latter and absent to the former; by contrast, the question that is (within the political fiction) so important to the torturer is insignificant to the victim in his or her suffering. In addition to the physical act of causing pain, torture has as its verbal component the interrogation, the question and the answer. The question is misrepresented as the motive for the interrogation, although it serves actually as the means for perpetuating the unfolding and dramatizing of the victim's pain. The answer is misrepresented as a betrayal on the part of the victim, who gives away more of his or her self with each scrap of information.

> However near the prisoner the torturer stands, the distance between their physical realities is colossal, for the prisoner is in overwhelming physical pain while the torturer is utterly without pain. . . . it is an invisible distance since the physical realities it lies between are each invisible. . . . The torturer's questions—asked, shouted, insisted upon, pleaded for—objectify the fact that he has a world. . . . [when juxtaposed with] the small and shredded world objectified in the prisoner's answers. It is only the prisoner's steadily shrinking ground that wins for the torturer his swelling sense of territory. The question and answer are a prolonged comparative display, an unfurling of world maps. (Scarry, 1985, p. 36)

The weaponry of torture converts the prisoner's pain into a tangible expression of power. This elaborates the motive for interrogation, so that the torturer can justify the act in terms of what needed to be done, no matter how repulsive it might have been. Quoting Hannah Arendt, Scarry says that this attitude does not reflect "what horrible things I did to people," but instead "what horrible things I had to watch in the pursuance of my duties" (p. 58). Torture does not simply follow from the motive, nor is the rationale for it having happened a mere excuse.

Putting this analysis alongside Milgram's work, it is possible to see that the infliction of (supposed) pain created a particular relationship between subjects and victim, or rather, that to understand what was happening, we need to acknowledge the special features arising from the juxtaposition of the experimenter's motive with the victim's pleas and sufferings. The power that is alluded to in the authority of the experimenter cannot just be seen as a matter of social status, for it emerges through the punishments administered in the course of the study. Both Milgram and his critics fail to discuss this special feature of the study, except to show why subjects broke off. The authority assumed to reside in the experimenter can be understood as being part of the power relationship emerging between "teacher" and "learner" during the course of the experiment; the screams of the victim, and his writhings when next to the subject, do not simply follow the shocks, but make the relationship into what it becomes. This critical alternative only arises once one begins to look at the nature of pain inflicted by one person upon the body of another. Nevertheless, as ordinary people, psychologists recognize that there is something special in this study; in consequence, they relate it in one textbook after another as an important demonstration of how people might behave if ordered to do so. These reports tell us about people's beliefs concerning authority, but nothing, apparently, about the moral basis for the objections to what occurs. The plane of bodily experience, which is the clue to the study's significance, remains opaque.

The Categorized Body

The study, conducted by Schacter and Singer (1962), on the labeling of emotional states is also frequently reported in texts of social psychology. It is interesting because it employed techniques of altering people's bodily states directly (through administering injections of stimulant drugs), and then making indirect arrangements for the subjects to assess their emotional states. Within this approach, the body is conceived in terms of the specific functions of the sympathetic system, so that the state of arousal that people feel and the context in which they find themselves are compared. The experimenters arranged that subjects given an injection of epinephrine (producing accelerated heart rate, tremor, faster breathing) were different-ially informed as to the nature of the drug and were placed in different social situations. Some found themselves in the company of a manic (euphoric) companion (a confederate of the experimenters), while others took part in an exercise with an angry person (also a confederate). The results showed that subjects were least likely to attribute emotional changes to themselves when they had been informed of the true nature of the drug's effects. When they were either ignorant of the drug's effects, or had been misinformed about these, the subjects used the social situation as the basis for interpreting their bodily state. Those in the company of the manic person reported greater euphoria; those with the angry person reported greater irritation.

This study is usually interpreted to show that people do not just have emotions, but that they label their bodily states in order to make them sensible. Also, because one effect of the drug was to produce undifferent-iated arousal, Schacter and Singer's study demonstrates the possibility that the different emotions that people feel do not belong to the body at all, but are the outcome of a labeling of diffuse feeling. While experimental support for the misattribution paradigm is limited (Cotton, 1981), the idea that emotions are social constructions has received even greater attention. This approach takes exception to the naturalistic view of emotion as residing inside the body. Instead, it argues that feelings are accounts that people give of patterned experiences in social life, as well as being sets of responses that they are expected to give in certain prescribed situations (Armon-Jones, 1986). When people speak of their feelings, or show their emotions, they do so as part of a sociocultural tradition that has schooled them in the appropriate responses to given situations.

The constructivist position is not identifiable with that of Schacter and Singer. Where Schachter and Singer were concerned with how people make sense of differences made in their bodies, not all constructivists feel the need to relate what people say about their feelings to the body at all. Neverthe-less, as in the Schacter and Singer study, the constructivist perspective emphasizes the cognitive basis of emotion, although unlike Schachter and Singer, its strong form dispenses with bodily perturbations entirely. Arguing that there are no essential bodily aspects to disgust or to jealousy, it rejects the body as the repository of emotion in favor of seeking the structure of feeling in forms of talk. This makes possible not only a pragmatic but also a moral treatment of the place of emotions in everyday encounters.

My purpose in citing this work is to show that even a radical critique of a topic such as emotion within social psychology can direct attention away from the body entirely, even if this is not the intention of authors taking this position (Harré, 1986b). It falls prey to what can be called a "cognitivization" of social life, in which all that matters is what people think about things and what they say about them. As one author of this approach has put it, "The principle underlying this work is simple: everything we know about our social environment is in some ways represented inside our cognitive system" (Forgas, 1983). This statement rather begs the question with the use of the words "know" and "is in some ways represented." That aside, it reflects a significant shift in social psychology toward understanding social life from the position of people as thinkers and speakers. The movement of this theorizing is away from what might be called "naïve empiricist", or "objectivist" descriptions of the "facts" of behavior. In taking a cognitive perspective, one subscribes to a further separation of mind from body in social psychology. As later chapters show, the body that can only be seen and reflected upon gives but a partial account of the world of physical existence.

The choice of the Schacter and Singer study for this section arose from its contribution to the revised assumption in social psychology that the body is pliable and formless. The idea of undifferentiated arousal being captured within mental categories of meaning (individual or social, as representations) makes the mind formative and powerful. The shape of feeling appears to come, not from biological determinants, but from society and the individual thinker. The question of emotion has been transplanted:

> We feel. We try to feel. We want to try to feel. The social guidelines that direct how we want to try to feel may be describable as a set of socially shared, albeit often latent . . . rules. (Hochschild, 1979, p. 563)

Physiology is denied a primary place in the investigations of social science; as a result, the physical existence of people becomes knowable only as a kind of story that people tell each other. Whether it is true, or how it is true, is a problem only to the extent that it is spoken by people in the course of their relationships with one another.

The objectivist (or nativist) position that this approach criticizes is identifiable with attempts to relate psychological experience to physiological functioning. In the field of emotion, the direction of influence (i.e., of causality) has been traditionally from the body to the mind; by this is meant that emotion can be reduced to, anchored, or located with respect to physiological mechanisms. In recent years, research into the workings of social stress has reversed this line of influence, now seeking to show how different sorts of relationship produce different changes in the body. For example, one review of the literature suggested that "environments characterized by higher levels of involvement will be associated with increased hormonal activity in their members" (Kiritz & Moos, 1974, p. 103). What this comes down to is that placing people in different social relationships leads them to show differences in various indices of physiological function. This whole line of research has been criticized as lacking conceptual integration, perpetuating a psychophysical parallelism through juxtaposing concepts from the realms of psychology and physiology. What results is either a kind of flicker-fusion effect, where the repetition of terms leads to their being seen as related, or else to the employment of a *double-entendre* (e.g., arousal), where the spheres of mind and body apparently coalesce into the same concept (Bannister, 1968).

There are, therefore, good reasons for social psychologists to be wary of attempts to link psychological and physiological concepts. The linking of experiences and ideas with particular indices of physiological functioning can add nothing to an understanding of how people make meaningful decisions or pursue a moral existence. The question remains, however, as to whether placing the accent upon thought and speech will in turn make the human body sensible within social psychology. As yet, this approach is still being developed, but there is reason to doubt that it will provide explanations that will capture the embodied aspect of social life. My reservations stem from the preference of this perspective for data from articulate individuals; the fact is that sometimes the most interesting things about the body are not spoken of directly at all, or at least, not by the individuals themselves.

While the body is unseen by much of social psychological research, it makes a covert appearance on occasions, as in the Milgram experiments. The Schacter and Singer work is exceptional in making the body (really, a part of it as viewed by physiologists), a key term of the research. However, their purpose in this was not just to pursue an interactionist analysis, linking ideas to secretory levels where possible, but to pry free an aspect of psychological experience hitherto attached to the body. The freeing of the emotions from the body is also a signal for social psychology's release from the need to attend to people's physical existence. The alternative offered by the constructivists is that we attend to matters of categorization and justification. However, just as this signal has been made, evidence concerning the body's place in social life is accumulating to the point where it can no longer be denied.

What can we say about the question of the subject in social psychology, with reference to the body? These three forays into the literature were intended to show that, whatever the differences between theoretical positions held in the discipline (and there are many), people's corporeal existence has been either ignored, glossed over, or interpreted as merely a vehicle for what they say and think.

The Biological and the Social

The question of why the body has been overlooked for so long by social psychology cannot be properly answered in one sentence; an attempt at such an answer requires an altogether lengthier discussion. However, at a superficial level, it could be said that the reason for this oversight lies in the traditional opposition between the biological and the social. What is of the body belongs to biology; what is social belongs to society and to people in relationships. Durkheim made clear this distinction when he wrote,

> A regulative force must play the same role for moral needs which the organism plays for physical needs. This means that the force can only be moral. . . . only conscience . . . can furnish the means to re-establish it. Physical restraint would be ineffective; hearts cannot be touched by physio-chemical forces. (1952, p. 248)

Durkheim's position, marked by his insistence on "social facts," is often taken to mean that sociology can proceed without any concern for the biologic individual. Later in this volume, I show reason to question why it is that sociology has made inquiries into the body in general, while social psychology has yet to turn its attention to this problem area. For psychologists, the problem remains that the individual is both organic and social in nature; there is an undeniable closeness about the double constitution of the person. Though acknowledged, it tends to get submerged in the disparities between the work of the physiological psychologist or the neuro-psychologist on the one hand, and that of the social psychologist on the other. We have divided up the individual along Cartesian lines and agreed to go our separate ways, discerning upon or in our subject matter only those things that are proper to the concerns of the relevant subdiscipline.

The leanings of the one approach—toward biology and its methods—and of the other—toward sociology and its concepts—result in an all but complete separation of the two universes of discourse. In part, we know which group of scholars we belong to because of the aspects of the person that we relinquish to others for study; what is "social" is what is *not* "biological" or "individual." In fact, the problem is not that simple, particularly for psychologists who study such things as personality (what of traits?) or those who study cognition (what of neural mechanisms?). As I show later, social psychologists are not free of the uneasy division of the biological and the social either, and one of the themes of the following chapters is the difficulties engendered by trying to construct acorporeal theories about people who palpably live in and through their bodies.

There are attempts to construct theoretical bridges between the social and the biological, and they are mentioned at this point only because they do little or nothing to help us to understand the body in society (Waid, 1984). For example, Hinde (1987) emphasizes how the predispositions of our bodies are subject to social influences brought about through teaching and learning. From this view, as from that offered by others concerned with this issue, the biologic is seen as a constraint that is completed by the possibilities that lie within the social sphere. For example, Richards (1974) cautions that social psychologists would do well to accept the limitations prescribed by our bodily nature, though he illustrates this with work from the field of developmental psychology, where the dictates of growth are incontestable. By and large, however, social psychology has eschewed the child for the adult.

The good intentions of the ethologist are spoiled (for the social psychologist) when reference is made to other species. When Hinde (1982) writes of the need for comparative studies to see where "man fits," "just as, by comparing our teeth with those of a range of animal species we can draw conclusions about the diet to which man was originally adapted, so can behavioural comparisons throw light on other aspects of our nature" (p. 202), he risks being rejected for ignoring what is special about human beings. The assumptions that would guide this rejection are, of course, as old as the debates about evolution itself. In the history of social psychology, they can be found in the acceptance of the distinction between the "biologic" and the "socially self-conscious individual," which Mead (1934) saw as roughly the difference between the conduct of the more intelligent of the lower animals and that of human beings. Where Mead went on to insist that, in individual experience, these are "cut by no lines of cleavage" (p. 347), the problems and possibilities flowing from this thesis have largely vanished from the mainstream of social psychology.

For many social psychologists, questions concerning the body do, I suspect, raise what Wrong (1963) once called the specter of biological determinism. However, this is not a charge to press; it is a situation to understand. Within a broad discipline that has made a home for psychophysical interactional research, the social psychologist is right to object that, whatever else they may be, neural mechanisms and hormonal secretions have no place in explanations of moral action. Nor, I would argue, is there any theoretical mileage in trying to achieve accommodations between social psychology and psychophysiology (Waid, 1984). More often than not, these involve a fitting of social theory around the "natural" substrate of the body. However, in all such cases, including the current predilection for stress research in the field of health psychology, inquiry rests upon implicit assumptions about the nature of society.

Young (1980) has argued that the discourse about social stress has coupled together an empiricist approach to research, employing methods for measuring both personality and physiology, with a set of values about the place of the (abstract) individual in society. These values are unstated but have the result of locating the explanation in nature rather than in culture and of somatizing it in individuals rather than in their social relationships. How is this possible? One reason is that the individual, taken as the personality subject to stress, is treated identically with the body that he or she inhabits. By this is meant two things: (1) the person *is* the body, and (2) personalities are measured in terms of common dimensions that objectify and abstract them. We might then learn that people with Type A personalities (believed to be prone to coronary heart disease), respond to certain situations with a characteristic style and with certain changes to their physiological condition.

(Friedman & Rosenman, 1974). What we do not know is the relative importance of these various indicators, or where and how to connect together the social and the bodily indices that have been determined.

The identification of person and body is basic to this kind of interactionist research. First, it circumscribes the mental and the physical within a common boundary, so that what is done, felt, or thought has, potentially, mental and physical correlates. This makes it sensible to correlate, statistically, measures from the two planes. Second, by applying a common method along natural science principles, it is possible to treat the physical and the psychological as if they are similar kinds of things to be studied. Effectively, there are then two spaces in which individuals can be located relative to one another; subjects are given scores on each kind of indicator. The result of this approach is to generalize not only about the body but about the person as well. In effect, there are no bodies as such, just common measures that vary with respect to the points (individuals) where they are assessed. The biological and the social are there in a form that simultaneously ignores the body as a unity and the individual as a being in society.

The preceding argument suggests that the failure of social psychology to study the body is more than a simple rejection of the biological standpoint. In effect, social psychology cannot entirely reject what it often tacitly accepts; that individuals are to be identified with their bodies. If this were not the case, then the argument put by Goffman (1959), that selves are the *product* of dramatic performances and not the cause of them, would appear noncontentious. As Harré and Secord (1972) have argued since, the idea that there is a single, consistent self that resides inside each single biologic entity is an institutionalized assumption. This means that it is possible to consider the person as playing a number of different, sometimes contradictory, but situated selves in the context of social episodes. The organization of the self is therefore no longer to be sought inside the body, in terms of traits, drives, or mechanisms but in the settings of people's social relationships.

This is a viewpoint at variance with the mainstream of social psychological research, which continues to seek general laws about human behavior and experience. For what are linked inexorably together are the generalized (i.e., anatomical) body and the abstract individual; these two conceptions mutually support one another in defining individuals as *essentially equal*. The subject matter of social psychology is a generalized person, both in mind and in body, so that each and all are presumed to be subject to the same laws in their different degrees. The biological conception of the body supports social psychology by underlining this parallel between the laws of nature and the laws of culture. How this is worked out in the various topics where the body comes under scrutiny is discussed in subsequent chapters.

In summary, we can say that the opposition of the *biological* to the *social* is only half the story in the attempt to explain social psychology's attitude to the body. Physical existence is ignored, not just because it is made up of physiological things, but also because it is subsumed within the idea that individuals share a common humanity. This is the tangible aspect of the general form that is ascribed to subjects who meet around a table, or who are asked to complete a questionnaire.

Studies on the Margin: The Body as Focus

In spite of the fact that social psychology has concentrated almost exclusively upon groups, attitudes and cognitions, there are a few examples where people's physical existence, or rather their physical differences, have been the focus of concern. These differences are not merely ones of quantity, such as weight or strength, but are qualitative distinctions by which the lives of those concerned can be distinguished. The few examples are interesting, in part, because they reflect work done at the margins of the subject, although they refer to whole sections of the population. I have in mind psychoanalysis, the study of the sick, of women, and of crowds. In each case, these reflect a subsidiary topic in social psychology, an area of research that is sufficiently on the fringe as to allow writers to discuss the relationship between it and the more generally accepted subject matter. At the time of writing, these relationships are in different stages of growth or decline. While social psychology's concern with psychoanalysis may be past its peak (Jahoda, 1972), its recognition of the place of women's studies in the broader debate concerning relationships and ideologies still has some way to go (Wilkinson, 1986). Equally, if not more important, these topics reflect the condition of groupings who arguably have a subsidiary place in society. In this section I want to introduce the idea that the body has made an appearance at the fringe of social psychology, within studies of individuals who are, in some important way, marginalized in the social world. Madness, sickness, crowding, and femininity are all subsidiary to their polar opposites—reason, health, the individual, and masculinity. Is it mere chance that it is in these topics that the body makes an appearance? Recently, Romanyshyn (1989) has argued that they represent the shadow of the technological culture of which modern psychology is a part, and that they point up issues that are obscured by the commitment to objectivity and the affirmation of equality. The body has been abandoned by psychology in its search for mechanisms of mind, but it returns as the medium, or vehicle, of issues that have been forgotten. For our purposes, we need to see how the body makes this reappearance in these contexts, both to anticipate the content of later chapters, and to reassess the mentalism of mainstream social psychology.

The Psychoanalytic Study of the Hysterical Body

Psychoanalysis continues to have an uneasy relationship with psychology, both in its social as well as its individual aspect (Jahoda, 1972). It has remained marginal to psychology for a variety of reasons, although the arguments against Freud's theory were being formulated from the time he was beginning to publish. One of the perennial difficulties for the academic discipline is the way in which psychoanalysis appears to span the mental and the physical. For many critics on the social side of this divide, concepts such as *instinct*, *libido*, *erogenous zone*, and *phallic stage* are sufficient evidence that Freud's theory is representative of biological thinking. It can serve as a countersupport to explanations (e.g., of aggression) that point instead to relationships or groups as moving forces in the scheme of individual behavior. This view of Freud's work is convenient for emphasizing the social more than the biological, but it is shallow and consequently incorrect. It is a good example of how the opposition of the social and the biological in psychological thinking preserves treasured notions of "the individual in society," while obscuring the body from view.

Reading the reports of early work carried out with Breuer, one is struck by the attention that Freud paid to the way his patients conducted themselves, both during therapy and in their lives outside. The idea that psychoanalysis concerns itself only with the relationship between particular ideas and specific organs falls short of the practice that Freud describes. In the case of "Fraulein Elisabeth von R.," who suffered from pains in her legs, Freud turns away from seeking the direct relationship between specific traumas and the locations of the pain. He says that, instead,

> I did, however, turn my attention to the way in which the whole symptomatic complex of abasia might have been built up upon these painful zones, and in that connection I asked her various questions, such as what was the origin of her pains in walking? in standing? and in lying down? (Freud, 1955, p. 150)

Freud goes on to relate the circumstances in which his patient stood, sat, and walked, as well as whom she accompanied, where it took place, what she thought and felt. Instead of focusing upon the specific anatomical parts where pain was felt, Freud sets the symptom in context by re-creating its setting. This setting has, as one of its essential features, the bodily conduct and experience of the patient, conduct that forms part of the biographic detail in which Freud is interested. He describes the symptoms as *mnemic residues*, a condensed record of the patient's lived experience in particular settings. The task that Freud sets himself, of understanding how the symptoms arose, is itself facilitated through his touching and listening to his patient.

> When I pressed her head she would maintain that nothing occurred to her. I would repeat my pressure and tell her to wait, but still nothing appeared. (Freud, 1955, p. 153)

Both in the accounts that his patients gave, and in his own practice, Freud was attentive to their bodily conduct and experience. The biographic accounts and the clinical relationship were aimed at elucidating the history of a condition manifested through the body, the transformation of trauma into somatic symptoms. This was a different approach to that of the physicians of the time, for whom "the patient was constitutionally a hysteric, liable to develop hysterical symptoms under the pressure of intense excitations *of any kind*" (Freud, 1955, p. 144, emphasis in the original). This view, which is recognizable as an extension of the medical perspective, which seeks pathology *in* the body, does depend upon biological assumptions. These are the terms that social psychology opposes in its own explanations. They are also the terms that Freud transcended in his theory and in his practice. Staying for a moment with the latter (Freud's practice), Mitchell (1974) cites Stephen Heath as saying that "Charcot sees, Freud will hear," (p. 298), developing this point to argue that what Charcot saw, classified, and dismissed as the shouting of hysterics was material that Freud would listen to as the reminiscences of people with a story to tell. As is discussed in the next chapter, there is a strong connection between the elevation of the seeing eye in culture and the presentation of the body as an anatomical object. Psychoanalysis goes against this movement, by listening to hysteric patients who tell their own stories. They are people embedded in particular social settings, who also *embody* desires and secrets in their conduct. Mitchell (1974) suggests that the condition of hysteria, with its dual manifestation in the mind and upon the body, was perhaps the inevitable seedbed for psychoanalysis. If that is so, then it is not accidental that Freud's theory addresses the body as it is experienced, whereas academic psychology perceives physical existence in terms of mechanisms or structures.

Freud's theory of conversion hysteria was, from the first, expressed in terms both of psychology and of physiology. This is at once true and yet a misleading statement, if by the latter we read it to mean that he expressed his ideas only in terms of either one or the other discipline. In the later developments of the theory, the metapsychology, Freud (1957) tried to be explicit about instinct, which, "from a biological point of view . . . appears to us as a concept on the frontier between the mental and somatic" (p.121–122). Instincts could be studied as the psychical representative of stimuli arising from within the organism, but their sources *inside* the body are, Freud insisted, beyond psychology. There is an either/or ambiguity about this analysis, which has bedeviled students of psychoanalytic theory ever since it was written (Jahoda, 1977). It invites a way of thinking that tries to connect mind and soma as mechanisms; yet it stands in contrast to the way that Freud reconstructed the experiences of his patients, experiences that could take place only *with or through* the body. The understanding of hysteria came, in part, from a recognition that conversion proceeded via a symbolic use of the body, not a mechanical association of ideas and physical states. There is no place to link the mind with the anatomy, because

> Hysteria is ignorant of the distribution of the nerves, and that is why it does not stimulate periphero-spinal or projection paralyses. It has no knowledge

> of the optic chiasma, and consequently it does not produce hemi-anopsia. It takes the organs in the ordinary, popular sense of the names they bear: the leg is the leg as far up as its insertion into the hip, the arm is the upper limb as it is visible under the clothing. (1966, p. 169)

Hysteria could not be understood anatomically, nor was it to be comprehended as the product of the patient's own thinking. The revelation of the erotic history of symptoms, of the aims of the sexual instincts in a world of strictures and temptations, meant that hysteria was itself symptomatic of a wider condition. When Freud told Elizabeth von R., at the end of her analysis, that

> we are not responsible for our feelings, and that her behaviour, the fact that she had fallen ill in these circumstances, was sufficient evidence of her moral character. (1955, p. 157)

it was more than a reassurance. Freud indicates here that the body is the site of needs, which we cannot negate, and it is the means by which we attempt to lead a moral life in the course of satisfying the demands of society. It is the body that bears the marks of failure in this struggle, which as symptoms are testimony to the stories that patients tell.

The reason for choosing to begin this section with psychoanalysis is that, apart from matters discussed previously, it dealt originally with the hysteric, the marginal person. Freud's later writings contained references either to others on the fringe of psychology's interest (e.g., the "pervert," the homosexual) or to matters that were declared marginal by virtue of their challenge to accepted beliefs about human nature (e.g., childhood sexuality). These points are sometimes coupled together in attempts to revise Freudian ideas, usually in order to deemphasize what have been seen as the biological, deterministic, and sexual nature of human beings. Criticizing these revisions, Jacoby (1975) talks of the values of neo-Freudians as being "scrubbed clean of their carnal and visceral origins" (p. 33). In a related argument, Holland (1977) views modern (i.e., post-Freudian) personality theorists as applying to their subject matter a principle of "positive generalisation"; this entails a shift of emphasis from the exceptional (neurotic) to the general (normal), and with that, a formulation of personality that either excludes or reduces the significance of the body. As already noted, Freudian theory is all too often cast in the role of the biological alternative to social psychological explanations. As a result, the body has been obscured, replaced by the biological–social opposition that can conceive only of bodies in general and of the mechanisms that constitute them.

What does psychoanalysis offer us, in the context of this discussion? It offers a view of people as moral beings, this morality being premised upon the meeting of desire and the social order. While the source of desire is within our physical makeup (and hence beyond psychology), its objects reside (though not exclusively) in the social world; while the social order is exercised through cultural and group practices, its effects are seen upon the body and through its conduct. These general statements summarize what Freud found in his treatment of his patients and in his attention to reminiscences simultaneously woven into moral tales and symbolized in bodily symptoms.

The Place of Women and Gender Relations

It is interesting to note that psychoanalysis begins with the treatment of women patients. This fact has been used to try to demonstrate that Freud's ideas are limited to a few middle-class people, in a city of dubious moral standards, in the nineteenth century. I want to argue, instead, that the attention that has been paid to the place of women in Western society has been aided by a recognition of bodily differences between the sexes and has helped to recover the body as a significant field of study for social scientists (Jacoby, 1975; Mitchell, 1974). The beginnings of psychoanalysis emerge from the people who suffer the repressions and dilemmas of their age—the women of the time. Given that Freud perceived the nature of desire as erotic, and that he saw the social structures that governed the behavior of the sexes as essentially repressive, the inequality of men and women was an important part of his writings and was to become an issue for feminists who were to come after him.

In a discussion of patriarchy, Turner (1984) summarizes the view that one main division of labor has been between the sexes: "men create enduring symbols, while women reproduce perishable bodies" (p. 116). The assumption of this basic inequality has extended to the ways in which (male) social scientists have conceptualized society, so that even Durkheim has been accused of having formulated his ideas to the exclusion of the situation of women (Gane, 1983). This realization does not precede, but follows, work formulating the place of women in society, using descriptions of women's bodily experience. Simone de Beauvoir has argued that

> The body of a woman—particularly that of a young girl—is a "hysterical"
> body, in the sense that there is, so to speak, no distance between the
> psychic life and its physiological realisation. (1972, p. 356)

By this, she means that women (a) are subject to bodily changes denied to men, (b) meet these changes with varying amounts of information, (c) are subject to privations because of these changes, and, as a consequence, (d) learn to value their bodies (and themselves) in particular ways. For example, the young girl's anatomy means that she has no direct knowledge of her "insides" and, at the time of menarche, is faced with a situation in which an unwanted change in her physical being is coupled with the knowledge that she is thereby made "unclean." This is one aspect of a life in which the young woman will learn to attend to her body in a way unknown to men. It is a "hysterical" body, in the sense that its changes and appearance will command her attention in relation to a male-dominated world that proscribes her activities on this basis:

> Because their bodily processes go with them everywhere, forcing them to juxtapose biology and culture, women glimpse every day a conception of another sort of social order. At the very least, since they do not fit into the ideal division of things (private, bodily processes belong at home), they are likely to see that the dominant ideology is partial; it does not capture their experience. (Martin, 1989, p. 200)

The debate about the place of women in society has inevitably centered upon the meaning of the anatomical difference between the sexes. In a world that bars women from certain occupations, and that places them in a subordinate position to men, the question arises, On what grounds are these distinctions to be made? The feminist movement has sought to show the role of biologist thinking in the advocacy of male superiority, which has pointed to the inherent weakness of the female body (so that women are not fitted for work), or to its unpredictability, which was thought to make women unreliable and irresponsible (Ussher, 1989). These judgments emanate from a patriarchy that did, and still does, find women, or rather women's bodies, dangerous. Historical analysis reveals that men have at various times equated women's sexuality with the devil's power and have seen the uterus itself as a magical threat to the male order (Shorter, 1984). In the nineteenth century, one response to women seen as deviant or difficult was to label them as suffering from the condition of the wandering womb—*hysteria*—and thereby to make the uterus a metonymic device for expressing all that was irrational, emotional, and ineffectual in their behavior. As Ussher (1989) points out, the effect of enforcing this category was to depoliticize the challenge that these women's outbursts or depressions expressed—in effect, to make "natural" something that was an aspect of social relations, and hence to make it signify nothing other than its own essential condition.

The designation of women's outbursts as hysterical symptoms partly lies in their being emotional—that is, expressed through the body. De Beauvoir compares these to the challenges of the male, which issue in a different use of the body:

> Even her outbursts of violence result from depths of resignation. When a boy revolts against his father, against the world, his violence is effective . . . he imposes himself upon the world, he transcends it. But it is not for the adolescent girl to impose herself, and this is what fills her heart with revolt . . . she can only destroy. There is desperation in her rage; when provoked she breaks glasses, window panes, vases—not indeed to conquer fate, but simply by way of symbolic protest. (1972, p. 377)

This description is not intended to endorse the containment of women within a pattern of behavior that it is their fate to enact; on the contrary, it reveals, through displaying the female condition, the form of relationship between men and women. This indicates the significance of the term *hysterical* as written in the first quotation taken from the work of de Beauvoir. It signifies at one time the situation of women and the means by which it is directly communicable, in the negation of the bodily condition to which society has allocated them. This is reflected in the space given by feminist scholars to women's experience of their bodies—to the menstrual cycle, pregnancy, sexual intercourse, sickness, attractiveness, and old age. No parallel literature exists (yet) for men because the masculine condition is to inhabit a world of their making, to transcend the privations of the body through work and politics. One contribution of feminist study, for social science, has been to unfold, through the stories that women tell of their embodied existence, the relationship of the sexes within society. This is done indirectly, in their own terms, by displaying the secondary place that women hold in the social order. It is only after this has been done that we are able to pose the general issues of gender relations. This is the message with which Martin (1989) concludes her analysis, in a chapter entitled "The Embodiment of Oppositions":

> We must not make the mistake of hearing the particularistic, concrete stories of these and other women and assume that they are less likely than more universalistic, abstract discourse to contain an analysis of society. It is up to anyone who listens to a woman's tale to hear the implicit message, interpret the powerful rage, and watch for ways in which the narrative form gives a "weighted quality to incident," extending the meaning of an incident beyond itself. (p. 201)

The task that Freud originally set himself, of interpreting the tale embodied in hysterical patients, is taken up by researchers who are attempting to unravel the stories told by any woman who ministers to the demands of a "hysterical" body in a patriarchal society (Bloch, 1987). Of course, there are other issues that arise out of feminist social science, although these are often grounded either in the debate about the legitimacy of the male–female biological distinction, or else make use of the language of the body (e.g., the phallus, the uterus) to symbolize the relations that they seek to make explicit. Upon reflection, it may be entirely consistent that social psychology, emerging as it did within ideologies framed by men, should have overlooked the body. Put another way, it is consistent with the view that the female body is the locus of irrationality and emotionality, a secondary feature in a world that prizes the competence of cognitions.

The Study of Crowds

Before leaving this topic, it is interesting to link it with one further marginal area of social psychology, the crowd. The study of crowds is as old as social psychology itself, and yet it remains a fringe interest in the discipline. Like the "hysterical" woman, the crowd has been regarded, following Le Bon (1896), as a mass of people who have surrendered themselves to their emotions. The image of the crowd as violent in its complaints, as irrational in its behavior, and as dependent upon the leadership of a strong man to guide it is not sustained by a reading of the history of social movements (Rudé, 1964). Nevertheless, these prejudices did and, one suspects, still do remain in the popular notions of the crowd as fickle and credulous. It continues to be an ambiguous entity in social psychology, so that, typically, students are told,

> Crowd behavior is characterised by suggestibility and irrationality, but this does not mean that crowds do not pursue primary objectives that might have some rational justification. Probably our greatest cause of confusion is our inability to predict the emergence or to explain the behavior of particular crowds. (Schellenberg, 1970, p. 211)

The search for rational justifications of such behavior are often in terms of the meanings that members of the crowd place upon their actions, a theoretical movement away from the physical setting that gives the problem its special significance. (See, for example, Marsh, Rosser, & Harré's 1978 analysis of the rules governing football hooliganism at British soccer games.) Instead of this approach, an examination of crowds in history (Rudé, 1964) shows that the destruction of property and the conduct of the crowd itself, as a body, indicate a form of protest not unlike that of the aforementioned "hysterical" women. By this, I mean that a study of what crowds do, the object of their actions, and the style of their conduct reveals a form of relationship to privileged sections of society that is unavailable to studies of them as rational individuals who just happen to express themselves as collectivities.

Moscovici (1985) has argued that the main model of social action in the crowd has been hypnosis, the technique by which individuals may be subjected to the influence of a dominant person. Instead of using the technique to remove a symptom, it is used in this context to engender a common frame of mind through the use of the body. Where symbols are deconstructed in psychoanalysis, they are subject to aggrandizement and mystification on occasions such as those that were organized by the Italian Fascist leader, Mussolini. Moscovici reminds us that these involved parades and assemblies in majestic squares, soliciting rhythmically chanted responses from huge crowds. The aim of these paraphernalia was, and in other countries continues to be, the subjugation of people by methods that engage them physically. The bodily condition of people in the crowd is both obvious in its importance and yet overlooked as well. The crowd remains on the margin of psychology because it does not readily yield to individual cognitive analyses, and unlike hysterics and women, it has no voice to speak of its situation. For this reason, the body of the masses remains obscure and, as part of this, the object of continuing prejudice, which ensures that its marginal status will continue.

Understanding the Sick Body

Disease is a universal phenomenon, but sickness is a cultural experience. In recent years, there has been a continuing effort to understand the situation of sick individuals, in order to place their condition within the scheme of social life. Virtually all of this work has been conducted by medical sociologists, working within a framework of interpretive research methodology (Anderson & Bury, 1988; Charmaz, 1983; Davis, 1963). The foci of these inquiries—talking to people about their symptoms and how they manage them in everyday life—lie well within the scope of social psychological research. The reason why it has been sociologists rather than social psychologists who have conducted the work is, arguably, that sociology has established theories of illness that do not rest upon the biological assumptions of the anatomists. By comparison, social psychology is still engaged in the process of working out the possible relationships between psychological and physiological variables, the latter taken at face value from the biological field. This is yet a further reflection of the different status of the body in the two disciplines. Where, in sociology, the body, as it is experienced, is being recovered as a datum (Freund, 1982; Turner, 1984), only exceptionally do social psychologists treat the sick body as other than the locus of physiological functions (Herzlich, 1973; Radley, 1988a). In this respect, psychological inquiries largely remain the handmaiden of medical ideology.

The view of physical symptoms as emerging ready-made, closed, and determinate has all but vanished from medical sociology. There is a recognition that the Cartesian heritage, by virtue of which it is impossible to speak of physical events and conscious experience in the same language, makes it impossible for us to hold a unitary view of illness. For example, in a detailed study of a set of symptoms known as "miner's nystagmus" (an involuntary oscillation of the eyes), it has been shown how this complaint was raised, contested, and negotiated within the sociolegal discourse of employment practice (Figlio, 1982). By carrying out a historical analysis of the relevant legal proceedings, it is possible to see how this particular condition was shaped by the medicolegal discourses of the day. Figlio argues that the practices associated with this discourse both discovered and envisaged the condition, as a result producing it as a discrete entity.

This form of historical analysis is rarely used by social psychologists, but it is significant in this context nonetheless. It offers a view of the body as engaged in particular social relationships (practices), which are themselves discerned through competing interpretations as to what the symptoms suffered by the body might mean. It also shows that the apportioning of life to preexisting symptoms on the one hand, and to social constructions or cognitions on the other, is inadequate in this regard. The Cartesian division into the (physiological) body on the one hand, and the mind of the free individual on the other, is an objectification of the situation through abstracting its components, and then seeing what impressions they make upon each other. This has the effect of obscuring and ultimately mystifying the problem (Young, 1980).

An example of the way that this objectification occurs has been given by Scott (1969) in his study of the socialization of the blind. He showed that workers for the blind hold that loss of sight is a severe condition, requiring that blind people submit themselves to a life of curtailed ambition. Their personal conceptions and their ways of understanding their lives through their experience of their incapacity are discredited by agency workers. This is followed by the blind being inducted into a program in which their bodily conduct is subordinated to an ideology of how the model blind person should act. In this way, the body may be deconstructed to enable it to embody a new ideology.

If social psychology is about how people live their lives, then suffering, disability, and overcoming disease are topics to which it should address itself; we have much to learn here. The debates within medical sociology are ongoing, though it appears that the significance of this field for the broader study of human relations is not in doubt:

> Sickness is not just an isolated event, nor an unfortunate brush with nature. It is a form of communication—the language of the organs—through which nature, society and culture speak simultaneously. The individual body should be seen as the most immediate, the proximate terrain where social truths and social contradictions are played out, as well as a locus of personal and social resistance, creativity and struggle. (Scheper-Hughes & Lock, 1987)

Marginal Status and the Body: A Summary

When introducing this section, I said that it would be concerned with topics on the fringe of social psychology. Those chosen for discussion are on the fringe, although they are in other ways very different from each other. Psychoanalysis has a unique relationship with psychology, both having provided it with a whole way of thinking about people and having achieved this via a methodology that psychology, in the main, has found not acceptable. The field of women's studies is no longer new, but it still has to establish its theoretical claims beyond the field of gender relations in general and of women in particular. In spite of being recognized as formative of the discipline, the study of crowds has remained peripheral as a topic for social psychological research. As for the sick body, this subject touches social psychology only as it is practiced by clinicians, and therefore, its influence upon the discipline is probably some way off, if it is to come about at all.

In spite of these differences, the four topics chosen share the common features of having addressed problems of people who are themselves marginalized within society, either as a whole or in some of its institutions. The mad, women, the crowd, and the sick are each in their turn subject to the organizing power of people to whom they stand in a subsidiary relationship. Of course, my reasons for selecting these particular topics, and not others, is that they serve my purpose of showing something of the place of the body in social life. Yet, they are not unrelated, because each one has shown that the study of the bodies of the people concerned has not been arbitrary.

Those concerned have presented themselves, in one way or another, as being salient members of society through a relation to it expressed in bodily terms. Hysterics symbolized the repressive nature of social life; women locate their conflicts with patriarchy in the reproductive functions of their bodies; the crowd revolts and protests through massing, moving against, and destroying; the sick, paradoxically, sometimes discover their social condition through the adjustments that they make to the demands of the healthy. In each case, the subsidiary relationship of these groupings is expressed, in part, through their ways of *embodying* it. There is an *immanence* in their relationships that appears not to characterize the dominant groupings, something that is falsified by reducing it either to anatomical functions or to personality characteristics of individuals or abstract groupings.

If we turn our attention to the dominant groupings implied by this analysis, we see immediately that the body appears to be different in each case. The rationality of the sane can be claimed by each one as a power, to be embraced as a credit to oneself. For the world of men, the body is a means to further ends, something to be transcended in the worlds of work and of political life. For the individual, the body is coextensive with the self, responsive and quiescent, as required. In the case of the healthy, the body is assumed, it is that which simply enables one to climb or run or work; in joining one to the world of health, it assumes a tacit existence. For these dominant groupings in society, the body would appear to be just such a tacit term, subsidiary to the ends that it enables them to reach. Note that this is a claim about the place of the body in the relationships between the groupings (sane/mad, men/women, sick/healthy), not about the experience of particular individuals. It suggests that the absence of the body from social psychology is not accidental, not an oversight, but a direct result of the discipline generalizing from the concerns of particular sections of society.

The form of this generalization is interesting. It is both inclusive and exclusive. By this, I mean that social psychology includes in its explanations the experience and behavior of these marginal groups; it does this by fiat. At the same time, it excludes the interests of these groups as they are expressed in terms of the means of expression at their disposal (e.g., the "outbursts" of the hysteric, the "emotionality" of women, the "irrationality" of the crowd, the "invalidism" of the sick). If, as we have seen so far, the body plays a key role in the relationships of these subsidiary groupings to society, then it is subject to a double exclusion—first as content and second (and more important) in its contribution to the form of this relationship. It is in terms of the latter, as the form through which the patient speaks, that psychoanalysis (i.e., as method) is unacceptable to psychology, as well as in terms of what the theory has to offer. Where the relationship also invites moral and political considerations, then traditional social psychology is faced with an increase in tension between the need to explain (include) and to minimize (exclude) the problems of these subsidiary groups. It is into the space created by this tension that a study of the body enters the debate.

The Way Forward: Recovering the Past

In this first chapter, I have tried to show, if this is not too clever a metaphor, that the ghost at social psychology's table is—the body. However, that body is not the one that is recognized as the legitimate field of study for physiologists. The idea of a biological substrate is the accepted view among social scientists, although it has not always been so. For that reason, the following chapter briefly examines some different ways in which the body has been ordered and experienced in the past and tries to indicate how the modern viewpoint came to be formed.

The modern position holds contradictory views about the body in psychological theory but attempts to resolve these in the acceptance of it as the locus of individual life and the material form of common humanity. As far as social psychology is concerned, the body is unique, as individuals are unique; it is common in the sense that it can be treated as a generalized entity. Neither of these views grasp the possibility that the body is also a social phenomenon. As the following chapters show, social psychology has purchased its sociality through trading the corporeal existence of its subject matter. It is this viewpoint—captured in the mental judgment of the social individual—that is threatened by the appearance of a *psychological body*, such as has been signaled in relation to certain marginal groupings. The threat to the traditional view lies not in the possibility of biologism but in the implications of a critical reappraisal of the subject that social psychology has assumed as its problematic. The task of this book is to explore this possibility further and to consider the implications of regarding the body with "a psychological eye."

In order to do this, the book uses the ideas presented so far to make a critical reexamination of some topics where traditional notions of the body either have been relied upon or have been allowed to continue undisturbed.

In each chapter, there is a review of the problem area, in order to see how and why the body has remained opaque. The intention is to make a series of excursions into the chosen topics, showing where and how a treatment of the body is essential to their explication. These excursions do not build up into a theory about the body as such, but reflected against one another, they point to the consequences for social psychology that the body's omission has brought about.

It is important to note that the word *body*, as a term held to describe an entity, a thing, is inadequate to our task. Already, the notion of *the body* as a generalized object has been rejected as the aim of our inquiry. This problem of terminology remains throughout the book. One reason for this is that each of the chapters tries to show, in its particular field, the ambiguities and tensions that have arisen through the inadequate conceptualization of the problem of embodiment. We cannot resolve these ambiguities and tensions here, if only because the book sets out primarily to display them, to open them up for critical inquiry. Therefore, it is sufficient to say that, when written in the following chapters, the words *the body* do not indicate a physiological entity, except where this is explicitly intended. In the light of this introduction, my purpose is not to try to fashion some new and unitary theory, but instead to go back over existing ground in order to (a) recover *the body* within social psychology, and (b) reveal the social psychology that its omission has consigned to the shadows.

Chapter 2

Subordination to a Democratic Eye

Students are used to being told that the separation of mind from body, and hence of psychology from physiology, was made decisive by Descartes, whose thinking allowed the body to be likened to a machine. While this is true, it also gives an impression too brief and too sudden to reflect the process by which the body would one day be placed outside of the reach of social psychological inquiry. In fact, the body continued to be of interest to scientists and philosophers alike in the two centuries that followed the work of Descartes. How it was of interest, and the progress of the investigations that it inspired, is the record of its transformation from significant figure to opaque background.

In 1775, Johann Lavater published a work setting out the study of individuals by physiognomic perception (Shortland, 1985). Physiognomy was defined as the mode of distinguishing a person's character by her or his outward appearance. It therefore stressed the surface qualities of the body and sought to make statements about what was "deep" and stable by the discovery of patterns and variations in what could be discerned by the eye of a skilled observer. In spite of Lavater's claims that "all parts of the body reflect all others to one who is observant enough to see" (Young, 1970, p. 14), these vague assertions were rejected by Gall, who nevertheless grasped the possible relation between surface sign and inner function. Young's (1970) analysis of the development of modern physiology is instructive, and I draw upon it to show the relationship between the emergence of this science and the fading of the body as a potential source of evidence. Gall is today remembered as the father of phrenology, and his reputation is tagged accordingly. However, as Young points out, he did attempt to replace speculatively derived, normative categories with faculties that could be observed in the underlying cerebral hemispheres. Gall's position, though preevolutionary, was that the brain was the proper seat of the mind. This organ, like others in the body, could and should be studied in order to understand its functional adaptedness to the environment. This way of thinking about adaptation set his psychology firmly in the category of biological science; mind, behavior, and character became functions of the brain. These functions were conceived upon faculties, with all the limitations of circular thinking that this involves. Nevertheless, they were envisaged by Gall as multiple and localized, enabling him to consider each faculty in relation to its "organ" in the brain and to its interactions with the environment.

Gall's work is significant, not just because it was central to the development of neurophysiology, but also because it emphasized the brain (via the surface of the skull) over against the body as a whole, *in the perception of the observer*. Where Lavater's physiognomy involved claims about the possibilities of becoming a skilful practitioner of the art of interpreting character (Shortland, 1985), the science of physiology restricted both the object of investigation and the form of observation possible. For a considerable time afterward, the dominance of the scientific attitude would ensure that debates about ways of seeing would be muted in the circles of psychological and physiological inquiry. Instead, the debate would center upon the functions of the brain, whether these should be seen as localized or residing in a unity of action. This debate was, for a time, conducted on the basis of the Cartesian doctrines of feudalism and the unity of the soul. These were no longer applied to the body as a whole but to the brain as the center of the nervous system. Flourens, whose career began as Gall's ended, held to a unity of the soul, which credited it with primary powers as opposed to sense-derived qualities, and these he projected onto a brain that must, therefore, also work as a unit. The subsequent history of the development of mind–brain research is one of the retreat of the soul from its seat in the body, thence to the nervous system, thence to the cerebral hemispheres, and lastly from the corporeal body entirely. This was a result of progress made in the experimental study of the sensorimotor function of the nerves in particular, allowing the brain to be conceived as being no different in kind from the remainder of the nervous system. By the end of the nineteenth century, a situation had been established in which knowledge had advanced to a point where "instead of allowing psychological categories to dictate to the brain, the categories of physiological analysis dictated that all thought and behavior were the result of the association and combination of sensory and motor sub-strata" (Young, 1970, p. 31). Not only had the "body surface" of the physiognomists and the "brain surface" of Gall (and phrenologists) been rejected, but the "deep" structures discerned by the anatomists had supplanted the categories of the earlier primitive psychology. In effect, the relative emphases upon psychological and brain categories were almost completely reversed, in the course of which the body, as a unity with a surface, effectively disappeared from view as a figure in its own right.

Young's account of the mind–brain debate during the eighteenth and nineteenth centuries documents how phrenology, though rejected in the form in which Gall presented it, nevertheless continued to influence the thinking of the physiological researchers who came after him. However, it was not in terms of the surface qualities of the body that the debate would be conducted. The possibilities of cerebral localization were taken up by Herbert Spencer, for whom the fitness of particular organs for their special function was commensurate with his views about the organismic relationship between body and society.

> We commonly enough compare a nation to a living organism. We speak of "the body politic", of the functions of its several parts, of its growth, and of its diseases, as though it were a creature. But we usually employ these expressions as metaphors, little suspecting how close is the analogy, and how far it will bear carrying out. So completely, however, is a society organised upon the same system as an individual being, that we may almost say there is something more than analogy between them. (Quoted in Young, 1970, p. 160)

The historical advance of society from its lowest to its highest stages was compared by Spencer to the process whereby the nervous system becomes differentiated as a result of its adaptation to the world. In this way, self-sufficiency, greater power, a higher moral sense, and distinct function occur together as part of a general process of "individuation." Underlying this process was the principle of adaptation, the survival of that which is most fitted to the function. Spencer believed that what he called the "experiences of utility" of past generations had produced modifications to the nervous system; these would be inherited by people in society as faculties of moral intuition, whose basis was therefore in the race rather than in the individual alone. These ideas of evolutionary associationism were significant in bringing together the tenets of inherited biological endowment together with sensationism; they provided the foundation for reflexology in psychology and, through the correcting ideas of Darwin, the establishment of what today is called "sociobiology." More to the point, Spencer shifted the analysis of experience from the individual to the race. In a reference to Condillac's method of speculatively adding senses to a statue of the human form, Young (1970, p. 178) quotes Baldwin as saying that Spencer replaced "Condillac's individual human statue by a racial animal colossus." That is to say, the nature of inquiry into the adaptation of the nervous system would no longer be by reference to the individual body, but to characteristics of the species. Once the broad function of the nerves and cerebral hemispheres had been established, this would enable the erection of a psychology that utilized comparisons across the nervous systems of different species. Within this psychology, there could be no place for the individual body as datum; its surface was penetrated and its unity destroyed by a view that had established a parallelism of mind and body and had given precedence to the latter.

Later on in this chapter is a review of the historical context in which the body is subject to analysis and reinterpretation. For the moment, it is again worth noting that the changing status of the body in psychology is tied up with changes in how people *see* the world and themselves within it. People's bodies were always there to be seen, but *how* they were seen, and by whom, was affected by the preconceptions of those who sought to establish a science of human behavior. At first glance, it may seem odd that the disappearance of the body from serious investigation presaged the disappearance of mind from scientific inquiry. However, once we are reminded that behaviorism grew out of American functionalist thought and comparative physiological research, it follows that what was to be observed by the new psychology was not even the anatomical body as a whole. Instead, the individuation of responses (to coin a Spencerian expression) required that specific movements be logged in relation to specific stimuli in the environment. The use of animals kept in restricted environments facilitated the narrowing of the psychologists's gaze upon those particular muscular contractions that were the object of training or observation.

Watsonian behaviorism's reliance upon psychophysical parallelism meant that the body, for a comparatively short period of time, reappeared as the repository of nervous and mental phenomena in harmony. This harmony was not to last for long. By 1919, Watson's erstwhile student Karl Lashley had shown that the thesis of there being definite connections in the brain could be disproved, as parts of the brain may take over the functions of other parts that have been damaged. Lashley later used a term (introduced by Flourens many years earlier) to describe this mass action of the brain—*equipotentiality*. At about the same time, Coghill (1929) published a book arguing that discrete responses emerge out of more complex responses by a process of individuation. The term did not have the same meaning as it had for Spencer; indeed, it questioned the idea of learning being a process of the addition or complication of associated responses. The idea of the working body as an assembly of discrete movements was under attack from several quarters. Bartlett (1932) had borrowed a concept from Henry Head, the British neurophysiologist, who was critical of the localization thesis. He had proposed instead that the central nervous system (CNS) models posture through the organization of what he termed a *schema*. Bartlett used this term to describe the organized set of attitudes that are involved in remembering, an activity that he proposed to be constructive. In an attack upon both faculty psychology and associationism, Bartlett argued that remembering, as with acting, involves the schemata in a whole, organized response, not in the resuscitation of specific traces in the brain or elsewhere. However, this whole response must involve more than the nervous system, as was then being argued by G. H. Mead, from the position of a "social behaviorist":

> Now behavioristic psychology, instead of setting up these events in the central nervous system as a causal series which is at least conditional to the sensory experience, takes the entire response to the environment. . . . It does not locate the experience at any point in the nervous system. . . . What the behaviorist does, or ought to do, is to take the complete act, the whole process of conduct, as the unit in his account. (1934, p. 111)

However, both Bartlett's and Mead's ideas were to have to wait some time until they were granted full attention. Even then, they were used to develop theories of a cognitive (Neisser, 1967) and of a symbolic interactionist (Lindesmith & Strauss, 1968) kind, respectively.

Meanwhile, psychology was to concern itself with variants of the debate concerning the relationships among stimuli, responses, and physiological conditions, such as drives. In all of this, the body remained a substrate for the individual movements under investigation. Indeed, with the failure to establish reliable connections between the mental and physical phenomena under study, the physiological evidence was declared irrelevant to proper scientific psychological analysis (Skinner, 1938). While not accepted by all researchers, this recommendation meant that the body was seen less as the natural and required support for psychological inquiry, and more as a separate field of study for physiologists. Any harmony between body and mind would, from then on, have to be recognized as a working assumption, rather than being claimed as the basis of empirical research. This did not prevent research continuing into the interactions between the physiological body and mental (and social) life, but it then proceeded on the basis of an agenda set by the findings of the neurophysiologists. For example, what began as experiments into cerebral dominance (Sperry, 1961) were transformed into speculations as to the differing life-styles of individuals considered as either "right-" or "left-brained" people (Ornstein, 1977).

To summarize, research into the nervous system resulted in a change in the way in which the body was perceived. From the standpoint of the (male) observer, this meant that his eye penetrated its surface to grasp the structures inside, particularly those deemed to be the location of mental life. The idea of looking on the body was superseded, so that it became instead a container of the active processes under study. This had the effect of making it into a thing, albeit a thing of a special kind. Perhaps this would be clearer to us today if we remind ourselves that it was not only the abstract mind, conceived of by philosophers, that became displaced; it was also the person who inhabited each particular body so considered who was effectively dis-located. The body of the anatomists was (and is) an objectified entity, a neutral, passive, and sometimes dead lump of material to be dissected and analyzed. When we speak today of "the body," it is to this generalized entity, abstracted from any particular personality, that we usually refer. In the realm of anatomy, on the operating table, in the clinic or laboratory, all bodies are equal in principle. However, it was not always so.

The Household, the Body, and the Public Domain

In this section, we have to go quite outside the bounds of social psychology to get a new line on the problem. As was pointed out at the beginning of this chapter, there are no ready-made concepts of the body to which social psychologists can link their knowledge, except those put forward in physiological terms. It is for this reason that it is necessary to survey the wider arena in which the concept of the neutral, equal body actually contradicted everyday thinking.

In the Athens of ancient Greece and at the center of the Roman Empire, ideas of equality existed alongside the practice of keeping slaves. For the Greeks, and for the Romans who came after them, this gross contradiction was premised upon a separation between the realms of the household and that of public life, the *polis* (Arendt, 1959). The household was the location for satisfying the needs of life itself, through the efforts of the man to sustain those under his roof, and through the woman's labors to reproduce the species. Arendt points out that the driving force of the household was necessity; to meet these basic needs, its members contributed according to their position in the age–sex matrix. The household was therefore accepted as a place of inequalities, reflected in the asymmetrical relationships between its members (e.g., man–woman, parent–child, brother–sister). By comparison, the *polis* was the sphere of freedom, accessible to men who had achieved health and wealth, in which they were free from the arbitrary rule of other people. Where the *polis* recognized freedom and equality, the household acknowledged the strictest inequality and the use of violence where deemed necessary (e.g., over women and slaves) to master necessity. This absolute distinction between the public and the private realms is a feature that has been transcended in modern times. Nevertheless, its relevance for understanding some of the paradoxes generated by current thinking about equality and the human body become clear by the end of this chapter. For the moment, we should note that what is being described here about the public and the private realms is not limited to ancient Greece or Rome alone. It has been argued, on the basis of anthropological data, that such a clear separation is characteristic of collectivist groups. Where high status is assigned to the public realm, and where this is populated by men, the house is seen as a "container" of women and goods, and therefore is to be avoided by the men wherever possible (Duncan, 1981). It is only as part of the process of individuation that the social sphere penetrates the home, so that it becomes a legitimate place for men to be and the house a status symbol for men to work on in order to improve its appearance for others.

These comments (elaborated upon in Chapter 7) show the need for us to loosen our modern assumptions about the place of people in the home, and about the home's place in society, if we are to grasp how relevant the body once was in signifying people's lives and prospects. The distinction between the public and the private realms once signified a clear distinction between those things that should be shown and those things that should be hidden. Arendt argues that the things that should be hidden comprised all things "serving the subsistence of the individual and the survival of the species" (1959, p. 64). It was the bodily part of human existence that needed to be hidden away in the household, which meant the women who gave birth and the slaves who attended to the needs of their masters and mistresses. Although in the modern age, the home has come to mirror the public domain and, in its turn, society has focused upon matters that were once regarded as highly intimate (sexual behavior being the prime example), it is still the necessities of bodily life that command strict privacy.

There is a further distinction that Arendt makes, between what she terms the "work of the hands" and the "labor of the body." This is relevant to the discussion of the separation of the public and the private realms because it is labor that is characteristic of how people must function in the cause of satisfying the necessities of life. Whereas *work*, as the term is used here, denotes an activity leading to a finished object, *labor* always signifies the process itself, of producing and/or consuming in the service of basic needs. Although modern usage of these two terms often confuses the distinction being made (notably the assimilation of mechanized work into labor), *labor* is still appropriate for such activities as chopping wood, hoeing a field, household chores, and, in its condensed meaning, the act of giving birth. The linking of the body with labor says more than that people labor with their whole bodies rather than with their hands, as does a watchmaker or a nurse checking a patient's pulse. It signifies a particular *mode* of action, of being, in which the person's activity is entrained with material changes in the world in a cyclical way. Not only is the activity circular, requiring repetition (e.g., feeding, cleaning), but it requires an engagement with one's own and other people's bodies, which marks it as basic and the individual as tied to its cyclical demands. The necessities of life impinge upon the body and are serviced through it being lent by people, to the amelioration of their discomfort.

It was to escape the privations of necessity, with which the household was identified, and to demonstrate publicly that one could do so that men in ancient times entered the realm of the *polis*. Slaves were appropriated in order to exclude labor from the conditions of free men and their families, and it was justified on these grounds. What condemned the slave to being regarded by the Greeks as somewhat less than human was not his or her bodily condition or outward appearance as such, but the condition of being tied to necessity. There were also other consequences of being condemned to the household. Slaves and women were less visible, and to the extent that their lives were filled only with bodily labor, they left no trace of their having been in the world.

The labor of the body was not productive of lasting artifacts or knowledge; these things were the stuff of the public realm, in which men strove through rhetoric and practice to make an individual mark upon their world. The *polis* was predicated upon the equality of its participants; the "body politic" supplanted, in their lives, the "body natural." Yet, this equality presupposed not only the inequality in the household, but also the existence of the majority of people as unfree, as tied to ministering to the basic needs of life. The contradictions inherent in discerning the uniformity of human-kind as a species and the distinctions drawn among peoples of different social, gender, and racial types are seen here in origin, though they extend right through the Renaissance up to and including the present day (Leach, 1982). Questions of freedom and of justice are modern issues too, not only because slavery still exists, but because age-old inequalities in the household became insupportable as the public realm penetrated further into the home (Harris, 1977). As for slavery in the New World, the household came to embrace within its boundaries the people who were subject to, but had not been part of the home. Some former slaves became voluntary retainers and quasi relatives of the host family in a fashion that suited both parties. However, the kinship terms sometimes used for them (e.g., "child" or "nephew"), which denote nurture and closeness to modern Westerners, convey authority and subordination in Africa and elsewhere (Kopytoff, 1982). The modern view of the household, as of the body, is a particular one; more than that, the two have been subject to some common influences during the course of social change.

The view of the body that we gain from Arendt's analysis is very different from that produced by scientific research in the eighteenth and nineteenth centuries, supported by the structure and values of modern society. The body appears as a locus of need and desire and as a site of unrelenting demands from which people are enabled, to different degrees, to release themselves. In the establishment of inequalities lies the basis for distinct experiences of bodily practices and for different social identities to be distinguished therein. Certainly, this analysis is aided by considering civilizations where the separation of household from political/public life is relatively clear, though I argue that the body also matters in modern life, albeit in a different way. As a qualification of what has been said so far about slavery, it is important to realize that there have been, and perhaps will be, several different forms of this condition. If, as Arendt argues, slavery was, for the Greeks and the Romans, a means of freeing themselves from necessity, it was not so for the merchants and cotton growers of the American South. Slave labor was integral with the emergence of an economic system based upon the acquisition of private property and the expansionist claims of the European states. In this scheme of things, the privacy of the body did not derive from its location in the household, but from the identification of one's body with the notion of private property. Just as we can appreciate the contradiction produced in the ancient Greek view of equality predicated upon the body free from necessity (when applied to people in general), so we can see the paradox in which the runaway slave Jim is caught, when he says to Huck Finn, "Yes—en I's rich now, come to look at it. I owns mysef, en I's wuth eight hund'd dollars. I wisht I had de money, I wouldn' want no mo'" (Mark Twain, 1953, *Huckleberry Finn*, p. 54).

For Marx (1977), the capitalist system had produced the "working man [sic]" as a being who, in being estranged from his product, was also estranged from his body. Formulated as alienation, this described a condition in which man was not only torn away from the product of his labor, but was constituted only as a worker who maintained himself as a physical subject. Far from the ideal of man acting freely as a member of a species in company with other men, estrangement reflected a relationship of servitude in which work—what should be his essential being—becomes a mere means to his physical existence. While the use of the term *labor* in Marxian analysis is not to be confused with the special meaning given to it by Arendt in her discussion of "the labor of the body," both of these authors point to the body being contingent upon social relationships that involve the material world.

At this point, it is sufficient to note that talk of slavery and of servitude do not so much denote particular topics for consideration, as it alerts us to the need to see people's lives as being shaped by, and in turn shaped through, their different bodily activities. It also points up the need to relinquish our conviction that, where people acknowledge that they all share the same kind of body (i.e., belong to the same species), they must treat each other as if they were of the same order of humanity. History teaches us that this is not so; even Marx benefited from the labor of his servants. This brings further into question the usefulness, for social psychology, of the notion of a generalized, commonly held, and ready-made body acting either as a passive medium (for thinking through) or as an unpredictable source of our animal nature (to control, or to give in to).

Medicine, Sickness, and the Anatomy of Disease

There are few times when people are more aware of their body than when they are ill. For this reason, the growth in medical sociology in recent years has directed attention to the need for explanations that can embrace both bodily ailments and bodily decay within social theory. Earlier approaches to the problem of sickness treated it as just another aspect of social life. A more radical standpoint has been proposed, which turns the relationship between medicine and sociology on its head (Turner, 1987). The traditional view sees sickness as beginning in physical ailments, and these ailments as being responded to and treated in a social context. From this alternative position, society is seen as providing the context within which changes to the body are sensed and then interpreted as symptoms calling for treatment. So, for example, whether individuals see a particular change or perturbation as something requiring a physician's attention is a matter both of cultural norms and of the degree to which the change can be accommodated within one's personal life (Zola, 1973). The symptoms or diagnoses do not have an a priori existence, even though in everyday life, people might speak of them in that way. This has been made clear as a result of historical analyses, showing that the emergence of a stable view of the anatomical body was a product of changes in the power and the knowledge structures of society over time (Foucault, 1973). It is on this basis that Turner (1987) suggests that the conventional view, that medical sociology came after the emergence of medicine as a unitary practice, is incorrect. Instead, it is possible to argue that medicine as a discipline grew out of social practice. We have already seen that the emergence of the neurological system as the seat of mind came about in relation to ideas about character and society. This was part of the wider movement during the eighteenth and nineteenth centuries, in which there was a change in the relationship between the suffering of people and the expertise of physicians. This, in turn, brought about changes in the way that people thought about their bodies, and, in effect, it formed the basis for the everyday notions on which social psychology came to base its research.

The story of illness during the past 200 years is one of a movement away from focusing on the corrupt body toward the linking of specific signs with internal lesions. The term *corrupt body* derives from the fact that, in earlier times, the ravages of plague and of smallpox left a visible transformation upon the body of its victims (Herzlich & Pierret, 1987). Sickness was seen as misfortune and was the reward for living a sinful life, so that redemption came through bodily suffering. This belief was not limited to the misfortunes heaped upon one's own body; after an accident in which his daughter had been badly burned, one nineteenth century father is quoted as saying, "Alas, for my sins the just God throws my child into the fire!" (de Mause, 1974).

Whereas today, people go to the physician for the relief of pain, in earlier centuries, they consulted a doctor to find comfort in their suffering. In a study of German women patients in the eighteenth century, Duden (1985) reports that they used the doctor's consultation as a confessional, so that by pouring out their story to him, they might gain further strength to bear their ills. These women had a language of pain and of what we would call "symptoms," but these symptoms did not connote a specific disease entity. At this time, there were several competing ideas about disease, its causes, and its cures, so that the doctor and the afflicted person negotiated a view of what the ailment meant and what should be done about it. Just as there were many theories of disease, so there were doctors who held onto different beliefs about its causes and cures. This meant that medicine at the end of the eighteenth century was as yet without the consensus, and hence the authority, that it commands today. In fact, the physician was in the position of having to win "the favours of his patron by individually proving his personal and professional suitability in the context of a primary face-to-face relationship" (Jewson, 1976). A successful consultation took the form of the doctor offering back to his client a recognizable and acceptable image of the condition as experienced. This meant taking into account the social and personal context that the illness embodied, so that the physician engaged a "sick person," not a specific disease.

Duden remarks that the story told by, for example, the cobbler's wife embodied a different experience from that of the lady at court; the state of people's (sick) bodies was inseparable from their status. The physician did not, and could not, separate the person from his or her condition (Herzlich & Pierret, 1987). This meant that even a century after Harvey published his studies of the workings of the heart, physicians who acknowledged his ideas were still in the position of prescribing treatments for patients for whom the "thickness," "curdling," and "movement" of the blood were linked to their feelings and daily concerns (Duden, 1985). The knowledge that the anatomists had made available could not be utilized within the existing form of physician–patient relationship; other changes had to come about before this could occur.

All this was to change with the adoption, in the late eighteenth century, of new techniques of observation and palpation of the body. These new clinical techniques, coupled with developments in the study of anatomy, were paralleled by the emergence of the hospital clinic as the base from which medicine was administered. The new knowledge of the inside of the body went hand in hand with changes in the doctor–patient relationship. Included in these latter changes was the move from "bedside" to "hospital" medicine (Jewson, 1976), establishing the clinic both as a center of occupational innovation (hence, high status), and as a means of surveilling and controlling people's lives through ordering their bodies (Armstrong, 1983). As a result, the ailing person was constituted as passive in relation to the authority of the physician's new skills, and the modern role of "patient" was established. These new skills concerned the diagnosis of specific diseases, each of which was to be located at some specific point in the anatomical structure. Diagnosis and pathology replaced experience and biography, opening the patient's body to the eye of the physician, while simultaneously abstracting it from the situated context of the sick person. The views of sick people about their condition became secondary, as did the conception of a personal body integral with the social world. In their place came the basis of medicine that we know today—pathological anatomy—and a conception of *the* body as a generalized space or medium in which could be plotted the newly classified diseases.

However, it is not true that anatomical knowledge simply followed changes in, or was integral with the emerging physician–patient relationship. Harvey had published his revolutionary ideas about the heart and movement of the blood in 1628, prior to the changes in medical practice, and foreshadowing the displacement of the doctor's gaze from the outside to the inside of the body. In an interesting analysis, Romanyshyn (1982) points out that Harvey's findings rested upon the observation that the septum between the two ventricles was occluded, thus dividing the heart in two and allowing it to pump "used" blood and oxygenated blood separately. Prior to this, and even for a time afterward, it was believed that the heart was a site for the transformation of venous into arterial blood, from which it would ebb and flow in the

body. The existence of interventricular pores in the septum was believed
to play a key part in this exchange. Harvey's demonstration of their absence
was material both to the downfall of this belief and to the establishment of
the thesis that the blood circulates around the body.

What Romanyshyn is keen to point out is that Harvey's work contributes
to a change in how people would come to see the world, not just the human
body. With respect to the latter, however, Harvey's vision is one of a heart
that is no longer unitary, but divided and acting as a pump, as if it were part
of a machine. This view shifts the gaze toward and highlights the location of
differences inside the body, which is now apprehended as a thinglike entity.
Simultaneously, Romanyshyn argues, differences once visible *between*
people in how they lived in the world, were relocated to differences *in* their
anatomy. We expand on this point later on in our discussion. At this point,
we need to note that what was occurring with Harvey's vision was repeated
later in the changes in medical practice; there was a shift in how people saw
themselves as human beings. The interiorization of life, its relocation inside
the body, meant that when differences appeared inside that space—differences of function, of disease—the ways in which people were distinguished
in how they lived out their lives were rendered equal. We have here another
version of the movement away from the body as a visible and living unity,
toward the apprehension of variation in the functioning of a generalized
physical entity, belonging to any-body.

Before leaving Harvey's work, it is worth noting a parallel between the
progress in his thinking and that in research on neuropsychology, as outlined earlier on. There, it is remembered, the trend was a continual retreat
from the privileged status accorded to the brain; from being the seat of the
soul, and hence regarded as essentially unitary in function, the brain came
to be seen in terms of the workings of the nerves and was ultimately understood as an aggregate of sensorimotor functioning. In a similar way, we are
told that Harvey revised his ideas in a later publication so that the heart no
longer held a privileged place in relation to the blood. Romanyshyn argues
that this occurred at the same time as the deposition of Charles I as King
of England, who claimed to rule by divine right. Reflected against one
another, these two events suggest that ideas about the body—physical,
royal, political—were in mutual transition. Speculations about this, however, cannot detain us at this point; what is important to note, nevertheless,
is that research and practice, which opened the body, divided, and appor-
tioned its functions, and demonstrated its machinelike status, made it impossible for people to continue to use it, to think of it, and some might say
to live in it, in ways that they had done previously.

From this brief overview, it is possible to see what Turner (1987) means
when he says that medicine and sociology emerged together out of common concerns and practices. The knowledge of the body as a system of
discrete and interconnected organs, subject to specific and classifiable
lesions, went hand in hand with the establishment of a medical profession.

Organized within hospitals, medicine disseminated research and clinical findings throughout a hierarchy of positions and rapidly elaborated into a number of specializations reflecting the new analytical view of the body. Following this line of thinking, it is easy to see why we should be critical of the assumption that the body is invested with a reality that is pregiven. In a similar vein, Armstrong (1983) goes on to make precisely the opposite point to that contained in this everyday assumption:

> The fact that the body became legible does not imply that some invariate biological reality was finally revealed to medical enquiry. The body was only legible in that there existed in the new clinical techniques a language by which it could be read. The anatomical atlas directs attention to certain structures, certain similarities, certain systems, and not others and in so doing forms a set of rules for reading the body and for making it intelligible. . . . In effect, what the student sees is not the atlas as a representation of the body but the body as a representation of the atlas. (p. 2)

Just as the program of scientific research diverted attention from the surface of the body to the nervous system, particularly the brain, so medical practice rendered the whole body opaque through the gaze into its interior. What became visible were the signs (symptoms) of classified diseases, figured against the background of a body whose owner's experience of it was now irrelevant. What became invisible, or rather difficult to apprehend or to express in a medical setting, was the person's experience of life within his or her body. Today, this situation has changed once more, with the reemergence of the patient's view (Armstrong, 1984). However, for the purposes of this argument, it is possible to see once again that "the body" that social psychology might study and explain is not a stable entity, but only becomes something that the discipline can address once it is accepted as an ontological problem. Indeed, rather than an entity or a topic, the body would seem to be more like an arena of experience and debate. However, this is too early a point in our analysis to discuss the potential offered by this prospect. Instead, we need to pick up the historical thread once again, but this time with respect to how changing conceptions of the body have involved the transformation of perspectives upon it. What were these perspectives, and how does the term *perspective* itself figure in the way that we take the body as given?

From Microcosm to Point of View

The medieval conception of the human body derived from the parallel that the Greeks had drawn between it and the cosmos; the unity of the cosmos lay in its bodily (animate) form, which aggregated its multiple elements, while the corporeal aspect of people was understood as a composite of the elements of which they were made up. While there were several forms of this microcosmic metaphor of the body, it remained as a dominant theme in the work of Renaissance thinkers. Barkan (1975) quotes Plato, who spoke of the heart "as the guardroom," from which the different parts could be alerted if threats arose, and which could act "as the noblest part to be leader among them all." By comparison, the stomach is "a manger" where the appetite is located like "a beast untamed" and is stationed far from the head so that it causes the least "tumult and clamour." Barkan notes that Plato thereby represents the body as a little world of conflicting powers, a forerunner of the image of *discordia concors* that would be dominant in the thought of the Middle Ages. This view of the body as uniting, harmoniously, a multiplicity of elements was achieved through figuring it via the analogous part of the cosmos. For example, quoting from Jacob Boehme (1575–1624), Barkan notes that the flesh signifies the earth "congealed and without motion; so the flesh hath no reason but is moved only by the power of the stars, which reign in the flesh and veins" (1975, p. 41–42). This view emphasizes the unchanging relations between body and universe and was part of the effort of medieval science to place humanity within the cosmic hierarchies. With the emergence of empirical science in the seventeenth century, this hierarchical vision was to decline, although the microcosmic metaphor continued to play a part in the re-envisioning of nature, which followed. George Herbert (1593–1633) could still express the relationship between body and cosmos as one of mutual support (from "Man," in Gardner, 1972):

> Man is all symmetrie
> Full of proportions, one limb to another,
> And to all the world besides:
> Each part may call the furthest, brother:
> For head with foot hath private amitie,
> And both with moons and tides

The way in which the cosmos and the body continued to act as metaphors for each other were by figuring their union with the world in terms of mortality and change. Leonardo da Vinci used aspects of the natural world to describe the movements of the blood, being an example of the increasing awareness upon change in the universe. As a counterpoint to this, the orderliness observed within a world of change was similarly figured. Attention has been drawn to William Harvey's dedication of his *De Motu Cordis* to King Charles I:

> The heart of animals is the foundation of their life, the sovereign of everything within them, the sun of their microcosm, that upon which all growth depends, from which all power proceeds. The King, in like manner, is the foundation of his kingdom, the sun of the world around him, the heart of the republic, the fountain whence all power, all grace doth flow. (Quoted in Barkan, 1975, p. 44)

Discerning motion and stability was a project of Renaissance thinking, in which the findings of the new empirical sciences were made sensible within the microcosmic metaphor. The result was an elaboration of the analogy between body and cosmos (and vice versa), as part of which the complexities and uncertainties about the universe became the condition of humanity too. When John Donne wrote that, if man is a world, "himself will be the land, and misery the sea" and "his matter is earth, his form misery" (from Meditation VIII), he was illuminating the way in which not only nature, but also "society is as fragile as the individual body, and the body is as prone to internal discord as society" (Barkan, 1975, p. 50). The inclusion, by analogy, of the newfound variability of the world into the body rendered it multiple, and thence potentially disordered and subject to inner conflict. As the reciprocal aspect of the metaphor, the ailments of the body could then stand for the condition of society, so that the idea of an unhealthy commonwealth became more than a poetic allusion; it indicated a social condition apprehended as real. As mentioned earlier in this chapter, by the time Herbert Spencer wrote, the analogy of society with body could be used as a unifying concept in the emergence of a theory of behavior.

The rise of empirical science did not result in a simple displacement of one way of thinking about the body by another. As shown previously, the new findings were first comprehended within and then ultimately transformed the microcosmic metaphor that had held the body within a certain scheme of things. That certainty was replaced by an *un*certainty about the place of humanity in the world. In spite of this, or perhaps because of it, the relationship of people with God was to be sought through the reunification of their complexity, a reappreciation of the *discordia concors*. This was achieved during the Renaissance by the outward expression of the human being as the measure of things, in the practical aesthetic of architecture. It was believed that harmony of form, of proportion, was to be found in the human body, and that its appreciation was an inborn sense. Architecture aimed at an expression of this form, and the satisfaction of a sense that went beyond the aesthetic to the religious. As Barkan notes,

> According to this vision, man's life requires a synthesis of the senses which is man's only means of knowing God. The church building is a man-made leviathan requiring all human skills in its construction and necessitating complementary skills in the observer. Thus the observer becomes himself an image of *discordia concors*, for all his varied capacities and senses are individually reached as he reads the church, which is a reading of his own body, in turn a replica of the cosmos (1975, p. 140).

Two ideas are introduced in this quotation, which are clues to a change that occurred in the way in which the body was apprehended. The ideas are contained in the words "observer" and "read," suggesting first the body as a locus, second the act of interpretation, and, common to both, the ascendance of the visual sense. The change to which they refer is a compound one, for it arguably involved both transformations in *the way* that people saw, and in the elevation of *seeing* as the primary mode of knowing (McLuhan, 1962). In medieval times, the sense of proportion alluded to in the preceding quotation was achieved by allowing light to shine *through* the windows that pierced the stone of the Gothic church. This "pierced technique" was compared by McLuhan to the exegesis of a scribal culture, which sought to release the meaning from the text, not to read meaning into it. So, in the Gothic church, light appears as an active principle, bathing the stone and the congregation together in the contemplation of their harmonic proportions. This quality of light *through* is contrasted by McLuhan to that of ecclesiastical architecture after Gutenburg (i.e., with the arrival of a visual culture), where light was shed *on* the church's interior so as to illuminate the objects it contained. This raised intensity of light, he argues, was essential to the emerging modern age, which sought to discern things and to read the relationships among them. Where the medieval room was comfortable (in a sense, meaningful) in terms of its proportions, its materials, and its form, the modern room could become so only inasmuch as, becoming a container, it could be filled with certain objects or activities.

The preceding distinction is between two different modes of being in the world, not just two ways of seeing things. Its relevance for a study of the body within psychology is that it alerts us to how our way of knowing ourselves as embodied beings has been transformed, producing an object for examination that appears ready-made. Perhaps the most documented change in ways of seeing during the Renaissance was the formulation of the technique of perspective drawing. This is the method often taught in schools today as the proper way to represent the world. Perspective drawing is part of the movement toward light being shed *on* things, which presupposes an observer as the active principle, who fills the space with objects. The rules for such a drawing were set out by the Florentine architect Alberti (1404–72), who wrote,

> In the first place, when we look at a thing, we see it as an object which occupies a space [so that when it is to be represented,] ... First of all, on the surface on which I am going to paint, I draw a rectangle of whatever size I want, which I regard as an open window through which the subject to be painted is seen; and I decide how large I wish the human figures in the painting to be. (Quoted in Alpers, 1983, p. 42)

The Albertian view begins with an observer, whose existence is assumed as prior to the picture, and from whose viewpoint the picture is then constructed. With the emergence of empty spaces to be filled with objects was coupled the appearance of the perceiver who defined his or her standpoint relative to them. The movement from the classical to the modern age produces the individual as subject, for whom a place must now be found relative to changing points of view. This focused attention upon the perceiver's intentions, skills, and techniques, which themselves needed to be located in the picture of the world. It also created the modern idea of the individual as subject and object, and it allowed for the development of the human sciences that would follow (Foucault, 1973).

It is important to note that this change did not happen everywhere at the same pace, or even in the same manner. In northern Europe, Holland particularly, artists embraced a mode of seeing that was made available by the *camera obscura*, informed by the writings of Kepler. In a closed and darkened room, light rays passing through a small hole produced an inverted image of the outside world upon the far wall. For Kepler, this was a way of comprehending the workings of the eye, but it also made possible a way of picturing the world which was *given*, so to speak, rather than ordered in the Italian (Albertian) fashion. In a penetrating examination of the Dutch and Italian traditions, Alpers (1983) has argued that the Dutch artists sought to represent the world in a way that privileged what was given, without prejudging or classifying what they saw. This was the basis of a seventeenth-century body of work (epitomized by the paintings of Jan Vermeer), which is characterized by attention to many small objects, to surfaces and their textures, to color, and to reflected light, rather than to a few large objects and their placement in a legible space. The northern European tradition was part of a culture that emphasized seeing, as contrasted with the Renaissance culture that emphasized reading and interpretation (Foucault, 1973). As part of the former approach, the Dutch tradition spurned the frame as basic to the picture, so that the scene appears to extend beyond the frame, and the location of the observer remains comparatively undefined.

The constitution of the subject in the Albertian picture—effectively, the perceiver taking up a perspective—places that person outside of the frame. The observer's body is unavailable for examination, except that it becomes part of a different picture, as it were, an object upon which another person could look. Within a discourse premised upon seeing as interpretation, the body is something to be inhabited only mysteriously, through the feel of everyday life; if it is to be known and understood, then it must be seen as an object, within a generalized space, the dimensions of which are provided by the gaze of the scientist. This is, in fact, the language of modern psychology, which seeks to discover laws (or at least, supportable propositions) that can tie experience to the generalized body, as a complex machine. The *subjective body*, which lingers outside of the Albertian frame, is as much a creation of this way of seeing the world as the objects that it renders distinct. However, within this way of thinking, where one talks in the language of seeing (Soltis, 1966), it remains, rather like the body of the sick person, intangible and closed to our investigations.

This distinction in art is introduced here to show not only that medieval and modern thinking overlapped but also that in the transition from one to another, different forms coexisted together. If we are to reconsider the body in social psychology, we need to avoid talking ourselves into a position where the modern view of the body appears inevitable and, though admittedly dominant, exclusive. Relating ways of seeing to literacy, McLuhan points out that people of nonliterate cultures, scan objects and images as we do the printed page, segment by segment. Thus they have no detached point of view. They are wholly *with* the object. They go emphatically into it. The eye is used, not in perspective but tactually, as it were. Euclidean spaces depending on much separation of sight from touch and sound are not known to them. (1962, p. 37, emphasis in the original)

The extent to which this way of seeing is recoverable by literate peoples is by the way here; what is important to note is that the dominance of the visual sense, and of the modern way of perceiving, is not immutable. To grasp this is to free ourselves, if only a little, from the assumptions that underlie the body as conceptualized within psychology.

The change in thinking that has been sketched out in this section shows a number of things. From being part of the cosmos that it reflected in proper proportion, the body came to be the measure for things ordered according to principles of human design. In the extension of the visual mode over the tactile, it came to be located within the empty spaces that the age of perspective made possible, and at the same time, it became a container, to be filled by the attentions of the anatomists (Devisch, 1985; Romanyshyn, 1982). This is what McLuhan (1962) referred to as "the homogenization of persons" as they moved from the medieval to the Renaissance world, and it is what we saw earlier on in this chapter as being the equalization of bodies viewed from the perspective of the new science of anatomy.

Foucault: Power–Knowledge Exercised Through the Body

Chapter 1 discussed four topics that are on the fringe of mainstream social psychology–hysteria, women's studies, crowds and sickness. The purpose was to show that their relationship to the traditional approach involved different treatments of the body; in short, that it becomes significant within these topics in a way wholly missing from the dominant sociocognitive position. It is not surprising, therefore, that the writer who has made the most far-reaching analysis of the body in history (Foucault, 1973, 1977, 1979) should also have chosen these themes for detailed examination. Foucault's work concerns the way in which power and knowledge in society work through each other, resulting in the constitution of the human subject that psychology (and the other human sciences) today takes for granted. In this praxis, the body has played a key role:

But the body is also directly involved in the political field; power relations have an immediate hold upon it; they invest it, mark it, train it, torture it, force it to carry out tasks, to perform ceremonies, to emit signs . . . the body becomes a useful force only if it is both a productive body and a subjected body. This subjection is not only obtained by the instruments of violence or ideology; . . . it may be calculated, organized, technically thought out. . . . That is to say, there may be a "knowledge" of the body that is not exactly the science of its functioning, and a mastery of its forces that is more than the ability to conquer them; this knowledge and this mastery constitute what might be called the political technology of the body. (1977, pp. 25–26; copyright © 1977 by Alan Sheridan, copyright © 1975 by Editions Gallimard, quoted by permission.)

This argument suggests that power is not exercised solely (or mainly) by privileged individuals over others but is something that extends through people, ordering their lives and at the same time investing them as agents of it. In order that this might happen, or simply as part of the extension of this power, people are discriminated as they are ordered, and they become more discriminating in their practice; the latter discrimination is, effectively, knowledge. For example, the use of social skills training by psychologists is aimed at remedying the nonverbal behaviors of individuals judged to be in need of help or guidance. This training is at once the exercise of power and a means of disseminating and extending knowledge about social interaction. While it has been argued that such training methods are derived from theory, the theory itself arises from the need to organize and normalize the conduct of individuals in society. For Foucault, then, power and knowledge directly imply one another; power produces knowledge, even as it constrains and orders; knowledge extends power but can also be the means whereby people resist it.

These ideas were worked out by Foucault in the context of several discrete studies, including the histories of madness, sickness, punishment, and sexuality. While the treatments of these topics are not all alike (he holds that there is no unitary process at work), the body is a key feature in all of them, being the locus for the application of power and the field in which knowledge is produced. Also, because there is no unitary process, the working out of power–knowledge relations upon the body takes place at what Foucault terms "innumerable points of confrontation," "focuses of instability," which allow for resistance and even temporary inversions of dominance. It is at these extreme points, where power–knowledge becomes "capillary," that Foucault has chosen to study it (Gordon, 1980).

In Foucault's writings, the body in history has been variously subject to separation (confinement), surveillance, discipline, and what has been termed *inscription* (Rose, 1988). For those who were mad, it was their inclusion with the idle and with the criminal that separated them from society. Their confinement, a physical ordering of bodies, provided the basis for the entry of physicians, who would distinguish the mad as "ill" and would separate them once again through attempts to discern, among other things, their physiognomy. In effect, the treatment of the insane depended upon their being designated as such and upon the working out of a system of classification for determining their forms of affliction. This required that they be confined, scrutinized, and constrained, according to the moral concerns of the day. It is sometimes thought that the liberation of the insane by Pinel, from what were effectively prisons for criminals and vagabonds, was a humanitarian gesture; in essence, however, it was the working out of a new form of power to which such people would, from then on, be subject.

The treatment of criminals also changed during the eighteenth century, moving from a form of punishment inflicted directly upon the body of the prisoner in torture and execution, to a system of correction instituted in the prisons. Foucault (1977) describes the former as a public spectacle, which followed necessarily upon the violation of laws identifiable with the sovereign's will, the source of power in the state. There emerged at this time a different view of crime, which was no longer seen as being committed against the king, but against society. The punishment that resulted was of a disciplinary form, which had as its center the idea of surveillance. Foucault used the model invented by Bentham as his ideal for this form of punishment. Bentham's Panopticon was conceived as a circular structure built in the form of a ring with a hollow interior. The circumference was made up of individual cells for holding the prisoners, who were overseen by guards positioned in a tower at the center of the ring. The essence of this system is that surveillance is exercised by a figure, of no intrinsic importance, who sees each and all but is seen by none of them. Foucault argues that this ideal is the form of the new disciplinary power, which extended beyond the prison walls into all of society after the eighteenth century. It is a *disembodied gaze*, which has its effects "on those who, knowing they are under surveillance, transform their actions and their identities" (Armstrong, 1987, p. 68). As Armstrong (1987, p. 69) has put it, this form of discipline provokes and works through resistance: "an up-raised hand to avert the gaze of surveillance marks the beginnings of a self-existence for the nascent individual."

This new discipline is one expression of the classical age's discovery of the body as object and target of power; it worked through the army, the school, and the hospital, as a counterpoint to the metaphysical writings of Descartes and the scholars who came after him. Foucault points to this new concern with "docile bodies" as follows:

> The historical moment of the disciplines was the moment when an art of the human body was born. . . . What was then being formed was a policy of coercions that act upon the body, a calculated manipulation of its elements, its gestures, its behaviour. The human body was entering a machinery of power that explores it, breaks it down and rearranges it. . . . Thus discipline produces subjected and practised bodies, "docile" bodies. (1977, pp. 137–138, quoted by permission)

Discipline was exercised through the normalization of judgment, which meant that the control of individuals was guided by norms of behavior to which they were taught to accede. Indeed, one of the functions of the clinic was to act as a base from which data could be collected about individuals, in order to discover the distribution of diseases in the population. The concept of the *norm* and the *deviant* emerged from this kind of endeavor. At the intersection of these two concerns—with the politics of the body and the politics of the population—Foucault located the issue of sex. He argued that sex, as a subject with its own autonomy, was a product of an increase in discussions of sexuality in the eighteenth century. (This stands in opposition to the idea that sex was wholly taboo in Victorian society.) He suggested that the multiple discourses on sex that proliferated during the nineteenth and twentieth centuries worked to multiply the possible forms of sexual expression, not to diminish and contain them. As part of this, however, the emerging human sciences were engaged in the work of inscribing within their discourses the variations in reproduction of populations and the various sexual practices of individuals. As Smart (1985) has put it, as sex became confined in its practice to the privacy of the home and the procreative couple, it simultaneously became a governmental matter between the state and the individual. With respect to the application of the human sciences to points of discord and contradiction, Foucault recognized the emergence during the nineteenth century of the "hysterical woman" as a fit subject for psychiatric treatment.

There is one difference between the techniques of surveillance of the sick body and that of sexuality, which bears upon a distinction made in the previous chapter, when we were discussing psychoanalysis. Where surveillance is primarily a technology of *seeing*, psychoanalysis is primarily a technology of *listening*. Armstrong (1987) has pointed this out, saying that this is best exemplified in modern medicine (arguably more so in psychoanalysis!), where the patient's confession constituted the reemergence of the patient's point of view. As a consequence, this apparent humanism is in fact the subtle workings of an even more intimate surveillance.

With this point, we are able to see where psychology fits into Foucault's scheme, as one of the human sciences that is involved in the ordering, surveillance, normalization, and inscribing of individuals' characteristics. This does not mean that psychology is engaged in a repressive activity, but that it emerged out of a need to understand the differences among people who were classified as different or as deviant.

> The figures around which concern centered often seem marginal to contemporary eyes: masturbating children and hysterical women, feeble-minded schoolchildren and defective recruits to the armed forces, workers suffering fatigue or industrial accidents, unstable or shell-shocked soldiers, lying, bed-wetting or naughty children. (Rose, 1988, p. 185)

In Foucault's work, we find support for the contention that the body, as a field of psychological study, is to be found at the margins of the discipline. There are two reasons for this. First, it has been argued that it is in the "capillaries" of society that there are likely to be found resistance to, argument about, and symptoms of the workings of power. Historically, this has occurred through the regulation of the body, so that where there are such resistances, these are likely to be signified in its terms and expressed physically. The body appears then as the site of moral and/or political struggle, as, for example, in the cases of the hysteric, the crowd, the feminist, and the sick. Second, the establishment of social psychology can be seen, in Foucaultian terms, as a movement toward describing not individuals but the spaces between them. By this is meant that the forms of their relationships to each other and to society become the focus of measurement and explanation. How these relationships are based upon the foregoing orderings of the body has now become mysterious to social psychologists, as it is implicit within their assumptions about the kind of subject matter they seek to study. Using Foucault's perspective, the social individual is constituted through the practices of a psychology that depends upon historical orderings of the body for its own existence. *The shadow in which the body remains obscured is cast by our own knowledge, our own practice, ourselves as social psychologists.*

Conclusion

The purpose of this historical overview of the body has been to locate the modern worldview as its product. We can now see that the body-as-physiological-substrate is just as much an outcome of social practice and inquiry as is the mind-as-social-process. With this established, there is no requirement upon us to tie together the findings of social psychology to the findings of the physiologists. Brief as it is, the foregoing survey is sufficient to show that this would be to trudge still further down a cul-de-sac in understanding the body and social theory. Instead, the remainder of the book examines those points within social psychology where issues concerning the body have arisen. These are not parts of the discipline that have addressed the problem of the body directly, for reasons that should now be apparent. Instead, the issues with which we concern ourselves either remain wholly unseen or are raised in ways that limit the possibilities for understanding the role of the body in social life. The book's purpose is to illuminate these problems and to expand the potential for thinking about a social psychology of embodied people.

Chapter 3

The Object of Scrutiny

The study of how people look at each other, and of what they deduce as a consequence, is the stuff of person perception research. This research tradition has been more concerned with how people see (i.e., with the perceiver) than with what they are looking at (Schneider, Hastorf, & Ellsworth, 1979). In this chapter, I relate this both to how the body appears and to how concepts in psychological theory depend upon unstated assumptions about its nature. Running through this work is a tension between person perception as discerning what is given in the face (or upon the body), and seeing it as a process of interpretation on the part of the perceiver. As this chapter shows, there has been a change in the balance of this tension over the years and, as a consequence, a change in how the body is perceived and depended upon by social psychologists in their theorizing.

Perhaps the best example of research which holds that psychological characteristics can be discerned upon the body is the work carried out by Sheldon (1940). Sheldon was not a social psychologist; instead, he derived his ideas from the project of the phrenologists and characterologists of the previous century. He acknowledged that they had the "rudiments of a plan" in mind, which only lacked the statistical measures that could give it an empirical grounding. His work aimed at providing what was missing, the measurement of various parts of the body. By taking the ratios of these measures, he defined three components—endomorphy, ectomorphy, and mesomorphy—which together specified the range of possible body types. Underlying this work was the same conviction that had been held by the phrenologists. There is a structural identity between the body and personality. This belief is still found in popular books propounding the reading of character from faces on the basis of the dictum, "as without, so within" (Davies, 1989).

Sheldon's methods—the photographic and anthropometric study of large numbers of men and women—are testimony to his belief that a study of physique bears upon a whole range of questions concerning people's personalities and their expression in everyday life. In developing his constitutional psychology, he was following in the footsteps of Kretschmer, who had made observations of his patients in terms of their physique. Kretschmer had identified three types of individual, corresponding to the different kinds of patients suffering from mental illness. In a development of this idea, Sheldon transformed it to cover three continuous distributions of people. On the basis of this work, he could generalize to the human population what Kretschmer had only been able to relate to his hospital patients. Sheldon could thus offer a method of measurement through which different social groupings could be compared on a normative basis. In Chapter 2, the point was made that the separation of particular groups of people was important in the formation of the human sciences, so that closing the door on the mentally ill opened these persons, metaphorically, to the gaze of psychiatry and psychology. Neither before nor since has the body been used in psychology as the central datum for understanding the variation of human behavior. This work, therefore, challenges the claim made at the beginning of this book that the body vanished as psychology developed. Nevertheless, the consignment of Sheldon's work to history by present-day theorists shows the rule to withstand this particular test.

Sheldon was explicit in his concern for establishing norms for men and for women, as well as for different racial groups. These, he conjectured, could be used to help make decisions about which constitutions were prone to disease, which women produce children most easily, and whether all of the somatotypes need to reproduce in order for people to be happy. He extended this list to include sickness, food needs, and the home environment, as features of people's lives that could be governed by a study of their constitutions. Finally, he carried out research into the somatotypes of delinquents, in order to study the relationship between criminality and constitution. In this research, we can see that, although he was not a social psychologist, Sheldon was engaged in social engineering. Having related various body types to particular forms of deviant behavior, he came to the question of punishment:

> The question of punishment of crime is one of the utmost delicacy. The tragedy of the matter lies in the fact that we have kept few records, because for one thing, we do not know *whom* we have punished. . . .
> It is possible that certain personalities *want* physical punishment, need it, and that such punishment is necessary for their balance and happiness, like exercise for the muscles. But it may be punishment administered to the wrong personality will change a useful and sensitive citizen into a resolute criminal. (1940, p. 258, emphases in original)

This quote shows that, far from having nothing to do with matters social psychological, constitutional theory was grounded in the assumption that the valuation of different groups and individuals in society could be mapped upon the body. These judgments were not for study (at least, not by Sheldon) but would guide the application of knowledge about the distribution of bodily forms. The problem was that such value judgments became apparent in the course of Sheldon's assessment of temperament, for he gauged the personalities of his subjects before taking the anthropometric measures (Hall & Lindzey, 1957). This, coupled with the lack of subsequent confirmatory findings, led to the demise of this line of research. What did emerge as a problem in its own right, however, was the very methodological weakness just mentioned. How do people form impressions of others, and come to attribute to them particular personalities?

To ask this question is to turn one's attention away from the person observed and toward the perceiver. Of course, this was more than a redirection of researchers' attention, because Sheldon's work stood in a long line of anthropometry, which situated the problem of human nature either upon the body (phrenology, physiognomy) or within it (biology). This was never an accepted part of social psychology, so that Sheldon's work was always of marginal interest to that field. However, before turning to the questions posed by students of person perception, it is worth noting that the assumptions of the constitutional theorists have always been alive outside of the discipline. In fact, one of the points that this chapter makes is that by turning away from the body, social psychologists have placed themselves at a disadvantage in being able to appreciate how these assumptions are employed in everyday life.

The body has been downgraded as a source of information. In their overview of the field of person perception, Schneider, Hastorf, and Ellsworth (1979) note, and by implication dismiss, the popular associations given to different physical features. They conclude that the list of physical features is "as endless as the list of personality traits" (p. 23), thus showing the body to be as multiple in its meanings as individual minds make it so, a pliable entity of only secondary interest.

In contrast to this turning away from the body, authors carrying out historical analyses have paid attention to specific representations of particular groups or individuals through the medium of the drawing and through descriptions of physique. For example, Gilman (1982) reports an attempt in the midnineteenth century to show that blacks were subject to particular forms of madness, "Drapetomania, or the disease causing slaves to run away, and Dysaesthesia aethiopis or hebetude of mind and obtuse sensibility of the body—a disease peculiar to negroes—called by overseers, 'rascality'" (p. 112). Such so-called illnesses emerged when the blacks' "slothful" nature was not encouraged with the hard physical exercise that working as a slave offered them. Gilman also reports how the case of William Freeman, a black who murdered a family in upstate New York, was used as the subject of a traveling panorama, which depicted him with an expression of mania. The conclusion Gilman draws is that the image of blacks as murderers and madmen became fused in these categories of exclusion. One is reminded of the study of rumor by Allport and Postman (1945), in which subjects were shown a picture of the interior of a subway train showing a black man and a white man standing together, the latter carrying a razor. When asked to reproduce this picture, half of the subjects transferred the blade to the black passenger. This was interpreted as a sign of the prejudiced thinking of the subjects involved. Gilman's analysis draws our attention to the possibility of the reproductions reflecting not distortions of one particular picture, which several subjects were shown, but the affirmation of multiple images, which had been made available for each of them in their social world.

A similar account can be given for the treatment of other subordinate groups who were (and are) seen as threatening, mysterious, and to be excluded. In France during the 1890s, the Dreyfus Affair provoked a barrage of attacks against Jews, some in the form of caricatures in the press. One example showed a Jew's head (and stereotypic facial features) with attributed racial weaknesses drawn, phrenology-style, upon areas of the brain (Kleeblatt, 1987).

The prostitute was also subject to visual representations that relied heavily upon the construction of a physical stereotype. Descriptions of appearance and of clothing were used to paint a picture of a woman whose overdeveloped sexuality had led her into moral decline and ultimately to degradation (Nead, 1988). Such physical classifications of deviancy served to mark the boundaries between the majority and the others, the ones who were to be either excluded or employed only in a minor capacity. They also told a moral tale, warning of the fate that would befall anyone who trod the same path. A particularly striking and effective use of this warning is given by Zola in his novel *Nana*, where the price of exercising her sexuality is visited upon Nana in the corruption of her beauty by smallpox. Illness is linked here with difference in order to distance and to control the "other"— the dangerous outsider.

This idea of the stereotype is different from the one normally put forward in social psychology. For the psychologist, stereotypes are features of thought, carried within individual cognitions; alternatively, they can be seen as expressions, or as creations that engender or preserve group differences and group identities. These two interpretations do not contradict one another, but they do emphasize different aspects of social existence, not least of which is the significance of the body. In traditional social psychology, stereotypes are held by people in their heads, the result of a process of judgment. So, for example, Gollin (1954) asked subjects to form an impression of a girl pictured first displaying sexually promiscuous behavior, then subsequently being helpful to less fortunate individuals. The findings were interpreted according to the degree to which subjects either compartmentalized or integrated the information. In fact, only one quarter of the subjects were able to form a unified impression, and this was interpreted as reflecting differences in individual ways of perceiving. That is to say, the study showed how individuals differed in their perceptions, but nothing of how they collectively relied upon images of prostitution to make sense of the film they were shown. Stereotyping is not merely a response to difference, but also how people inscribe distinctions upon each other. Physical appearance is important as the medium in which the various others—be they sick, mad, sexually profligate, or black—can be juxtaposed bodily or can have qualities condensed in their facial expression and in their deportment (Gilman, 1985).

In Chapter 1, we saw that it was through a study of marginal groups that the body became important to psychological explanations, although it remained very much on the fringe of the discipline's interests. Now we see that this emergence was not out of a vacuum, but from a social world in which the dominant majority had always used bodily differences as ways of making distinctions among groups, and in which they continue to do so. This was also true of the use of photography as a social record:

> If, in the last decades of the nineteenth century, the squalid slum displaces the country seat and the abnormal physiognomies of patient and prisoner displace the pedigreed features of the aristocracy, then their presence in representation is no longer a mark of celebration but a burden of subjection. (Tagg, 1988, p. 64)

Photographic images are not just evidence of history; they are historical. The ways of looking, the means of looking, and the purposes for which images were collected all attest to qualitative distinctions in social life and to powers that create them and put them to one use or another. In contrast to this state of affairs, social psychology changed its focus to one of (a) how individuals perceived the other person in general, (b) with what accuracy they did so, and (c) under what ideal conditions.

Perceiving the Other Person

The idea that there might be a natural linkage between what people are inside and their physical makeup underlay the work of the physiognomists. This was the starting point for psychological research that studied how accurately people could perceive the personalities of other individuals from photographs of the face alone. The research record is brief and comes, we are told, to an early and unsuccessful end (Schneider, Hastorf, & Ellsworth, 1979). Interest soon shifted to understanding the processes by which the perceiver either forms impressions or makes interpretations. One exception to this has been the work of Ekman & Friesen, (1971), who have provided evidence for there being some universal ability for people to judge emotional expressions. The extent to which certain gross expressions are universal is still a matter for debate (Ekman, 1977), given that successful identification has followed careful specification of what the face should show in the photograph.

The research into how accurately people could judge another person's personality was, in an important sense, different from the interest of the physiognomists. It shifted the focus of inquiry from the face itself to the character of the perceived person; it was rare for psychologists to study the relationship between personality judgments and the facial features themselves. However, it has been demonstrated that people will form a common stereotype if given particular photographs, although no specific associations of physiognomy to personality have been found (Secord, Dukes, & Bevan, 1954). When discussing the finding that people do form particular stereotypes of photographs, these authors looked to cultural factors for an explanation. They suggested that responsibility for the meaning placed upon facial features might be due to images available in art, in fiction, and in motion pictures. Anticipating the aforementioned historical studies of blacks and of prostitutes, they suggested that the source of such stereotypes, the cultural valuation of certain sets of features, may lie in the relationships between more and less powerful groups in society.

Interest in the face as the main source of information about the person is not new, and studies of its communicative capabilities provide us with explanations of why this should always have been so (Ekman & Frisen, 1969a). In the time before photography was established and allowed us to have reliable representations of how people looked, there was always a doubt about the extent to which a portrait or bust did justice to a particular individual. This was especially so in the case of important individuals, whose likeness had to bear the special burden of symbolizing what they stood for. For example, in the case of George Washington there was grave concern about the resemblance of the various paintings and busts to what the real man had been like (Schwartz & Miller, 1986). This arose from the fact that these representations served as vehicles of inspiration and encouragement to many ordinary Americans. This work could only be done well by the portraits that most resembled Washington, and could only be undermined by marked variations in the representations available. Schwartz and Miller make clear the difference between the view of Americans in the midnineteenth century and that of the social psychologists of today. Where social psychology sees pictures of people as matters of appearance, depending upon angle, lighting, and passing expression, the portrait (or bust) of Washington was believed to be an instrument of moral virtue because it expressed what was essential about the man himself ("as without, so within"). In such a world, facial features become concrete expressions or markers of what society deems significant, and can be used to make statements about the values and interests held to be important by the dominant groupings of the day.

This point has already been made in the context of how group differences are marked. My reason for restating it here is to show that, in redirecting attention away from accuracy of perception to the perceptual process, social psychology endorsed the movement away from caring about how or when the body mattered. Instead, what made a difference were the distinctions to be found in the eye of the beholder; not the object, but the way of looking became of primary concern.

We need to reflect for a moment upon this idea that social psychology cared less about the body and more about the process of seeing. In truth, the discipline shifted its concern along the lines laid down by a cultural movement that drew it along in its wake. Personality was no longer something to be read out from the body in a kind of exegesis; instead, it was read upon it in terms of an active process of interpretation that depended upon the perspective of the observer. In a world now replete with reproductions of visual images, changing and repositioning by moment and context, the idea of being concerned with a true representation is one that we find difficult to grasp. Yet, to understand this change is to put conceptual brackets around person-perception research and to comprehend it as itself *a* way of looking, not as simply *the* study of "what is there."

To make this cultural and conceptual movement clearer, we examine one more example from a world in which resemblance was a matter of concern. In her study of Dutch art in the seventeenth century, Alpers (1983) points out that the artists' concern to describe things as they were had led them, among other things, to a tradition of portraiture that was not paralleled in the painting of southern Europe. Within the northern tradition, artists were exhorted to attend to the differences between features of people and things, so as to render them in their natural individuality. Alpers notes that this belief that everything was created to be different from everything else was severely tested by examples of striking resemblance, such as in the case of identical twins. She cites an example, noted by an artist of the time, of a crowd of people pursuing a nobleman through the streets of London on account of the fact that he had a remarkable likeness to the king. Alpers comments that the artist does not see this mistake as a matter of appearances, made possible by the kingly look of the nobleman. On the contrary, he draws the conclusion that even the recognition of a king is a matter of individual identity, that one must look even more carefully upon the person to identify that which marks out the individual person. The modern view of the "emperor's new clothes," which demystifies royalty as a matter of bearing and props supported by popular belief, would have been alien to artists of that time and place.

The acceptance of failure to establish accuracy in the perception of personality can be seen as social psychology's final break with any interest in physiognomy. Indeed, the acknowledgment of a lessening of interest in judgmental accuracy (Bruner & Taguiri, 1954) was used to legitimate the theoretical approach that was to dominate the field up to and including the present day—attribution theory (Heider, 1958). It is interesting to see what happens to the body in Heider's scheme, though it must be said that this was merely the endpoint of a long history of emphasizing the eye over the hand, in spite of the previous dominance of behavioral psychology.

Using Brunswick's lens model as a guide, Heider proposed that person perception involved forming an "image" of the "distal stimulus"; the former is the percept, and the latter the other person "with his needs and intentions." These two terms are separated by the "mediation," the behavioral manifestations, in which is included the body of the other person. Heider poses the problem of person perception as one of achieving a constancy in one's image of the other against a background of changing circumstances and behavior. As a result, "the interaction between a person and someone he is observing, can be described as going on between two foci separated by the mediation which can, to some extent, be neglected in the description" (1958, p. 29). The neglect of the mediation was in favor of constructive processes presumed to lie within the (anatomical) body, in the perceptual mechanisms wherever they might reside.

The research studies that grew out of Heider's theorizing privileged the eye. It was assumed that the social world is composed of individuals who look, discern, and attribute intentions, as it were, from the center of one to the center of another. This judgmental eye is often disembodied in attribution studies; the subjects read or hear about a person and then summarily decide upon that individual's disposition. Because the aim of the work is to understand the process of attribution in general, it is of no consequence *who* sees, just that the conditions under which particular attributions are made can be specified (Kelley, 1967). These conditions might include the relationship of the observer to the observed, as well as that of who is actor and who is observer (Storms, 1973). In either of these cases, however, the primacy of looking is preserved, even to the point of claiming that people know their own behavior in a manner similar to outside observers (Bem, 1972). From this perspective, acting in the world is having a special but not a privileged point of view, and one's body is a source of weak and indeterminate cues that cannot be relied upon.

Attribution research depends upon variations in perceptual standpoints for its rationale. These different standpoints are seen as exclusive—the observer or the observed, Observer 1 as compared with Observer 2. Therefore, what people see depends upon variations in the mediation caused by the adoption of different perspectives. The difference between being an actor or being an observer is seen as one of point of view, involving such things as informational biases, differences in self-monitoring, and the salience of information available to each party (Jones & Nisbett, 1972). That is to say, what is special about action, quite literally about using one's body, is transformed into whether one is the watcher or the watched. This is, arguably, a serious distortion of the common experience of being involved in social relationships, in favor of preserving a theory of seeing at a distance.

The local proximal stimulus—what one sees "at the eye"—Heider regarded as being determined in part by the mediation. Sometimes, we are aware only of the disposition of people, such as that they are displeased, but we are not sure why. At other times, we can say what it is about the mediation that brings us to a particular conclusion, such as that we know they are displeased because of their tone of voice. Polanyi (1967) has suggested that such an example reveals that we identify a disposition by *relying upon* the person's features (or tone of voice). Attending *from* these *to* the inner disposition of the person, simultaneously gives these particulars their meaning. He uses the example of a blind man who uses a stick to find his way. The awareness of the stick in the hand (proximal stimulus) is transformed into a sense of the objects that are touched at its point. He attends to the object by relying upon the feelings in the hand; these in turn are meaningful with respect to the objects (distal stimulus) that they signify. Polanyi calls this "tacit knowing," meaning that we must rely upon some particulars in order to know other things. Where meaning tends to be displaced away from ourselves—onto the distal object—tacit knowledge is disclosed in our reliance upon all kinds of proximal relations for attending toward such distal objects. Like the stick in the hand of the blind man, or a tool in the hand of a skilled mechanic, particulars on which we rely change their appearance. They are incorporated, as it were, into the body, so that we "dwell in them" (Polanyi, 1967) as we attend to other things from them. This is the way, Polanyi suggests, that things are made to function as a proximal term in tacit knowing. Also, at the base of this relationship between distal and proximal terms is the body itself—the body that we feel in terms of the things in the world, and from which we attend to those things. The realm of the proximal is crucially the realm of the body. (An extended discussion of this point is made in Chapter 6.)

How has attribution research conceptualized the relationship of distal and proximal stimuli so that it privileges the eye and promotes a disembodied social existence? To continue with the example of the stick as a probe, it is as if experiments were conducted in which subjects had placed in their hands different sorts of sticks and were asked to make judgments as the stick was moved (by the experimenter) over an object. Altering the size, shape, and length of stick, as well as the angle of approach, would provide data as to how varying the mediation affects the final judgments that people make. However, this would mean treating the various features of the stick as if they belonged only to the outside world, not examining how they might change in experience as the person did or did not come to rely upon them. In the same way, by giving subjects things to do in experiments (e.g., have a conversation with another subject), investigators have missed the intentional aspect of social relationships, in which individuals rely upon things (e.g., feelings, knowledge) in order to fashion or to discern something about the other individual. It is on this point that Buss (1978) has argued that attribution research has studied not *actor*–observer differences, so much as *sufferer*–observer differences (i.e., the watcher and the watched).

The privileging of the eye, the concentration upon the distal object, and the concern with the perceptual process in general have all been emphases that have obscured the body as a key term in our understanding of social relationships. Heider's work can be seen as important in diverting attention away from the question of accuracy of perception, by removing the difficulty of how distal and proximal stimulation were related. His answer was that they were not related, in the sense that particular behaviors (e.g., a raised eyebrow) did not always mean one particular disposition, such as surprise. The message was that mediation is ambiguous and equivocal, so that the proximal stimulus is unreliable. As a consequence, the research agenda made its primary aim the study of how dispositional attributions were made. Even intentions, which in Polanyi's terms could refer to the basis from which people act toward each other, were reduced to things discerned by a perceiver; from the center of one person to the center of another would mean precisely that.

Heider, in common with Goffman (1959), used the ideas of the Austrian sociologist Gustav Ichheiser when framing his theory of social relations. Ichheiser (1949) had anticipated the failure of perceptual accuracy research and set out a thesis concerning the tendency to misperceive personality, which antedated the arguments of the situationists (Mischel, 1968). Ichheiser claimed that personality was not to be understood as something inside people, somehow belonging to them, but derived from "impressions" that were attributed to them by others. "Impressions" were therefore of social origin and were to be distinguished from "expressions" presumed (like emotions) to erupt from the body. What made these attributions possible was the visibility of the person's behavior to others; personality was shaped in the public arena, not in the privacy of the person's body.

Ichheiser proposed that characteristics are attributed to people on the basis of social status and group membership, so that individuals can (or find they must) take on what he called "sham" qualities. Other characteristics are adopted by people on the basis of positions that they occupy, so that they can claim particular abilities or moral credits for themselves ("pseudo" qualities). For Ichheiser, misperceptions occurred because of general tendencies to assume that what was seen was the "center" of people, not their actions embedded in a context. This was the point on which Heider drew in his analysis of interpersonal relations. However, Ichheiser also proposed (and this Heider overlooked) that "sham" and "pseudo" characteristics are fashioned in the crucible of social differences, particularly in relation to issues of power and of disadvantage.

Goffman (1959), too, drew upon Ichheiser's work in order to set out a theory in which explanations of the self were relocated away from the individual body to society. Selves were characters that individuals had to establish on the basis of performances, to sustain through consistent actions that would lead to their moral claim to be such and such a person, these claims being subject to legitimation by other people. Unlike Ichheiser, Goffman saw the body as a vehicle for the establishment of selves, even though it might "give off" cues that might be inconsistent with the character being claimed at the time. Unlike Heider, Goffman viewed social life as constructed through forms of dramatic realization, requiring people to manage their impressions in an active way; they were not limited to perceiving each other in attempts to discern each other's "centers." Indeed, in attribution theory, where the accent is upon the dispositions that the perceiver reports about the other, in Goffman's theory, emphasis is placed upon the ways in which the proximal stimulus can be arranged—in effect, how to create, through judicious use of the body and one's surroundings, an impression in the eyes of the other person.

In spite of Goffman's shift of emphasis from the "impressions" of the other to the "expressiveness" of the actor, his analysis leaves the body in an ambiguous position. As both a "performer" and a "character," the individual is subject to cues that he or she 'gives off," as well as being the author of those thus given. The body remains a not-altogether-controllable vehicle for the establishment of impressions in the eyes of other people. Within this view, the body is shown, for the first time in social psychology, as the site of an ambiguity concerning the management of its given, biological workings in the cause of fashioning an acceptable, legitimate claim to moral status. Nevertheless, when it comes to an ordering of priorities, it is the internalized social eye that constrains and transforms the eruptions of the natural body.

I cite these authors because they fostered, intentionally or otherwise, a conception of the individual as inessential, by which I mean subject to constructive processes either in other individuals or in society. In attribution theory, the behavior of the perceived person is not seen as the raw material that it had previously been assumed to be; the proximal term in this process, sited at what Heider called "the periphery of the body," is structured by central processes that are cognitive, not corporeal. Within Ichheiser's incipient social constructionism, the body and its expressions are inappropriate objects for sociological analysis. For Goffman, the body is incorporated within the moral requirements of players in social episodes that have a ceremonial form. That is to say, the body is both a vehicle and a site for the establishment of selves, which are subject to consensual agreement. (This point is explored further in Chapter 4). To summarize, for Heider, the body vanishes; for Ichheiser, it is irrelevant; and for Goffman, it is manipulable in the service of making impressions.

What kind of view of the person can be inferred from these positions? It is one of people who are subject to being labeled by others in society (Becker, 1963; Scheff, 1966). Behavior becomes something dependent upon context and upon the perspective of the perceiver. There is no self other than one that is determined through social negotiation, and the selves that individuals might own depend upon their being able to establish them through impression management. The body, in this scheme, is a plastic entity, to be shaped and molded by the press of social expectations and the characters that inhabit it.

This is a modern view and can be recognized as such by comparing it with one now largely abandoned. My purpose in making this comparison is not to show that one view is wrong; it is to demonstrate how, in coming solely to a position of social constructionism or attribution, the social psychologist is disabled in any attempt to understand the body as anything but a secondary feature of everyday life. The feeling of freedom from biological determinism that might accompany this movement only adds to questions of the body being unattainable from this perspective.

We saw in Chapter 2 that social psychology shares in the modern conception of the equality of individuals, in how they should govern their lives, and in the dignity that should be afforded to them. Berger, Berger, and Kellner (1974) have proposed that this view is fundamentally different from that of hierarchic societies (such as those that existed in medieval times). It is also different from the view of people in societies where strict inequalities among groups exist. In these societies, they argue, the etiquette of everyday life consists of relationships founded upon honor. Honor, unlike dignity, operates upon the principle of "to each his/her due", but extends from the individual to his or her family and to the whole community. It may apply strongly to those in positions of high status but will also apply to those who are lowly, such as men who should show manliness, and women who should exhibit shame. The moral order is borne by people according to their institutional roles. In contrast, modern society poses the solitary self as the bearer of rights, which are infringed only with loss of dignity.

> In a world of honor the individual *is* the social symbols emblazoned on his escutcheon. The true self of the knight is revealed as he rides out to do battle in the full regalia of his role; by comparison, the naked man in bed with a woman represents a lesser reality of the self. In a world of dignity, in the modern sense, the social symbolism governing the interaction of men is a disguise. The escutcheons *hide* the true self. (Berger et al., 1974, p. 84 emphases in the original)

This means that the form of modern society has given rise to a way of thinking that poses the individual self as primary. Just as the person no longer occupies, essentially, any place in the social structure, this person has no essential self for others. We may act one way to one person, another way for somebody else. The characters we play are relative and are context dependent. The attributes that others grant us depend upon their vantage point and upon what we show to them. The body no longer carries, primarily, the marks of people's status in society; instead, it carries the symbolism, the marks of the kind of personality or self that they might try to present or that others might grant to them. What is called "impression management" is the attempt by individuals to make their bodies, as part of their general presentation, the living aspect of the mask with which, in that setting, they would like to be identified. As later chapters show, this linking of the body with the self has far-reaching implications for how the body is conceived of in everyday life, and for how it is portrayed in the media.

By itself, person-perception research could not divert attention away from the body; it was part of a larger movement in psychology, which emphasized the cognitive above and beyond the behavioral. What it did for social psychology, however, was to assert the primary importance of "central processes" in the observer. Also, of course, every individual was an observer of other individuals, each one applying common rules of attribution from distinct and relative positions. To speak, as Heider (1958) did, of the "centers" of individuals was to make use of a metaphor in which people formed not so much a society, as a myriad of percievers who reflected to each other constancies of perceptual meaning. However, the reality of their dispositions could no longer be sought inside the people themselves, for this essentialist thinking had been abandoned. Selves were not bound within bodies, even though they might be located there by perceivers. Attributions and stereotypes served as explanations of how people came to be seen, or to see themselves, as limited, or incapable, or culpable. Bodily distinctions such as gender, race, and physical handicap are examples of matters that can be seen as differences with social dysfunctions that can be traced to false perceptions. The emancipation from socially imposed roles that this position invited, in the name of equality and dignity, involved a further turning away from the body as the source of difference and distinction.

Body Image and Attractiveness

The emergence of the concept of the social self (Gordon & Gergen, 1968; Jersild, 1952) made it possible to view the body as an aspect of a person's self-image. Rendered an object of perception, it could then be related to other conceptions of self on equal terms (Feldman 1975; Zion, 1965). Part of this interest in body image was fueled by studies carried out in the clinical domain, although these drew, in their turn, on the new psychology of impressions and appearances. Consistent with this position, it was then argued that earlier notions of a single body image needed to be replaced with a concept of a multiplicity of body images, deriving from "others' appraisals and reactions to one's appearances and actions" (Van der Velde, 1985). These images were considered to have social functions, in providing people with the means of projecting a desired appearance, of maintaining such a view over time, and of hiding things about the self, which individuals did not wish others to know. This is a view that can be traced directly to the work of Goffman (1959) and back to Ichheiser (1949) before him.

Once separated from the mind in social psychology, the body was recovered in part by being made an object of perception. This was not the living body, as much as the physical body seen and objectified through the comparisons its owner might make with the physical characteristics of other people. The development of methods for objectively measuring differences in such perceptions allowed comparisons to be made of individuals who were considered deviant in one respect or another (Collins, 1986). Groups that drew interest include women diagnosed as either obese or suffering from anorexia nervosa, who could be shown to differ from normal persons in their estimations of their body shapes or sizes (Garner, Garfinkel, Stancer, & Moldofsky, 1976). This provided for cognitive explanations of bodily disturbance, which themselves were taken at face value. By this is meant that the normative basis of judgments of body shape and size remained a tacit feature of work that sought to appraise body perceptions in an objective manner. It was the woman's view of her physique, taken as a separate object for reflection, that characterized this approach, a perspective that abstracted her body from its life settings and social situation (Orbach, 1978).

Within the terms of a social psychology of the perceiving person, the body becomes another accoutrement of the self. It is something that, in being an object for appraisal, is there to be acknowledged or disavowed, identified with or sensed as alien, and manipulated in the course of establishing effective relationships. It is known through the eye alone, or at least through the eye as a metonymic device for the mind, which then understands only what it sees.

The study of facial attractiveness has relied upon physiognomic features to attend to other aspects of social relationships. This line of work is interesting, not only because it reflects one way in which social psychologists have approached such problems, but also because it is symptomatic of a contradiction in the status that psychology accords to people's bodies. The early work in this field showed that individuals judged to be more attractive were more popular with their dating partners (Walster, Aronson, Abrahams, & Rottman, 1966) and had more socially desirable personality traits attributed to them (Dion, Bersheid, & Walster, 1972). Since then, there have been numerous studies attempting to link facial attractiveness to such things as satisfaction in marriage, persuasiveness, advertising, and attribution of responsibility for criminal misdemeanors. At the beginning of their review of work in this field, Bull and Rumsey (1988) quote one of the main researchers on attractiveness as stating that there would be more work in this field "if society were not so enamoured of the idea that because a person's appearance ought not to make a difference, it does not" (see Berscheid, 1981). The study of facial attractiveness is fraught with the problem of squaring people's notions of equality and fairness with evidence that good looks bring better treatment, if not in all cases, then in a good number. It is a withdrawal from this thorny problem that Berscheid (1981) sees as the reason for social psychologists having ignored the effects of appearance upon relationships and liking.

The sensed unfairness of facial attractiveness relates to the repudiation of phrenology and to the denial of the powerlessness of individuals to steer their own fate. Not all writers in this field take this view, however. Wilson and Nias (1976), for example, in a book entitled *Love's Mysteries*, discuss the resistance to studying attractiveness in the following terms:

> Recently, however, the most common objection has been that the research only draws attention to a source of handicap that would be far better played down or entirely forgotten. This "ostrich" attitude has been expressed most vehemently by women's liberationists, who of course oppose beauty contests for the same reason. While their political aims are well intentioned, perhaps laudable, the brief of the social scientist is to study the behavior of people as it actually is, rather than as he or anyone else would like it to be. (p. 2)

Unhampered by any critical theories, these authors go on to show the different ways in which attractiveness has been found to relate to people's social behavior, particularly in the choices of opposite sex partners by men and by women. There is no felt contradiction in this approach, for the differences in people's facial appearances are taken for granted, each person being marked with a greater or a lesser degree of appeal. While Wilson and Nias do report evidence about the different parts of the body that men and women find important in potential partners (e.g., the breasts, the legs, the buttocks, the eyes), these are treated focally, as images of body parts that can be judged in isolation. From this perspective, the body is one (very important) property of the individual, to be made the most of in one's attempts to find a mate.

The preceding position is not typical of research into attractiveness, which often explores situations where bodily differences ought not to matter but do, and settings where these ought to make a difference, but do not. An example of the first kind is the finding that people will judge an attractive woman more harshly if she is believed to have committed a swindle than if she is believed to have committed a burglary (Sigall & Ostrove, 1975). The explanation put forward is that swindling somebody is regarded as the abuse of one's natural advantages, whereas burglary is not related to looks. An example of the second is Goffman's (1963) report that stigmatized people (e.g., the facially disfigured) are treated by others as if they are "normal," provided that they do not attempt to claim the full rights of a "normal" person (e.g., to kiss the other person). Both of these cases illustrate the contradiction that is expressed by social psychologists in terms of whether attractiveness should be studied, and whether it is or is not a trivial problem. These examples show, however, that this is not merely a concern with methodology or research ethics but reflects the ambivalence that modern society accords the body. In a world of free individuals, each would be able to pursue a life or career through the effective presentation of self. When joining and leaving social groups, matters such as height, body shape, or facial attractiveness should be external characteristics of decreasing relevance to the work and interests of these groups. Such is often the aim, if not the actual case; we try to deal equally with each other in spite of differences that are noted. This contradiction between the belief in egalitarianism and the knowledge of corporeal inequalities is part of people's everyday experience. To recognize this is not to underline the need for more studies of attractiveness but to indicate that we should explore the cultural way of seeing in which this research tradition is enfolded.

These points form the background to objections that have been made regarding research into attractiveness. They center on the claim that (a) it exposes behavior contradicting the ideal that individuals are equal, (b) it robs the self of free play in fashioning an image for others, and (c) it undermines the malleability of the body in the service of presenting oneself socially. The point is that people never were equal, and an understanding of the part that the body plays in this inequality is essential to revealing the possibilities for change. For example, it has been shown that people associate physical attractiveness with high status, particularly ascribed status. Reporting this finding, Kalick (1988) notes that in one old New England family, the son was advised by his mother to marry a girl only after he had inspected her family portraits, in order to ensure that she came of stock with good bone structure. This is not a matter of mere attractiveness, but of a concern that the values of a privileged social class are embodied in a particular physiognomy. In that sense, this example makes the body salient in a way that research on facial attraction does not do. It raises the possibility of inquiring into how society not only sees differences in physiognomy but inscribes, maintains, and even cherishes them.

Paradoxically, attractiveness research colludes in the suppression of the body as a legitimate subject for social psychological study. How does this come about? The very use of the term *attractiveness* is an abstraction from the settings in which people live together. It poses this as if it were a quality that is distributed in the population, dispensed in different quantities to each individual for their lifetime. Treated as a general trait, it marks each individual as more or less pleasing to another individual, so that the study of its effects involves an analysis of the variations in the points of view of the perceivers involved. This approach is consistent with what was said earlier about person perception. The body is treated as a proximal term, which remains implicit in the judgments made about persons by other perceivers, each treating the other as individuals in a free market of attraction and repulsion. While there has built up a literature on the place of such judgments in different social settings, and between people in different relationships to one another (Bull & Rumsey, 1988), the look of the perceiver has remained primary, and the assumption that attractiveness applies to all individuals in the same way has, with one important exception, been adhered to.

The exception is that group of people who are disfigured, in one way or another. The inclusion of facially disfigured people acknowledges that they are different, and studies of how they are perceived, how they perceive themselves, and possibilities for ameliorating their situation are now documented (Bull & Rumsey, 1988). However, these studies are not addressing the same problem as those of facial attractiveness and for this reason can be used to show the limitation of attractiveness research. The study of the facially disfigured is the study not of individuals in general, but of a stigmatized group in society (Goffman, 1963). A comparison of the concepts shows this difference. Attractiveness is the unmarked term relating to the general trait, so that we can ask, "How attractive is [any person]?" In contrast, disfigurement is the marked pole of an opposition (Greenberg, 1966), which means that it is impossible to ask, "How disfigured is [any person]?" because the question already refers to an excluded minority. In fact, the opposite of attractiveness is not disfigurement, but ugliness; the opposite of being disfigured is to be unmarked. This distinction can be seen to refer to a difference in the ontological status of the face. In one case, the physiognomy remains proximal and the differences are relied upon to be there (i.e., an attractive person looks different to an unattractive person, though we need not specify exactly how). In the other case, the features are known distally (e.g., the livid scar), and indeed the identification of the person as disfigured rests upon these aspects of the physiognomy being specifiable in this way. We can easily see how these two concepts are different, by looking at cases where they are joined together. For example, a woman regarded as beautiful may be scarred in a motor accident; her beauty is then flawed, but she does not necessarily become ugly. In the universities in Germany, there was a practice of dueling in order to gain a scar from one's opponent's sword. This might enhance the man's attraction for young women who regarded it as a sign of bravery. My point is that the movements between these two ways of seeing, related to the differences in physiognomy, and to distinctions between social groups, begin to show how the body is both relied upon and becomes figured within social relationships.

To conclude, social psychology studies attractiveness as a trait attributed by individuals to each other, so that the body remains implicit in a kind of self-fulfilling prophecy of categorizations (McArthur, 1982). When that happens, questions to do with the body remain folded back inside the generalized perceptual schemes presumed to lie inside the heads of the people concerned. The contradiction between equality and difference then becomes a question of competing beliefs or attitudes that perceivers hold and how these might be subject to modification. Such research participates in, rather than illuminates, the contradictions that it raises. In the endorsement of some images as attractive and of others as ugly, it locates the problem in the individual body under scrutiny. In the study of the conditions under which attractive people are perceived in different ways, this approach also locates the problem in the attributional processes of the observer. Both of these positions assume attraction to be a fixed quality, something independent of the social process. It could be said that having rejected phrenology as a scientific system, social psychology has turned to investigating its workings in the population.

The conditions under which attractiveness is made salient, to whom and by whom its criteria are applied, and the means by which the marks of difference are inscribed upon the body—all these things then remain occluded from view. The problem needs to be turned inside out in order to understand it; physical attractiveness as a trait description should be taken as a product, not a cause of social relationships. We need to ask instead about the way that group differences are made to designate objects of desire and of repulsion, and how bodily distinctions are made to signify as part of this process. Given these comments, it is hard to see how any inquiry constrained by the assumptions of the research tradition of person perception could satisfactorily address the aforementioned issues.

This critique points away from the individualized perceiver toward an appreciation of the differences between groups of people in how they watch and respond to the look of others. We turn to this in detail in the section that follows, examining the differences between men and women in the way that they observe each other, and the implications of this for social psychological theory.

The Look of Men and Women

"Nothing," Simone de Beauvoir (1972) wrote, "is more equivocal than a look." A look can exist at a distance and seem respectful yet it can also take possession of the image that it captures. De Beauvoir made this point when discussing the contradiction that many women feel when being looked at by men, a contradiction that is not shared by males. Men and women do not just see different things when they look at each other, but they look in different modes. The young girl, in traditional culture, is brought up to be an object of men's attentions, which she must win through attentions to her own appearance. This is in contrast to the socialization of boys, for whom the winning of her favors comes through their activities in the world. To be gazed at and admired is, de Beauvoir argues, the dream of many young girls, and the aim of some older women, too. The aforementioned contradiction arises from the fact that what men see in women is not primarily grace or beauty, but sexually attractive bodies, or more specifically, desirable parts of the body.

How men regard women and how women view men are important matters to consider here because they challenge the assumptions that underlie the psychology of attractiveness—that everybody looks and judges in the same way. In his analysis of the use of images in art and the media, Berger (1972) pointed out that the traditional relationship of men to women has been one of the keeper to the kept, and that the production and use of images need to be understood in the context of this historical fact. These images of men and women are reflections of their social presence, and these are of different kinds. Berger argues that a man's presence is dependent upon the promise of the power that he embodies. Large or small, this power relates to activities or to spheres in the outside world; it is exterior to him. In comparison, a woman's social presence expresses her attitude toward herself and defines what can and cannot be done to her. It is intrinsic to her person and is there to be read in her gestures, clothing, facial expression, and physical surroundings. Upon this difference is predicated the relationship of men as lookers upon women, and the relationship of women as being surveyed by men, as part of which women watch themselves being looked at.

Berger has argued that the history of the nude painting in Western art is premised upon these two relationships. The female nude is not merely a woman naked, but a woman naked as a spectator sees her. This device—of the woman who sees the spectator watching her—is used along with others, such as the model holding a mirror, to construct her as a sight for the eyes of a surveying male. In glamour photographs as well as in paintings, she is a conventionalized figure who, in being set on display as an object, sets aside her own status as a naked individual. The counterpart is the spectator, which the image presumes to be a man, a clothed but invisible stranger who is able to take and to possess the image as he surveys it. What he possesses, if only in imagination, is the submission of her social presence (what can and cannot be done to her) to his potentialities, no matter how large or how small they might be.

This form of argument has been extended to an analysis of pornography, where the objectification of the model is amplified by the concentration upon parts of her anatomy. The spread thighs, the proffered breasts and the thrust-out buttocks are evidence of the model's openness to scrutiny. Her performance (for that is what it is) reverses the presence of a naked individual into the image of a thing, of the flesh of anywoman and of all women (Griffin, 1981). Set in a painting or picture that a man might own and keep, the image calls out a look the aim of which is to reaffirm that the watcher acts while the model is there to appear as the quintessential being for him.

A comparison of things that men and women find erotic is worth undertaking, if only to show that women not only react differently to images but that looking is for many of them a secondary sense. It has been argued that where men's pinups of women are likely to be anonymous and naked, women's pinups of men (even in all-female areas) are likely to be of a particular person, clothed (Faust, 1980). There is an identification of the woman with a self who she might be for that man, not necessarily for men in general. Many women respond more readily to sounds and particularly to touch, a modality that is culturally diminished for men. Faust (1980) has suggested that the skin is not classed as a sex organ because the haptic response of the categorizers (mainly men) is so muted. The discrepancies between what men think women admire about their physique and what women say they admire (Wilson & Nias, 1976) is evidence to the fact that women do not look on men as men look on women. Where men have negative attitudes toward women, this effect would appear to be amplified, insofar as the men express strong preferences for an idealized masculine physique (Maier & Lavrakas, 1984).

The dominance of the visual mode, which characterizes the male attitude, becomes, when adopted as a premise for studying people in general, an unwarranted bias. It assumes that women look at men as men look at women, and therefore that judgments can be made within that modality comparing the preferences of the sexes. It is not merely that touching and hearing should be studied as well as vision, but also that the ways in which relationships are mediated through the senses, and the consequent ways in which the body is sensed and deployed, are matters that come within the psychologist's reach. Once acknowledged, this position makes possible a study of the qualitative differences in perceiving with special reference to gender. Equally important, it undermines the notion of this being a single process whereby a common eye surveys a generalized body.

One example that highlights such a difference is the case of women's clothing, particularly items such as corsets and high-heeled shoes. It might be thought that corsets and the fashion for tightlacing were just a form of control once inflicted upon women by men, a kind of imprisonment in clothing. This view does not stand up to extended analysis, where it has been argued that, while corsets were indeed an expression of male control, they also provided some women with a source of bodily pleasure and with a means for deploying their sexuality (Kunzle, 1982). Within the male perspective, corsets enhance the woman's bust and hips and cultivate a youthful appearance through the image of a slender body. Although such items of clothing have been discarded by many women as being too uncomfortable, some women who wore (and still wear) corsets have found that they can provide intense kinesthesic stimulation. Kunzle (1982) reports the experience of thoracic constriction by some women as "breathtaking" and erotic; Faust (1980) is explicit in her description of the sensations that were afforded by the high heels and girdle that some women gave up only after considerable indecision. We see here that an item that constrains the body serves different purposes for the woman and for the man; he sees, she feels. Similar points are made by both authors for the wearing of high-heeled shoes, which serve to emphasize the woman's sexuality for a male observer and to help one of Kunzle's respondents "feel in constant contact with my body" (1982, p. 19). Like high heels, the tight skirt requires women to walk in a "provocative hobble," so that men discern sexual invitation (and by implication, licence) through the use of an item that, like the corset, simultaneously expresses constraint in the deployment of the body.

In making this comparison of men and women's experience of corsets and high heels, I want to stress two points. First, the comparison shows the limitation of trying to understand the body only as it is given in images, or to the distant perceiver. (Chapter 6 discusses in more detail the living body, its deployment and its experiences, particularly from a phenomenological viewpoint.) The primacy of the visual mode would appear to derive from the male perspective, in which "the" body—any body—is to be understood in terms of what is seen of it or in it. The second point to be made is that this comparison is not intended to suggest some easy complementarity between these two relationships, men to women, and women to men. The woman walking in the high heels or wearing a tight skirt is not doing it just for (or mainly for) kinesthetic pleasure but within a situation in which she is also trying to make a particular impression. With this, we are brought back to the point with which we began this section—that a look is an equivocal thing. De Beauvoir suggests that when (young) women show their legs and their décolletage, they draw the stares of men, which flatter and hurt the women simultaneously. These stares, which are too penetrating (for the aforementioned reasons), disrupt the pleasure that a woman might gain from having captured a man's attention and can destroy it in the lust that a stranger expresses in his manner.

The feeling that de Beauvoir identifies as arising in the young girl who reveals too much of herself, or who draws unwanted attentions from men, is that of shame. Clearly, this feeling is dependent upon the cultural norms that are elaborated upon the relationship of women to men, as part of which will be a consciousness of women about their situation. Shame is an emotion that is often tied up with being seen, revealed, open to the scrutiny of others. It is also associated with conduct to do with one's body, but not exclusively to do with sexual matters. In some cultures, being seen while eating is a cause to feel shame. Therefore, it is not the transgression of some particular law, or the showing of a particular part of one's body that underlies shame, but to exist in a state whereby one's "bodilyness" (Fischer, 1964) is exposed, so that one has fallen from the world of subjects into the state of mundane things (Sartre, 1957). It is what Griffin (1981) has termed "the humiliation of *being* flesh" (p. 59). The nude model who is perhaps seen as shameless by a man looking at her photograph becomes for him simultaneously an object of contempt and one of increased eroticism. However, from her point of view, there might be no shame to earning a living where she poses and acts up for the camera, establishing her subjectivity in the "art of glamour." As Berger (1972) has said, nudity can be a form of clothing.

From these remarks, it can be seen that the scrutinized body cannot be understood as if it were a thing merely subject to inspection, available equally to all who would view it. The problems of appearance and attraction are bound up with culturally established differences in the ways in which people relate to one another. By choosing gender as our focus, we have seen that any social psychology that builds its analysis upon objective judgment is prey to missing important differences in how people see, and the extent to which seeing is, indeed, relied upon. More than this, to speak of the body as an object of person-perception research is to deal with an entity so abstracted from the various situations of social life as to be incapable of extending our understanding of what happens when people are in each other's physical presence.

Body Images in Society

The mechanisms for reproducing visual images has meant that the modern world is flooded with pictures of the body. While for some time advertisers have used models to sell goods of various kinds, today, the body itself has become the object as well as the vehicle for mass advertising (Featherstone, 1982). People's views of what they ought to look like, in and out of clothes, has never been subject to a greater range and intensity of messages. Whatever social psychologists think about questions of appearance, there can be no doubt that these are shaped by groups and classes in societies who have the opportunities and the means to press their interpretations. In the realms of beauty culture, of clothes and accessories, of sporting goods and of health-related items of all kinds, images of the body are used to exhort individuals to aspire to this or that shape or condition in the cause of health and good looks. There is now a moral demand for people to show themselves to their best advantage, to look after their bodies, and to please the eyes of all with whom they have dealings day by day. It follows, therefore, that to meet these criteria is to enjoy an alignment of one's condition with others with whom one would identify, an alignment achieved perhaps during a workout with a group and then confirmed in comparisons made against outsiders who do not exercise (Redican & Hadley, 1988). The coming together of the two discourses of health and beauty constitute a formidable channeling of people's views upon how they should treat their bodies, and how a healthy body should appear. (See Chapter 7 for a detailed discussion of this topic.) Part of the message is that desirable body shapes are those that are naturally good; indeed, the appeal to nature in many advertisements and articles concerning a healthy body attest to the fact that the normative basis of these messages is deliberately obscured. It is not surprising that the overweight have now been joined by the unfit in being made to feel guilty about their failure to progress in improving their bodily condition (Orbach, 1978; Yates, Leehay, & Shisslak, 1983).

The exposure to the plethora of images seen on television, at the movies, and in magazines means that people's views of what they should look like, of what is attractive, are matters of historical import. The invention of photography changed our way of seeing, just as television has altered our views about what we see. Photography and moving pictures made available models with whom people all over the world could identify. The movie star, and later the rock star, became simultaneously mysterious with the reproduction of their images; they also became untouchable, so that their images, pored over in their tens and hundreds, became the only source for determining what they are (or were) really like. (The continuing interest in pictures of Marilyn Monroe, in her appearance and her attraction, is perhaps the best example of this.) As part of this aggrandizement of the image of the stars, their admirers adopted their dress, looks, and mannerisms to create a style. What was attractive was thereafter no longer the body as given, but the body that echoed a recognizable image. On the television and in the streets, what we see are echoes of such images, not just the look of anatomical bodies or physiognomies.

We need to ask ourselves how images that promote particular body styles work; what is being arranged for others to see and, reciprocally, what form of perceptual experience is involved? Taking simple photographs first, such as those that any family or group of friends might take of one another, there is a strong tendency for these to be posed to show the members to be part of a group that is "healthy, happy and handsome" (Beloff, 1985). Such pictures play down oppositions and conflicts, much as do those that are portrayed on the front of women's magazines. By omission rather than inclusion, the woman on the front cover suggests a homogenized world of femaleness, stripped of its color, class, and economic variations (Ferguson, 1978).

This idea of omission is central to the explanation that Barthes (1972) put forward for images acting as myths. He used the example of a picture from the front of the magazine *Paris-Match*, showing a young black soldier saluting the French flag, the *tricoleur*. This could be read as showing the endorsement by members of the then-French colonies of France's ideologies. Barthes argued that the picture works to present precisely this meaning. It does this by draining the (image of the) black soldier of his history, which is omitted from the display. By itself, the form of the soldier giving the salute is shallow, Barthes says, and impoverished. However, once filled with the concept of French imperialism, it becomes replete with meaning, as myth. It must be understood that the soldier is not a symbol of the French empire, for he has too much physical presence, as a young black; nor is he just one example of a French soldier, for he is standing for something altogether wider and more elusive than the French army. The mythical status of the picture is achieved through the removal of the black soldier's cultural biography from his physical image, and its replacement with the intended meanings, which, says Barthes, tend to naturalize the French empire.

We can use this idea as a way of understanding the way that bodies are used in advertising various products or in promoting particular relationships of people to their world (these two are not wholly separable). Just as the soldier carries over into the picture his blackness and his young manhood, so the female model in the advertisement carries over her age and her femaleness. In the course of the pose or the action, the history and situation of the woman's image is removed in order that it be replaced with the meaning of the concept—the idea that the picture is trying to sell. The real world, which is stolen from the picture or commercial, is returned to the physical image as style. It works as myth when it appears natural and when it speaks for me or how I would like to be.

Another application of this idea might help to illustrate the point made earlier about the nude or glamour photograph presenting a generalized object to the spectator. The woman's body—her physical presence—is not that of an individual person with a biography; she is not a naked individual. In Barthes's terms, her physical form is emptied of its history in order that it be suffused with the ideology of pornography. She is not an example of a woman, nor does she symbolize womanhood; instead, she indicates in her postures and on her flesh an idea to do with possession, subjugation, and eroticism. The poses of the model, her collusion in the display, are the means by which her body becomes an instance of a message that attains a mythical quality, in the terms that Barthes uses the word *myth*. Male dominance condemns her body, her "look," to be nothing more than its instrument, while she displays herself in the name of this same domination. While nothing is hidden, everything is distorted.

The converse of this situation is exemplified by the woman photographer, Jo Spence, who has photographed herself naked on a couch, at 43 years of age, in a comparison with a similar picture of herself at 8 months old. The restoration of the body to its owner in this way is both salutary and disturbing to those who would see it through the eyes of a spectator of pornography (Beloff, 1985).

From these examples, we can see that what is omitted from advertisements, as well as from posed everyday photographs, is the history of the situation. Emptied of this, the bodies of the individuals can smile and posture so as to promote a myth of beautiful and successful people, or of happiness and community. Goffman (1976) used the example of a company selling its product through filming a well-dressed, happy-looking family at an expensive beach resort. He argued that this was, in principle, no different from an ordinary family arranging to take photographs of themselves, well-dressed and happy, enjoying their vacation at an expensive beach resort. In many walks of life, people try to look their best, or to look like someone by lending their faces to a look and their bodies to a style.

Again, we need to reaffirm that this argument relates to a particular historical period. The work of Berger et al. (1974), mentioned earlier, suggested that the adoption of personas is a modern phenomenon; in a traditional, strongly hierarchical culture, the idea of style does not appear. Only in a culture where individuals look to their own agency, rather than to society's institutions, does the concept of style become figured and constitutive of ways of appearing and attracting that were not there before.

Conclusion

In this chapter, we have seen that social psychology moved away from its brief and tentative excursion into looking at the body (perceptual accuracy studies) in order to establish the perceptual process as being of primary concern. Studies such as Sheldon's, in which the physical structure of the body was a datum giving direct access to personality, were abandoned. More than this, such studies represent the antithesis of a modern social psychology, which holds that all matters, including the corporeal, are subject to construction and to interpretation. The result of this has been that the body has all but vanished in theories of person perception. In its place has been established a world of generalized perceivers, for whom the body is recaptured only as another kind of percept, an aspect of self, a body image. One sign of the contradiction that this involves is revealed in research into attractiveness, where the assumption of equality that underpins the generalized observer is challenged by the patent inequalities of bodily form and of physiognomy. A tension is produced that is irresolvable within a theoretical position that cannot confront the body as anything other than an object of perception.

The development of person perception in its various forms has been away from an understanding of who sees, of how they see, and of the significance of seeing in the social world. Instead, the assumption of people as *essentially* individual perceivers has led to the situation and the biography of the perceiver–perceived being omitted. Important aspects of this background include gender and social position. This chapter has shown, with respect to gender, how attention to the body as the source and site of perception reveals questions that are occluded by the traditional person-perception approach. That approach puts in place of those inequalities the propensity for individuals to employ the body as an accoutrement of the self. This establishes people as individuals whose bodily existence is a matter of appearance, which can and should be molded according to the requirements of the day. At the same time, bodies become sites in a world where the arrangements and the opportunities for display are beyond the bounds of traditional social psychological theory.

This chapter deliberately draws a parallel between the social psychology of person perception and the work of myth in image making. It has been suggested that myth operates by draining the history of the imaged person and replacing it with a message. In social psychology, we have done something very similar, in removing from our subjects differences in their ways of seeing and of being seen. In the place of these differences has been positioned the individual who attributes and makes impressions, this being presented as if it were the natural form of social life, the nature of social existence. Arguably, this is also a myth, one sustained by the omission of the body, with its distinctions and inequalities, from the focus of the research effort.

Chapter 4

The Character of Movement

Perhaps that part of social psychology easiest to identify with research into the body is the field of nonverbal comunication. There is, by now, a considerable literature about people's gestures, facial expressions, postures and vocal characteristics. As yet, there has not emerged from this mass of evidence an overall, explicit view of the body as a medium of communication or of expression. Instead, there are several different approaches that, taken together, make an incoherent statement about bodily conduct and communication. In keeping with the approach established in the book so far, this chapter examines the assumptions that underlie certain approaches to the study of nonverbal communication. The argument is made that, in general, this research effort has often proceeded on the basis of narrow and inadequate views of the body. As a consequence of this and the dominance of the experimental method, we now know much about the use of various parts of the anatomy in social situations but still have only a tentative grasp of the body as a social entity.

From Culture to Communication

The beginnings of research into the body from a cultural standpoint were tied up with a new way of looking—or rather with the possibilities held out by the use of photography. In the course of their field trips together, Margaret Mead and Gregory Bateson had taken a great number of photographs. These showed individual members of the tribes that they had studied going about their everyday business together. This photographic record was, therefore, a valuable resource for understanding culture through the variations and commonalities in the bodily conduct of the peoples concerned. The attempt to make use of this material was published in a report entitled *Balinese Character: A Photographic Analysis* (Bateson & Mead, 1942). Of course, Bateson and Mead were not the first anthropologists to describe differing or special uses of the body, but their publication marked the beginning of an approach using a particular methodology, with a view to making bodily life central to social analysis. The inclusion of the word *character* in the title of the work reflects the terminology of the time; it also shows a concern with the total, unique form of a society that could be reflected in the everyday conduct of its people. Bateson and Mead did not focus upon the body in Balinese culture but described the forms of cultural practice that are given in the way that men, women, and children use their bodies in family life, in work, in play, and on ceremonial occasions.

It is reasonable to speak of the "character of movement" in relation to these observations because they view the body as reflective of culture. The body is seen as the locus of traditional practices concerning birth, child rearing, courtship and marriage, everyday survival, and death. However, these matters, which are more easily considered together in studies of pre-industrial societies, become separated in social analyses of modern societies whose character cannot readily be discerned. Perhaps it is not surprising that a shift away from the anthropologists' viewpoint should mean a change in how the body was considered in social analysis. More to the point, the emphasis upon ways of recording people's movements served to structure the research agenda so that general patterns in the body's use could be established. As a result, the description of the character of movement gave way, over the years, to the inscription of the body's communicative potential.

The main work of this chapter concerns some of the issues that arose from this relocation of interest, and which still structure much of the thinking of modern social psychologists about the body. Before turning to these, we need to say a little about some of the broad strands of research that followed from the work of the anthropologists, and about their different theoretical and methodological assumptions.

Birdwhistell (1952) acknowledged his debt to Bateson and to Mead when presenting his work on kinesics, the study of the microculture of movement in social relations. Birdwhistell's approach drew heavily upon their emphasis on the patterning of action in everyday contexts, giving special attention to methods for the detailed study of movement. His orientation to the use of the body in social life also owed much to the writings of Sapir, who had embraced the cultural analysis of behavior within an explanatory model of speech. By regarding speech as having a series of levels, it becomes possible to analyze these so that we can "put our finger on the precise spot in the speech complex that leads to our making this or that personality judgement" (Sapir, quoted in Birdwhistell, 1961). Similarly, a careful analysis of body motion should also reveal those levels in the system where culture exerts a common influence and where individuals make characteristic contributions. This depended upon parallels being drawn between the articulation of words and the movement of the body, both conceived as systems of communication. By the rigorous application of a scheme for the identification of postures and of movements of different parts of the body, Birdwhistell was able to identify what he termed *kines* or significant movements, and their dependent association into *kinemorphs*, these being strung into meaningful acts with junctures identifying "internally meaningful material."

The promise of this approach was that it would provide a detailed and methodical analysis of how people use their bodies in social relationships. At this point, I note the differences between Birdwhistell's work and that of the anthropologists. Instead of providing a description of the embodiment of culture, what has been called the "structural" approach to nonverbal behavior offered instead the prospect of isolating recurrent patterns of movement (Duncan, 1969). While there is scope within Birdwhistell's scheme to allow for differences between the individuals under observation (e.g., mothers and children), there is a tendency to see all bodies as subject to the same behavioral possibilities, and thence to having the same capacities. This involves, by use of a notational system for recording movement, change on the part of observers in their way of looking at the body. Instead of seeing *cultural practices* made by people, one looks at *movements* made with parts of the body. As Birdwhistell himself pointed out, patterning in the parakinesic data "appears in the body–motion system of all American movers" (1961, p. 94). The meaning of what people do can then be read in the structure of such movements carried out by people together, focusing directly upon the body as the medium in which the problem is given. This means that, while small phases of action can be studied in terms of recurrent patterns, the meaning of these actions (upon which interpretation must always rely), remains beyond the category system employed.

To take a more recent example of the structural approach, Kendon (1975) used a notational scheme to analyze the kissing of a couple seated on a park bench. His interpretation, however, relied upon words such as "fierce," "passionate," and "playful" to frame the facial interchanges that he had recorded. The point is that, while there is much that might be learned from detailed comparisons of bodily movement in social life, the rendering of the body into a field of patterned movements necessarily leaves outside of its terms criteria essential to its analysis; these criteria concern the cultural significance of the movements that have been made. In the case of Birdwhistell's work, carried out almost exclusively on Americans, the significance of movements has remained a cultural background feature shared by investigators and subjects alike.

While the idea of conduct having a natural history was taken from the work of anthropologists, so too was the assumption that its patterning required a different sort of explanation from that of physical phenomena. Among theorists who were concerned with problems of control and of systems theory, Bateson (1958) had in his earliest publications set out the basis of schismogenesis, and what was to become the double-bind theory of schizophrenia. In this work particularly, and in the field of cybernetics generally, the conceptual focus shifted from causal effects of one thing upon another to the relationships between bodies, to fields of mutual effects summarized as "systems." This conceptual shift was used by Scheflen (1964) in his approach to the study of posture within psychiatric consultations. Scheflen's work is introduced at this point because he, like Birdwhistell, contributed to social psychology's view of the body as operating within a patterned sequence of moves that make up a meaningful episode. Scheflen (1964) used the study of posture within conversation to show that the body's movements can be analyzed as mediators of what is considered to be essentially a communication system. Changes in smaller and in larger units of posture are described alongside developments in the progress of the interview taking place. Using the analogy of the linguistic system, the hierarchy of "points" (e.g., head tilts), "positions" (e.g., a postural shift) and "presentations" (e.g., leaving the room temporarily) is set out in relation to the clinical significance of these elements. The meaning of any particular posture is not to be found in the individual, by reference to motives or to causes, but to the context within which it takes place. The body is therefore a medium for the expression of signals that derive from the culture concerned, and it lends its movements to a system of exchanges, the patterned form of which the participants have learned as members of that culture. In being removed from the realm of motives and animal expressions, the body in Scheflen's "behavioral systems approach" becomes effectively a conduit for an exchange established upon its redundant code; for example, people sit in a congruent manner or stand so as to include (or exclude) others entering the room.

Both Birdwhistell's and Scheflen's work illustrate the influence of anthropological writing upon the analysis of body movement. Both authors reflect the concern that the body be studied in natural contexts, although it should be apparent from the little said previously that there is a bias toward those contexts being essentially about communication. Unlike some studies located within the anthropological literature, this communication is not grounded in specific actions or gestures. To that extent, comparisons of particular actions across cultures (e.g., posture—Hewes, 1955, or gestures of respect—Firth, 1978) become secondary. What is it, then, that the bodies of the participants are communicating in the work of Birdwhistell and Scheflen? It is information about the exchange itself; the body has become a medium for communicating things within and about the situational context of the individuals concerned.

A rather different perspective upon nonverbal behavior is gained from the work of Argyle and his colleagues, working in Britain (Argyle, 1969, 1983; Argyle & Kendon, 1967; Kendon, 1967). This derived from the work of psychologists carrying out research into skill acquisition in the work setting. In the 1950s, stimulus–response theories were critically undermined by the concepts of cybernetics, the new science of information and control. Essential to this approach was the concept of feedback, through which a system could maintain an output (a behavior) directed to achieving a predetermined change in its relationship with its environment. From this perspective, skilled performance is defined as "performance that is nicely adapted to its occasion," and "an individual engaged in interaction is engaged in a more or less skilled performance" (Argyle & Kendon, 1967). This involves people in watching others for signs that their behavior is not provoking a disturbance or otherwise leading the exchange away from their desired goal. If interaction becomes a performance, it does not do so in the aesthetic sense. Instead, its key element is control, through which social relationships become regulated exchanges and their constituent moves become skills to be acquired and adaptively employed.

Over the years, this research perspective has given rise to studies of how different channels of nonverbal communication (e.g., gaze, touch, proximity) function in the course of social interaction. The word *function* is appropriate to describe how, from this perspective, the body in social life is seen as a means whereby individuals make an adaptive fit with each other. Stand people close together, and they will avert their gaze in order to reestablish a desired level of intimacy (Argyle & Dean, 1965); mask their eyes so that they cannot see each other's expressions, and their conversation will be disturbed (Argyle, Lalljee, & Cook, 1968). This work falls within the category that Duncan (1969) called the "external variable" approach to the study of nonverbal behavior; it links variation in specific channels of bodily communication with differences in other (external) psychological variables. In this respect, it is different from the structuralist approach of Birdwhistell, in that it shifts attention away from the body as a medium of expression (in the broad sense of the term) to the body as a means of communication and control.

Although regularly cited in the literature, the structuralist approach has been recognized to have remained largely programmatic (Spiegel & Machotka, 1974). The experimental approach, on the other hand, has become differentiated into the study of posture, gaze, proximity, touch, facial expression, and gesture. This difference between the two approaches is also reflected in the method of study that each adopts; where the structuralists, in the tradition of anthropology, study whole episodes, the social psychologists use the experimental method. Argyle (1975) has argued that experiments are needed to study small and rapid movements (e.g., gaze and eye-blinks) that require special equipment, and to determine the answers to questions of causality (e.g., whether forms of bodily expression are innate). As a result, the movement from the natural setting into the laboratory has meant that the body has come under close scrutiny; rather, it should be said that the communicative potential of certain parts of the body has been studied in great detail.

Research into the communicative role of the body includes work embracing cross-cultural and ethological perspectives. Included here are studies of gesture (Ekman & Friesen, 1969b) and of the facial expression of emotions (Ekman, 1972, 1977). For these authors, the categorization of gestures has been a central problem. Building upon the work of Efron (1942), they have attempted a classification of gestures according to their communicative function. One of the results of their analysis has been the realization that body movements or discrete gestures do not contain their own meaning, but depend for this upon the context in which they are carried out. For example, a clenched fist might be classed as an "emblem" where its meaning is shared within a culture, or as an "illustrator" where it accompanies speech to emphasize the meaning that is given by the speaker at that moment (Ekman, 1977).

In their work on the cross-cultural meaning of facial expressions, these authors have claimed support for the view that emotions (as shown in the face) have both universal and cultural features. This theory suggests that people in all cultures experience the same bodily reactions to certain basic emotions (e.g., fear, pain), but that the expression of these feelings to others is subject to what they term "display rules" (Ekman, 1972). From this perspective, the body becomes a site for the containment or the revelation of feelings that are given in physiological response to events. This is not unlike the position put forward by Goffman (1959), who likened the "eruptions" of the body to information "given off" by the performer. In this case, the effective presentation of a performance depends upon the judicious use of such information, suppressing those responses that would contradict the "character" being put forward and allowing the display of others that might further the claims made in that name. Compared to both the structuralist and external variable approaches, the work of Ekman and Friesen has been concerned with the origin of expressions, and not only with their deployment in social interaction. Though subject to cultural constraints and usage, the body remains for them a site in which meaning is also originated. This meaning cannot be transferred to culture or to individual minds, but exists in their theory as an irreducible quality of the body considered as a biological system.

These three positions—the structuralist, the external variable, and what I call the "universal/cultural"—are representative of the approaches that have been made to the study of nonverbal behavior. I have presented them, albeit briefly, because I want to show them as strands in the debate about the place of the body in social psychology. Each one raises different issues. The structuralist approach sees in the pattern of movement a regularity that, if sufficiently analyzed in its structure, could reveal the meaning implicit within it. The question raised here is whether nonverbal behavior is part of a code not unlike that of the linguistic system. The external variable approach, which must include much of the experimental research in social psychology into nonverbal behavior, has investigated the function of the different channels by which we can communicate with the body. This question concerns the extent to which the body, viewed as a complex of different channels, is to be understood as a regulative device for coordinating or manipulating interaction. Last, the universal/cultural approach raises questions about the degree to which the body can be understood by identifying it with the emotions and with their expression.

The purpose of this chapter is not to analyze these points in isolation, but to argue that each of the approaches has had the effect of simultaneously raising questions about the body and of limiting the scope for providing the answers. How has this happened? I suggest that their common focus upon the body—its movements, expressions, and spatial distribution—has been part of a narrowing of attention to particular kinds of exchanges. Many studies focus upon two-person conversations, or upon small groups. While there is nothing wrong with this in principle, the coupling of this scrutiny with questions of communication (aided by the experimental method) has meant that the body has been seen essentially as a means for the sending and receiving of messages. Focusing more upon the face and upon those gestures and signals accompanying speech, "the body as part of culture" has been displaced by "nonverbal behavior as part of communication." Paradoxically, this has been aided by the different strands of research contributing to the problem field. From surveys of this topic, it might appear that the contributions of psychologists, anthropologists, linguists, communication theorists, and ethologists would guarantee breadth of vision. This does not automatically follow. In fact, one of the problems in this field is that the diversity of approaches has been used to juxtapose different findings to suggest that they can be sewn together to create a broad perspective on the problem. This only obscures the differences where they exist, and keeps our attention focused upon the body as a signaling system, when we might be questioning some of the assumptions that underlie this approach and the limitations of the work carried out so far.

Nonverbal Behavior, Speech, and the Question of a Code

The conception of the body implicit in research into nonverbal behavior is that of a complex signaling system. The model for this communication system is, naturally, spoken language. Of course, the ethological perspective views the human body, like those of the animals, as a means of communication that has evolutionary features. However, the fact that language is unique to humans has been taken as further support for its use as a model for the study of how people communicate with gestures and expressions. It has been pointed out that it was Sapir, not Darwin, who realized that body movement is coded and that this code has to be learned for successful communication (Birdwhistell, 1968). The attempt to understand nonverbal behavior as a coded system has meant that comparisons have been drawn, simultaneously, between gesture and language, *and* differences have been noted between the two (Argyle, 1975; Hall, 1963; Leach, 1972). Language and bodily communication have been seen as familiar, in that they can be understood in terms of the same kind of analysis. The clearest example of this is the claim that movements can be analyzed into units, the compound forms of which can be studied using the methods of the structural linguists (Birdwhistell, 1968). Differences between language and bodily communication are often discussed in terms of their different function in social interaction; words convey messages while bodily movements and expressions serve to regulate the interaction itself.

In spite of the distinctions that have been drawn between the two systems, there has been a tendency to analyze bodily communication in the terms used to understand spoken language, and to focus upon conversations or similar contexts involving speech. This has meant that researchers have asked questions concerning such matters as the importance of nonverbal information in spoken messages (Argyle, Salter, Nicholson, Williams, & Burgess, 1970), and its place in the regulation of conversational turn-taking (Beattie, 1983; Duncan & Fiske, 1977; Kendon, 1967). This has been accompanied by the free use of analogy in talking about the body in social life, so that phrases such as "body semantics" (Abercrombie, 1968) and "the syntaxes of bodily communication" (Argyle, 1975) have entered the literature. In effect, the very term *nonverbal behavior/communication* is testimony to the fact that the body's movements have come to be seen as first and foremost an accompaniment to spoken language.

In this section, I try to show the consequences of this position for an understanding of the body in social life. Its limitations were appreciated some time ago, when it was claimed that the very title of Hinde's (1972) book, *Non-Verbal Communication* was a "logocentric manoeuvre" (Benthall, 1975). By this was meant that the academic world, which is concerned with words, had tried to subsume a phenomenon that defied inclusion in its verbally centered terms. Before taking up this argument in more detail, I want to address a related issue concerning the use of the terms *behavior* and *communication* as they are used alongside the term *nonverbal*. In an important commentary, Wiener, Devoe, Rubinow, and Geller (1972) showed the fundamental weakness of research designs that assumed that distinctions made by observers about someone's bodily movements constituted an instance of nonverbal *communication*. They argued that, to accept an observer's judgment that a particular gesture or posture is communicative, when the actor is unaware of having made the movement or of when a judgment has been made, is to fuse the notion of *sign* with the notion of *communication*. In this way, anything that one person can select about another's movements or expressions becomes a communication; and if so, it must communicate something, even if the actor does not know what it is. The danger of basing a program of research upon this assumption is that one begins to seek for a code within which to make these movements sensible. Wiener et al. argued that the existence of a code cannot be deduced from such studies, but remains a working assumption, a supposition. This assumption is more likely to receive support in contexts involving verbal communication (as often used in research into nonverbal behavior), where movements with shared meanings are likely to be made.

In their paper, Wiener et al. went on to specify what they considered to be the logical requirements for gestures to be organized and understood in a code that has languagelike features. Among these were that the behaviors must have referents, and that the referents of the behaviors must be known and used by the group. What these authors took up only in passing were those behaviors that do not satisfy their definition of communications. In effect, while their critique had a special purpose in suggesting that only a certain class could be called "communication," it also had a general effect in calling for an understanding of nonverbal behaviors that are, in their terms, not communicative. Essentially, there is more to bodily conduct than communication of a languagelike kind.

Seen from the outside, a person who acts *in such a way as to* do something may sometimes be indistinguishable from someone who acts *in order to* bring it about. Mackay (1972) cited the example of the schoolboy with spots on his face; the boy's appearance informs his classmates that he might have measles, though he does not intend to communicate this to them. Better to say that, like the person who blushes, his spots are a symptom, not a communication. Wiener et al. make the same argument, using accent as an example; accent informs but it is not normally employed as a means for sending a message about oneself. To make the argument relevant to the body as a whole, we can even consider the portrayal of gender through bodily comportment in these terms. The way in which men and women walk is not necessarily a communication of maleness of femaleness, symbolizing either their place in the social structure or their biological relationship to one another. It may be, like the spots or the accent, a symptom not a communication (Goffman, 1976).

One more example offered by Mackay is useful in showing where we might look further to reorganize our view of the relationship between nonverbal behavior and nonverbal communication. He considers a person sailing with the international distress signal at the masthead. When offered help, the person claims not to know the flag's meaning but to be flying it because it looked attractive. Mackay says that the person *seemed* to be communicating and *was perceived* as communicating, but was not in fact doing so; s/he was only *exposing*, not using the communication signal. This raises the question of intention to communicate, and in so doing shows that communication is not a field or set of actions but a context of behavior. It is, in Bateson's (1987) terminology, a difference that makes a difference. Returning to the previous example, in a *different* scenario, if the schoolboy is perceived by his classmates as deliberately parading his spots before them, his appearance is likely to provoke a different reaction from his fellows.

Given these qualifications, it is a poor view that sees the body as an assembly of channels, each of which has sign potential in relation to one or another social situation or relationship. To know that some people stand nearer to or further away from a partner than others, or that gaze varies from one situation to another, tells us little about how and under what circumstances these signs become communicable, or are made to be so. The findings appear meaningful to us, the readers of such studies, because we share with the experimenters an (observer's) understanding of what the chosen situation is about, and of the aims appropriate to individuals in such circumstances. The more interesting question concerns the way that people arrange that their actions are seen as communications for others, or else allow those actions to remain as information to be used for inference only (Goffman, 1959).

The very term non*verbal* indicates that this is behavior to be identified in relation to the spoken word. While distinctions have been drawn, for example, between paralinguistic and extralinguistic behavior (Abercrombie, 1968), the focus has remained upon the body as a supporter of conversation, or as something integral with speech production (McNeill, 1985). This approach does not address the body as such, but assumes it to be a physical expression of cognitive processes more adequately articulated in speech. In effect, the nonverbal pole of this opposition has remained unelaborated in social psychological research, being a shadow only of the unmarked verbal label. The restriction of the majority of research settings to two-person conversations or meetings, coupled with attention to faces, eye contacts, and gestures has allowed this narrow view to continue almost without challenge.

There are, of course, many forms of bodily conduct that are not about conversation, although they involve symbolism; dance, sport, lovemaking, war, and play to name some major examples. The difference between these acts and conversation is that they are presentational, or nondiscursive (Langer, 1951). The meaning that they carry lies in their being performed, and they have a strong semantic aspect precisely because of this. The description of gestures as being iconic is partly a recognition of this fact. By comparison, spoken language involves the use of arbitrary symbols that digitize our experience of the world, being concerned with boundaries and objects (Bateson, 1987; Wilden, 1980). By virtue of its grammatical structure, language is strong in syntax but weak (compared to gesture) in semantics. To say "I love you" effectively is not to pronounce the words correctly, but to show in one's manner the strength of one's feelings. What we call "strength of feeling" is a clue to the difference that Bateson (1987) proposed between language and action. Where language is digital (dualistic, measurable in discrete units), bodily gestures and expressions are analog (continuous, measurable only on continua) in form. This means that they are conveyed, not through propositions and denials, but through increases and dimunitions in magnitude. This, however, means that when we speak about such matters, we are forced to communicate in arbitrary symbols. These are better suited to discrete ideas than to something that is a continuum and the essence of which is ambiguity. That is why it is difficult to convey, in words, degrees of pain or to describe adequately our feelings. It is also the reason that we often find it difficult to convey the meaning of bodily movements in words alone, where to do this effectively requires that the sentiment attaching to the action must also be described.

The implications of this argument for the study of the body as a system for making nonverbal signals are profound. They suggest that efforts first to digitize it by analyzing separate movements, and then to ascribe meanings to these, misses the essence of how we do communicate in this way. By extending to the body the properties that properly belong to language alone, researchers are in danger of misconceiving not only the role of gesture in conversations but also the place of the body in social life. It then appears primarily (if not only) a support for the communication of verbal message; or else it is granted the form of language itself, in which its separate parts are severally and jointly presumed to carry their own coded messages. The failure to establish such a code is the legacy of this protracted program of research. Alternatively, the body is seen as the repository of emotional expressions, which means that instead of locating the code in the social world, there is the possibility that it is rooted in an invariant (biological) structure that we all come to learn.

None of these possibilities have led to anything like an adequate understanding of the body in social relationships. The remainder of this chapter broadens the analysis to show how, as a consequence, each of these claims to an explanation of nonverbal behavior is further undermined.

The Determination of Emotions

One aspect of research into nonverbal behavior has been the attempt to determine the degree to which expressions are universal or are culturally formed (Eibl-Eibesfeldt, 1972; Ekman, 1977). The recognition of emotion has been a focus of interest, especially the degree to which people can recognize emotions in the faces of people from cultures other than their own. In summarizing one line of work, Ekman (1977) offers a "neuro-cultural" account, in which the response systems identifiable with different emotions are subject to modification in terms of the display of the cultural rules concerned. Essentially, however, this explanation uses concepts such as "response system" and "affect program" to suggest the bodily side of emotion, the cultural aspect of which lies in the kinds of elicitors of these responses and in the social rules for the management of their expression. In these terms, emotion is a particular form of response, and the body is the repository of the different programs of response available. In their methodology, Ekman and Friesen (Ekman, 1972) have conceived emotion as something to be judged in the face of one person by another. This suggests that the feeling expressed by one person is credited to that individual through the judgment of another. This viewpoint proposes the body as a site for emotional display, such emotions being integral with the workings of the body as a physiological system. Even though they are subject to cultural interpretations, from this perspective, emotions are responses of individual behavioral repertoires.

At a commonsense level, this idea of emotion as a complicated response to circumstances lacks the one thing that is significant about feelings in social relationships; they are engaging, they make a difference. So, to have a friend break down into tears when talking with you is not merely to *see* sadness, or to *recognize* an expression of distress, but to be caught up in a new relationship with that person. Emotions do not just lie "in" or "on" our own or other people's bodies, because they are expressive of the *relationship* that we have to each other. This is not an argument for removing emotion from the body in our explanations (Harré, 1986b), but for recognizing the place of the body in the different ways that feeling is evoked in social life. It is surely a mistake to see emotion as a separate class of behaviors, distinct from other kinds of action, when it is arguable that much, if not all of people's everyday experience is colored with feeling.

The point made in the previous section—that bodily expressions involve analog (rather than digital) communication—is important in this context. Analog communications are iconic, in being either directly or indirectly related to the things that they indicate. In Bateson's (1987) terms, analog communications express the *relationship* between people or between individuals and their environment, or as Watzlawick, Beavin, and Jackson (1967) said, they "set context." Examples of how relationships can be invoked in this way include the raised fist, the caress, the cold handshake, or even the crouching and tail-wagging of the family dog. In these cases, the use of the body is made mysterious by the convention of applying names to these exchanges, thus making them appear as entities with discrete boundaries. Once given names, as emotions, and located inside one or other of the parties involved, it then becomes necessary to try to explain them on this basis. Once misconstrued as discrete entities, subject to the same rules as digital communication, there follow vain attempts to understand feelings within the logic of words or of processes that operate according to digital principles.

I now take the position of affect being relational. For example, to become angry with another person is to impose a setting within which one's words and actions are given a particular significance, invoking a relationship that makes a claim upon how the other people should treat you. This evocation of relationship is achieved through the body, in what might be called a "concrete realization," to contrast it with the use of the arbitrary symbols of language. To impose such a setting—either deliberately or otherwise—is to experience a qualitative change both in oneself (e.g., anger) and in one's situation; then there are people and things that appear negative, or things that one wishes to change or to eradicate. A similar account was given by Sartre (1971), who used the example of a man who hears that he will shortly meet someone he loves, from whom he has been separated for a long time. He is filled with joyful anticipation and dances and sings with happiness. Sartre argues that the need to possess the desired object is so strong that the man makes use of his body as an instrument of incantation in order to grasp it directly. His joy is "magical behavior" that embodies a relationship within which his loved one is possessed all at once, symbolically. About the man's body, Sartre says,

> The various activities expressive of joy, as well as the muscular hypertonicity and the slight vascular dilation, are animated and transcended by an intention which envisages the world through them. (1971, p. 72)

This view emphasizes the body not as expressing an emotion that it already contained, but as setting out an *attitude* embracing the man, the loved one, and, indeed, his world within a symbolic relationship. This view can be extended to all feeling, so that emotion signifies something of people's mode of relationship, as whole individuals, to their social and their physical worlds (Levy, 1984; Radley, 1988b).

The example of the man who dances for joy lies somewhere between the two extremes of the person who is gripped by emotion and the individual who does or says something with feeling. In the first case, the person is apparently taken over by the emotion, and on these occasions, we speak of the individual in the passive voice; people are consumed with love, are overcome with anger, are driven to despair. In the second case, the feeling is something that is dramatically employed by the person, who is concerned to color what is said or done. Although we might sometimes confuse these two instances, in everyday life, we not only recognize them as different, but we experience them differently. As actors, the anger that one feels in a rage is not the same as the anger that one invokes in order to send one's child off to bed. Where, in the first case, the person is identified with the emotional relationship, in the second, the emotion has a gestural quality insofar as the parent's raised hand is indicative of possibilities within the family rule structure.

In order to distinguish further between how the body is employed in each of these examples, we can make use of the distinction between *having a posture* and *making a gesture* (Lamb & Watson, 1979). A person who flies into a rage can be said to be posited by the relationship; that individual, from the flushed face to the whitened knuckles, can be said to be "all posture." By comparison, a ballet dancer uses graceful steps or powerful leaps to evoke in the audience a sense of pity or of wonder. Using the whole body to create this sentiment, it is not necessary for the dancer to feel these actual emotions. What is important is that all of the dancer's body is deployed in the symbolic communication of the relationship or theme that conveys feeling to the audience. In this way, the dancer can be considered to be "all gesture." The evocation of feeling, its referent, and the coordination of bodily experience are quite different in these two situations. In the former case, emotion is expressed *through* the body of the angry person; in the case of the dancer, it is evoked *with* the body in relation to a symbolic sphere to which the movements give vital expression.

This distinction between acting through the body and acting with it is but a makeshift conception that allows us to see that emotions are not a separate field of human experience. One of the consequences of treating emotions as a subclass of behavior is that they are implicitly opposed to rationality, and with that, they are underpinned by the separation of mind from body. In this, the commonsense view that has exerted its influence over psychology for much of its history, emotional expression is synonymous with physiological eruption, whether it be of laughter, of crying, or of movement. This makes it impossible to understand things done with feeling and, for our purposes, to understand the role of the body in these expressive acts. Langer (1951) has made the distinction clear in her treatment of significance in music. She argues that music is not self-expression (an outpouring of felt emotion), but the formulation and representation of sentiments, ideas, and moral tensions. It presents these issues in the forms of a "logical picture," the aim of which is an invitation to insight, not a plea for sympathy.

Langer's analysis is consistent with the idea that the body communicates analogically; the logic of music (and of other art forms) involves a rationality that is based upon pattern, not upon discursive propositions. This rationality involves a formalizing and a distancing of the person from the material. It is this psychical distance that allows the composer to articulate complexes of feeling that language can hardly name, let alone analyze; "we do not compose our exclamations and jitters." (Langer, 1951, p. 222). Where emotions expressed through the body, as in rage, are reflective of the person and the setting in which this takes place, such is not the case with music. The feelings that are evoked in the playing of a concerto, for example, do not depend upon emotional disturbances in either the composer or the players. What then does the playing of the music allow? It enables the listener to *conceive of* the forms that the composer has set out. In this, it is quite different from the sign given in the attitude of the person approaching us with red face and clenched fists; these are *symptomatic of* his (or her) relationship to us, and something with which we have to deal.

The power of music and other nondiscursive activities, such as dance, is that they communicate ideas that spoken language is inadequate to express. As pointed out already, this is also true for emotions that are simply felt. In particular, gestures are capable of expressing contradictory feelings, as well as ambiguous ones. Koestler (1964) analyzed the phenomenon of weeping to show how it is different from crying. Where crying is a self-assertive emotion, weeping is a self-transcending or participatory emotion. It does not tend toward action, but toward quiescence; it signifies a relationship that is lived out in the act of shedding tears. These may be tears of joy, or of relief or of both at the same time. Similarly, gestures may become part of such feeling, as when a bereaved woman sinks her hand into a glove belonging to her dead husband; in doing this, she gains some comfort and closeness through what is also an intensification of her sorrow. These are simple examples of what can be complexes of feeling that are very difficult, if not impossible, to analyze adequately with words. The point that Langer makes about music, which can be extended to other nondiscursive presentations, is that it is peculiarly fitted to the communication of *the idea* of such complexes of feeling.

I now return some of these points to the idea that the body is a repository of certain basic emotions, or more explicitly that particular facial expressions are universally associated with particular emotions (Ekman & Friesen, 1971). While it is interesting to know how members of one culture judge the facial expressions of another, it can tell us little about the ways in which these emotions are employed, separately or together in everyday life. Given what was said previously about the body being able to communicate forms that language can only haltingly set out, the linguistic naming of separate emotions and their being distinguished one from the other is no basis upon which we can understand how the body is employed in the communication of sentiment. As was mentioned earlier on, the logocentric attitude has dominated research in this field, perhaps because, as Langer remarked, "it seems peculiarly hard for our liberal minds to grasp the idea that anything can be *known* which cannot be *named*" (1951, p. 232).

Gestures, therefore, are expressive in two senses of the word. They are symptomatic in being indicative of the relationship in which people stand together; that is why a frown or a turning away of the head may be "felt" by the other person as an insult or a threat. However, gestures can also communicate a meaning that depends upon a world of symbolic forms, where individuals have the capacity to conceive of feelings that they do not presently own. The problem with research into nonverbal communication is that the coexistence of these two meanings of expressive gesture has rarely been realized; rather, where they have been distinguished, the two forms have been quite separated. This has led to two distinct subthemes. One concerns the expression of spontaneous emotion, with all that entails about the workings of culture upon a biological substrate. The other has involved the attempt to read gestures as if each one denoted something particular or were put together in a languagelike fashion.

Next, I elaborate upon the capacity to conceive feelings using symbolic forms. Things done *with* feeling, or where there is a psychical distance involved, indicate what can be called "virtual self-expression," having a *virtual* power to affect us (Langer, 1953). The actor on the stage can evoke in the audience a sense of tragedy that neither s/he feels "really," nor the members of the audience retain outside of the story to which they attend. However, it would be a mistake to see these performances as mere storytelling. The expressiveness of the actor or the movements of the ballet dancer are portrayals of relationships, of our sense of these as feelings; they do not refer to distinct things, although these may be present in a known storyline.

I make these points about the stage in order to draw a comparison with the expressiveness of selves in social life. This argument, best represented in the work of Goffman (1959, 1961), proposes that the roles that people play are not spontaneous expressions of real selves that lie somewhere inside them but are performances, the form of which is sensible only within a social drama. What we call "social selves" are the product of performances that "come off," and their owners are credited with the virtual powers by which these performances are sustained. For Goffman, the body is the vehicle by which individuals may foster a particular character; that is, in our manner, we give certain messages. At the same time, we give off information that may or may not be consistent with the character that we are attempting to put forward. Hence, the body is the site of expressive features that are both symbolic *and* symptomatic. The universal task for members of society is to contrive an appearance of social poise, as part of which is the need to show control of one's body and its functions. Put in this way, the relationship between these two expressive features suggests that what is "given" as a communication is what is symbolic (e.g., a cultivated manner), while what is "given off" is symptomatic (e.g., eating greedily). However, while this is often true, it is but one way in which these two features are expressed by the body.

The reason for exploring expressiveness within the dramaturgical metaphor is to show more of the relationship between the two features that have been distinguished. The idea of dividing the body into its symbolic and its symptomatic features is tempting, and there is evidence that its various parts are differentially subject to voluntary control (Ekman & Friesen, 1969a). However, in order that an effective performance be fashioned, it is necessary that such things as level of involvement, keenness, and proper concern are reflected in the person's manner. This means that it might be appropriate to show shock, or pleasure or outrage, and for this to be seen as heartfelt—as spontaneous. In other contexts, for example in the case of flirting or love-making, what are seen as the lusts of the body must sometimes be muted or transposed if the individual is not to be seen as brutish.

The psychical distance to which Langer drew attention was paralleled by Goffman (1961) in his discussion of role distance. This concept is relevant to our discussion of the body, for it sets out some of the requirements for role performances involving virtual expression. Goffman introduced this concept through the example of the merry-go-round, where one can see riders of different ages astride the circling horses. For small children, the ride is a challenge and somewhat of a feat of endurance, given that they have to cope physically with staying on the ride. For older children and teenagers, their casual attitude of not holding onto the horse, of turning around or laughing with friends, is testimony to their not being mere riders of wooden horses. They are concerned to demonstrate to the people standing by that they have mastered the ride, and the fun that they have is part of making this obvious. This example of the younger and older children indicates that, for the former, the ride has a reality, a substantive quality that is missing from the experience of the latter. The older children treat the merry-go-round in a ritual fashion, the ride having more of a ceremonial quality about it.

This difference between acts that are substantive and those that are ceremonial is basic to Goffman's accounts of social life. Referred to the body, it parallels the distinction drawn between symptomatic and symbolic gestures. In the case of the rider on the merry-go-round, the laughing and the exclamations of joy might not reflect his or her spontaneous feeling but the tenor of a performance whose purpose is to communicate an attitude of easy accomplishment directed toward the people watching. By comparison, the small child who clutches at the pole attaching the horse to the ride shows in the strength of grip and concentrated expression that he or she is grappling with an issue of balance. This does not mean that in either case there is, for the older child, only virtual expression, and for the younger, spontaneous (or symptomatic) expression, even if this is how it is seen by the casual bystander. In the case of the little child, there is the need to contain his or her anxiety and to endure what is meant to be a pleasurable activity. In the case of the adolescent rider, all of the taunts and joke gestures depend for their validity upon him or her staying on the horse. To fall off would be to dispel the image being fabricated.

Bodily communication, therefore, is not best thought of as being coded messages from one individual to another, or as the eruption of emotion (read more or less accurately) in the face or demeanor of a person being perceived. Instead, it is taken up in rituals that both draw upon and demand that appropriate feelings be shown; emotion is not merely a response to situations, but is also a requirement for certain situations to be defined in a particular way. The party and the funeral are well-known contexts of this kind, where the participants are expected to contribute or to lend their bodily attitudes toward a proper definition of the setting concerned. The problem with thinking of emotions as a separate class of expressions from, say, communicative gestures is that we are then inclined to categorize a given exchange or action as being one thing or the other. We then imagine that we see ritual devoid of feeling, or else emotional expression, the function of which is presumed to be some cathartic effect.

Take for example, the cockfights of Bali described by Geertz (1972). In these fights, two cocks are matched in a contest that will mean either death or severe injury to one of them, and the loss and gain of money placed in bets by the onlookers. While it goes on, those watching are caught up in cheering on their preferred bird, participating at second hand in a contest that Geertz describes as one of "untrammeled rage."

Upon its conclusion, there will be winners and losers, with all of the exhuberance and deflation that accompanies these outcomes. At one level, here is an occasion for extremes of emotion to be shown. However, at another level, Geertz argues that these contests are ritual exchanges, with precise rule structures. The cockfight is like an art form in being presentational. It does not exist to control or to alter the status of the participants in the real world, but to render everyday life comprehensible. It does this by becoming, "an image, fiction, a model, a metaphor, the cockfight is a means of expression" (Geertz, 1972). How then do we explain the emotions of the people taking part? Certainly there is strong feeling present, but the competition does not exist because of this, nor is the feeling a mere consequence of the cockfight. As Geertz puts it, "its function is neither to assuage social passions nor to heighten them (though, in its play-with-fire way, it does a bit of both), but, in a medium of feathers, blood, crowds, and money, to *display them*" (1972, my emphasis).

In this situation, which can stand for many similar types of occasions in Western cultures too, the emotions of the participants should not be taken only as forms of spontaneous self-expression. We should not mistake ritual for feeling. However, to recognize the virtual qualities in the emotion of the Balinese cockfight is not to deny their substantive features. As with any presentational episode, it has to be enjoyed, savored, or suffered, in effect endured; and part of this endurance is the lending of the onlooker's body as a medium for the display. The relationship of struggle and the shifting balance of the contest are known *with* the observer's body, *through* which the ritual pattern is established, grows, and fades.

Clearly, this argument depends upon the identification of ritual elements in social life, or rather upon the establishment of different forms of ritual in everyday exchanges. In spite of Goffman's claim that life is a ceremony, there are distinct differences between the way that the body is employed in the ballet and in the office. Even if these are claimed to be of a fundamentally similar kind, in offering elements of both spontaneous and virtual expression, we need to say how these situations are different in the way that the body is used in displays that are enacted. To overlook it, or to relegate it to a secondary place in the analysis of interaction is, in the light of the foregoing discussion, unwise. Even Goffman (1959) is guilty of this when he argues that we need to abandon the equating of the self with the body, and to see the latter only as a peg on which will be hung the collaborative efforts of the social circle. Although this proposal is part of the wider argument that the self be seen as a social product, it nevertheless reduces the body to being a passive (though irreplaceable) vehicle in the ritual exchange process. This actually undermines the idea that the body is crucial in the establishment of the social self. It can also be seen to fall short of what is required of any explanation of the part that feelings play in the course of everyday relationships.

Feelings and emotions are not reducible to codified forms typical of linguistic communication, nor are they best thought of as disturbances of the physical form, whether universal responses or open to cultural modification. The nature–culture debate is a diversion from the main task of understanding the place of feeling in social life. Instead, we need to recognize that emotion is integral with society, in being both constitutive and indicative of the relationships of which it is seen to be a part (Radley, 1988b).

Status, Intimacy, and the Channels of Control

As applied to Western culture, the study of nonverbal behavior has emerged as a voluminous inspection of how the parts of the body are variously employed in different situations, or between different kinds of individuals (Argyle, 1983; Henley, 1977; Heslin & Patterson, 1982; Kleinke, 1986). For example, studies have been made of the arm positions and head tilts of people asked to communicate either a positive or a negative attitude (Mehrabian, 1968a, 1968b); of the role of gaze in the communication of status (Kleinke, 1986); of eye contact as it varies with proximity and intimacy (Argyle & Dean, 1965), and of head nods and body leanings as communicators of persuasion in counseling sessions. The purpose of these experiments would appear to be not only to discover the differences between the use of the body in different situations, but also eventually to lead to some theory of the place of nonverbal behavior in social life. The first aim has been more than adequately satisfied, in that the literature about these matters is large and grows year by year. The second aim cannot be said to have been achieved; there is no comprehensive theory that embraces these findings apart from the implicit assumptions that made the studies meaningful in the first place.

A convenient example is offered by Kleinke (1986) in his review of work on gaze. This overview discusses gaze as something that serves to establish or to reinforce dominance, to search for information, to share feelings of warmth and liking, and to act as a stimulus for eliciting escape and avoidance—to name but a few of the functions discovered in experimental studies. How can this be? At one level, we know that this range of gazing is possible; everyday knowledge tells us so. At another level, that of psychological theory, there is the problem of how *a single thing*, such as gaze, can be used in these many different ways.

The reason for stressing the unity of gaze in this context is to underline the fact that the experimental study of nonverbal behavior renders the specific aspect under scrutiny into an objective entity. The definition and measurement of gaze become issues in the need for investigators to isolate and vary the same thing in their experiments (Stephenson & Rutter, 1970). In effect, a working consensus emerges through the operations that are agreed for the measurement of gazing. Gaze, in being stripped down to an observable behavior, can then be entered into any study design as a dependent variable. Its relationships to the various external variables chosen to give it meaning (e.g., intimacy, persuasion, status) reemerge from the design in the form of statistical measures that then require interpretation.

This means falling back upon the everyday knowledge of what it means to be intimate, or of lower status, or a good conversationalist in order to return significance to the findings. One is pushed back repeatedly to other features of the situation (external variables), the subtle interactions of which will, it is believed, explain the difference between a yearning gaze and a cold one:

> The functions of gaze will be better understood when the influence of context and personal factors (e.g., race, status and motives) are delineated. . . . The challenge for researchers is to outline conditions under which gaze expresses (or is viewed as expressing) intimacy. (Kleinke, 1986, p. 82)

The unchallenged assumption in all this is that there is a single entity called "gaze," which remains the same in all of the different contexts studied, and that this single thing is seen differently only because of its interaction with other contextual variables that define the different situations. This assumption is shored up by the adoption of the experimental method and the belief that data are not those that are given, but are those that can be seen. The body is to be studied with the eye of a scientist, who discerns upon it the variations that will reveal its true meaning. One defense of this approach has been that psychologists (as opposed to sociologists and anthropologists) need to study microscopic movements such as eyebrow twitches, involving the use of the laboratory (Argyle, 1975). In effect, however, what is being pressed is the requirement that the experimental method be preserved and that the body be studied as something amenable to its devices. This is not, as it appears, a point of methodological difference, but a reaffirmation of an epistemological position.

Where theories of gaze have been put forward, they tend to reflect the body as an aggregate of sign systems that is essentially functional rather than expressive in nature. The role of nonverbal behavior in social interaction becomes one of setting and sustaining a level of involvement through the operation of gaze as a means of acquiring feedback on one's conduct (Argyle, 1969). In a similar fashion, this feedback process has been proposed to be linked with a cognitive–affective assessment of the physiological arousal that discrepancies create (Patterson, 1982). When studied in connection with speaking, nonverbal signs are taken to be cues, the function of which is to smooth the progress of the conversation (Duncan & Fiske, 1977). In all of these cases, the explanation offered presumes that the body serves a regulatory, compensatory function. It can serve this homeostatic function because its parts are conceived objectively, as separate channels that are deployed in the service of other higher operations, such as the sharing of ideas.

Discussions of how these channels connect with people's ideas and with the changing social contexts in which they operate are vague. This is the price to be paid for reducing the expressive aspects of the body to regulative, mechanistic systems. Kleinke (1986) suggests that the way forward is to include the work on gaze within what is called the "paradigm shift" toward cognitive processes. In this recommendation, all traces of the expressive, social, and intentional aspects of gaze (and the body) are abandoned. One is returned to a psychology in which once again the body is merely the physical extension of a mind conceived as being a subtle, but objectively knowable information system.

Where the anthropologists began by looking at culture *through* the body, experimental social psychologists have ended up looking *at* the body *from* their own cultural assumptions. No satisfactory theory of social action is ever likely to come from this latter endeavor, for it consists of dissecting movement according to the presuppositions that researchers have about "an intimate exchange" or "a situation of dependency." This results in the correlation of bodily particulars with the situational differences that give them meaning. It is as if one were to stand very close to an Impressionist painting and a Renaissance painting and attempt to locate the different styles wholly in the detail of the brushwork. In *principle*, we may know the difference between these two art forms in the technical differences; in *fact*, we comprehend them as distinct forms through the (virtual) powers of perception that the different distributions of paint make possible. Apprehension of the form is fundamental to knowledge of the detail. It is no more possible to build up a psychology of the body from specific movements or channels (even by calling them "elements of social behaviour," Argyle, 1969) than it is to comprehend a school of painting in terms of brush technique alone.

The idea that nonverbal behavior has a regulatory function rests upon the notion of control. While it has been recognized that control and expression are dual aspects of bodily communication (Argyle & Dean, 1965), there has been a tendency over the years to amplify the control function at the expense of the body as a medium for expressing intimacy. This has been made possible, in part, by analyses that have separated these two aspects of bodily communication. Edinger and Patterson (1983) drew a sharp distinction between what they termed the *social control* and the *intimacy functions* of nonverbal behavior. (Note that in these terms, intimacy is also assumed to be functional, *like control*.) They defined *social control* as "attempting to influence or change the behavior of another person," involving "a deliberate, purposeful response designed to promote a change in the other person's behavior." In contrast, these authors defined intimacy as "the underlying affective reaction toward another person," shown as a "spontaneous manifestation" of behavior. Having separated the two functions in this way, they are able to proceed with a discussion of nonverbal behavior as social control only.

From what has been argued earlier on in this chapter, such a division of bodily communication severely undermines the ecological validity of the problem in question. We act both deliberately and spontaneously, so that it is artificial to divide actions into one or the other as if they carried their status within them. For example, in greeting a person, one might smile, lean forward, and touch their arm. Is this behavior expressive or controlling? In their review, Edinger and Patterson (1983) describe an experiment that varied touch of this kind, which they interpret in terms of social control. In this study (Fisher, Rytting, & Heslin, 1976), a library assistant touched people lightly on the arm as they returned books to the library. A touch of this kind can be expressive from the point of view of the person carrying it out, as it is an intimation of friendliness. It can also be controlling, in the sense that, if done deliberately, it can facilitate a positive impression. The interpretation that it is the latter only is based upon placing, albeit implicitly, the conscious intentions of the experimenter into the actions of the library assistant. The fact that some subjects in the experiment perceived the assistant as friendly, but did not report being aware of the touch itself, only goes to show that the determination of it as an act of control or as one of intimacy depended upon the intentions and the perceptions of the people concerned. By virtue of the assistants being collaborators with the investigators, the touch is rendered controlling through the duplicity with which it was carried through.

My point here is that the study of expressiveness involves an appreciation of the intentions of the people concerned, something that experimental social psychologists have found extraordinarily difficult to study (Wiener et al., 1972). It also involves an acceptance of the position that whether bodily conduct is perceived as expressive, controlling, or a mixture of the two will depend upon the responses of the person to whom it is directed. By this, I mean that there is an openness to conduct; we intimate with our bodies, inviting a relationship that might or might not be endorsed in the actions of the other person. A hand outstretched in greeting awaits the response of the other person for its intention to be completed. If this response is not forthcoming or is in some way foreshortened, then the act of greeting will take on a different form. At what point it becomes an act of control or an expression of friendliness cannot easily be determined. It certainly does not lie within the movement itself, unless we beg the question entirely by calling it a "friendly greeting" or by judging it solely in terms of certain predicted outcomes inferred to be contained within it.

Perhaps there is one further reason why the control function of nonverbal behavior has been more often the subject of study than the body's expressive features. This derives from the aforementioned logocentric view that has dominated the study of nonverbal communication in social psychology. This inclines to the study of ego functions, involving issues to do with mastery of ends and with rivalry with other people. Expressive gestures that intimate relationship are analogical in form and, like other libidinal features, are homologous with the erogenous zones that operate according to principles of inclusion, exclusion, and receptivity (Bateson, 1987). In a social psychology dominated by issues of cognition, it is perhaps not surprising that the body should be seen as operating on the principles of ego functioning, as the means by which one person's thoughts might triumph over those of another.

Channels of Communication and Bodily Control

The use of the term *channel* has become widespread in the literature on nonverbal communication. It is generally used to refer to the communicative possibilities that are derived from different parts of the body. The face in particular (Ekman & Friesen, 1975) has been the subject of detailed study, as have the use of the eyes (Kleinke, 1986) and the effects of posture and proximity (Mehrabian 1968a, 1968b). The merit in making special studies of particular channels of communication needs to be offset against the risk that these will detract from an overall examination of nonverbal behavior as a total system. It is clear that when people interact with each other they do so using most, if not all, channels simultaneously. This means that the various modes of communication are there to support or to modify each other, as well as being available as substitutes for others should the need arise, such as when signaling levels of intimacy (Argyle & Dean, 1965).

This point has often been recognized in the literature, although the remedy has tended to be seen as the need for a multichannel approach. This is consistent with the experimental attitude in which the body has been analyzed into its separate elements. Once having separated them out in this way, there is a necessity to put them back together to see how they work as a single system. Arguably, however, the composite of a number of channels reintegrated together is not the same as viewing the body as a whole. Indeed, there is a considerable difference between the view of the body as the connective tissue supporting eyes, hands, and face (or whatever) and the perspective gained by seeing it as an entity in itself. In the first case, the body remains a supporting substrate for particulars that are granted focal meaning; in the second, it takes on a different meaning in the light of what it portrays about the social system of which it is a part.

This latter view has been elaborated by Mary Douglas (1971, 1973) on the basis of material from anthropological studies. She has argued that the position adopted by experimentalists, who see the body as being like "a signal box, a static framework emitting and receiving strictly coded messages" (1971), is a misunderstanding of its social form. Instead, the body mediates the social situation of which it is a part; it does this by becoming the image of the social structure, presenting itself as a medium through which the form of the society—its rules, its moral concerns—can be appreciated. Douglas's analysis owes much to Durkheim and to the British sociologist Basil Bernstein (1971). It is concerned with the controls that are immanent in the social system and with how these operate through bodily conduct. The body is not, therefore, an individual structure, a means for one person to signal his or her intentions to another. It is a medium that expresses the controls and the boundary conditions of the society. Taking this view, we are brought back once again to the body as something with the aid of which we can understand culture.

Douglas (1973) makes two main assumptions. The first is that the style appropriate to any message will coordinate all the channels along which it is given. She develops this idea with respect to the relationship between verbal and bodily communication, arguing that there is a natural tendency to express social situations of a particular kind in the appropriate bodily style. By *natural*, she appears to mean something like "functionally effective," not biologically governed. In one sense, her proposal is not too different from Goffman's (1959) claim that an effective presentation demands consistency of information *given* with information *given off*. Where there are discrepancies, there will be ambiguity and possible rejection of the intended message. The concept of style seems to me to offer another, more powerful interpretation than the one given to it by Douglas. It indicates not just that channels are in greater or lesser agreement, or just that verbal (social) and bodily messages are consistent, but that they are coordinated with respect to a *virtual* power to be discerned in them. This use of the term introduced by Langer reminds us that the expressive use of the body cannot be reduced to issues of consonance and dissonance alone.

Douglas's second assumption is that the scope of the body as a medium of expression is limited by controls exerted by the social system. If the body is seen as a source of interruptions, from sudden movements, through laughter, to coughing and breaking wind, then the expression of these things will be subject to the thresholds set by the culture about bodily relaxation and control. There are societies where there are relatively high thresholds set for bodily expression, where, for example, religious devotions may include dancing or falling into trance. These behaviors are prohibited in societies that set relatively low thresholds for bodily expression, in which verbal means of communication are usually preferred to physical expression. These thresholds are indicative of what Douglas calls the distance between the "social" and the "physical bodies."

This distance, in its turn, is an index of the range of pressures and classification in society. In a complex society, subject to civilizing influences (Elias, 1978), this distance is marked by a disembodiment of sensibilities, in which bodily expressions are modulated and controlled. By comparison, in societies where these controls are weak, the distance between body and society is relatively small, so that social concerns are more directly expressed in a physical way. The essential point is that this difference in levels of control refers to varying contextualizations of behavior that regulate the distinctions to be drawn between the physical and the social body. Society does not operate upon the body; the body reflects the controls of the society of which it is a part. Where Geertz (1972) drew attention to the metaphoric role of the body *in* ritual practices, Douglas makes a special point of noting its role as expressive *of* the ritual order in any given society.

We do not have to agree with Douglas about the need for consonance between the physical and social bodies, in spite of the fact that there appears, more often than not, to be such consistency. Within a culture, for example, we see people endorsing joy at parties and sorrow at funerals in their comportment. There might well be pressures upon individuals to conform in this way, but there will also be occasions when their bodily expressions can serve as their only means of articulating revolt or dissent; hysteria can be seen as one example. This, in turn, can lead to such individuals being misunderstood and vulnerable to sanction.

How do these ideas bear upon the notion of the body as a multichannel system? They suggest that the use of any particular channel cannot be understood in terms of the physical body alone. Whether people laugh out loud or sit in quiet concentration is indicative of the scope there is for them to communicate in that way. Note that this is not merely saying that people act differently in different situations; it is saying that the use of the body reflects its scope as a legitimate way of knowing the world in that culture and of communicating that knowledge to others. This repeats, at a general level, the more specific argument put forward by Ekman and Friesen about cultural display rules. However, where they saw these as controls upon the body, limiting the message about the feelings of the individuals concerned, Douglas offers an account of how these same behaviors can be taken as expressing the relationship of the individual to the group. It is not the selection among a fixed set of behaviors or between the use of one or another channel that provides variation in bodily communication: it is the way that the person chooses to act in the context that his or her body helps to define.

Two distinctions can be drawn between this perspective and that of the experimentalists. The first is that bodily movements or expressions are not comprehensible as communications between individuals. They need to be seen as expressive of the system of cultural controls to which they give public, visible form. One cannot answer questions about whether the eyes are more important than the hands in a particular situation, or whether a discreet cough signals one thing or another, without some cultural view of this kind. When social psychologists talk about the need to study variations in nonverbal behaviors in the light of changing situations, it is to this that they refer, but in an ad hoc manner. Focusing upon the careful measurement of movement, one can discern difference, but not why that difference is significant. Frankly, to say that gaze depends upon context and that this requires further study (Kleinke, 1986) is hardly to move beyond Mauss's (1972) statement (made in 1934) that "we should attribute different values to the act of staring fixedly: a symbol of politeness in the army, and of rudeness in everyday life." What Douglas offers is a theoretical framework (only briefly sketched out here) within which the significance of such differences can be understood. What is communicative about a stare or a touch comes not from a universal code that is shared by all individuals, but from its place in a symbolic order, the outward form of which is expressed in ritual differences. These may lie on either side of boundaries between episodes or ceremonies, each varying in the scope with which the body may be used as a legitimate way of communicating. (Compare a laugh in church with a laugh at a party.) Boundaries are also created between individuals, so that there is differential scope for those concerned to vary or to enlarge upon their bodily display.

A second distinction between the approach offered by Douglas and that of the experimental social psychologists lies in their conceptions of bodily movements. The latter conceive of nonverbal behaviors as technical movements or expressions that can be isolated, objectively described, and modified. This is consistent with the analysis of communication as a multichannel phenomenon, with these channels being assumed to have some elemental status in relation to the whole body. In contrast to this view, the contributions of Douglas, of Mauss, and of Geertz show that the technical aspects of body movement are often caught up in magicoreligious acts. To reduce the ceremonial to the substantive is to obscure the expressive and the virtual features of bodily life that give it its special characteristics. One is then in a position of being unable to discern how and when there are shifts in the use of the body as a medium of expression, as a means of communication, and as a vehicle for the execution of techniques. That nonverbal communication might vary in these ways has been pointed out by social psychologists, but they have restricted themselves to listing these differences without any sign of their being able to embrace them within a single theory.

Concluding Comment: Culture, Character, and Control

It might be said that the study of nonverbal behavior in social psychology has broached the question of the body, but has not breached the everyday assumptions on which that study is based. This was what was implied by the statement that experimentalists have looked at the body through culture, rather than at culture through the body. It might be thought from this that the study of nonverbal communication is no longer concerned with character and culture, but this deduction would be mistaken. The progress of research in this field has led to its assumptions becoming visible in the form of its application to everyday problems. Nowhere is this more clear than in the emergence of what has come to be called "social skills training" (Argyle, 1984; Trower, Bryant, & Argyle, 1978). This is claimed as the scientific study of nonverbal behavior in the course of helping people to be more effective. In fact, it is the application of scientific methodology in the service of bridging the gap between an individual's desires and the requirements of social or group norms. It therefore depends for its effectiveness upon the intentions of the trainee and upon the values of society, both things that have been absent from the research agenda (Radley, 1985). In this way, character (as the desires of the trainee) and culture (in the form of the values inhering in the aim of training) are implicit terms in what is a program that claims its rationale on the basis of its practical effectiveness.

Arguably, the use of social skills training gives to nonverbal behavior research a credibility that is spurious, and to the body a status that is false. Social skills are not fundamental aspects of bodily communication but appear so only through a shared viewpoint of trainer and trainee, within which particular behaviors become tangible, salient, and modifiable. Looking *at* the body, issues and problems that derive from its relationship to society can be located upon it. Discerning a repertoire of social skills does not mean that an invariant nonverbal reality is there to be discovered. It means that social psychologists and others have taken up a practical attitude (as trainers) within which bodily movements are constituted as skills. What began as a metaphor, treating nonverbal behavior *as if* it were a physical skill, has become literal, real. This has other consequences. The establishment of what is now seen as a universal capacity means that every individual, having better or worse social skills, has a moral duty to deploy these effectively in the service of self and group. We are told that "we pick up bad habits of perception and interpretation [with] large and serious gaps in our repertoires of skills. . . . We simply stop trying to improve ourselves" (Soucie, 1979, p. 213).

As part of the study of nonverbal behavior, social skills training is important in giving a scientific credence to the disciplinary movement in society, of which psychology is a part. This is not simply a matter of controlling the body, to bring errant individuals within the norms of the majority. Its appeal and its claim lie in the fusing of efficiency with contentment, achieved by the way that skill development mediates the fit between person and role (Rose, 1989). In this way, the smile of the airline hostess blends the aims of the airline, the needs of the passenger, and her own job satisfaction in a tangible expression of a skill well learned. The point made here is not that agencies should cease engaging in training, but that social psychology should at least be aware of its part in fashioning a technologized body that it risks later "discovering" as the natural form of things. Were this to happen, social psychology's theories would be based upon a pitifully narrow conception of the place of our physical existence in social life.

Chapter 5

The Embodiment of Group Relationships

The study of small groups by social psychologists is traditionally identified with questions of decision making, cohesiveness, and leadership (Shaw, 1976). In recent years, issues of identification with the group and of majority or minority influence have emerged as central problems (Brown, 1988). Rarely, however, has the body entered as a topic for legitimate inquiry. This could be because the typical setting for such studies has been the group of subjects sitting around a table discussing a topic given them by the experimenter. In that situation, the bodies of the subjects remain things upon which they rely in order to join in the discussion or to make decisions, as required. This does not mean that physical existence has been entirely overlooked; the nonverbal communications of group members have also been recorded in experiments that have interpreted gestures and postures as indicative of individual attitudes toward others or toward the group as a whole (Bales, 1958). Of course, there have been studies carried out outside of the laboratory, but these have relied upon the bodily dispositions of the subjects involved in order to report differences in roles, attitudes, or types of behavior (for example, the classic study by Lewin, Lippitt, and White, 1939). This attitude is typical of the approach of social psychology as described in the first chapter of this book; in being wholly relied upon, the body remains invisible. Exceptions to this state of affairs include groups of individuals whose behavior is sufficiently different or sufficiently important to be a matter of social concern. The prime example is the case of children, whose behavior is a matter for debate and control, and whose groupings merit special treatment (Shaw, 1976).

The body entered the sphere of group relations in what might be called a "mundane" way, in terms of the age–sex matrix. We are aware of the constraints upon group membership placed by a person's age and gender (one should add race as well), so that they might be allowed access to one group but not another or might find that their continued membership of a group is no longer regarded as appropriate. In the localization of a group's composition in terms of such differences, these fundamental aspects of their social existence are accorded the status of background features to support the study of other variables of group life. However, even when treated as variables in the study of group differences, these discrete and abstract categories do not bear upon questions of the members' bodily existence. For example, to study how men and women differ in the way that they make group decisions relies upon assumptions of gender that are never made clear and that are unlikely to contribute to an understanding of the body in group life. In one sense, this is not surprising, as the demarcation of groups in terms of the everyday categories of the age–sex matrix can easily become an exercise in elaborating our assumptions, not one of exposing and exploring them. This can be justified, on the face of it, by appeals to the need to understand more about children, or about the social life of the elderly, or about the relationships of men and women.

One way in which bodily differences have been noted (if not studied) in group life is in terms of external status characteristics. For example, Strodtbeck, James, and Hawkins (1957) used artificial juries in order to study the effect of different kinds of group compositions, upon the process of reaching a verdict. They found that, among other things, men were more likely than women to be voted foreman of the jury, to retain their opinions in the course of discussion, and to take a greater part in reaching a decision. Gender is here treated as social status, as another characteristic that individuals bring with them, either from the wider realm of society or from their positions in other specific groups. It indicates the constraints and the opportunities that people variously afford others of their own and of the opposite sex, and hence the ways in which groups are organized around inequality. External status characteristics are features that are considered to have existed prior to the formation of the group and to continue to exist unaltered in the course of the group's activities. This continuity is presumed to be located in the fact that individuals bear these social differences either in or upon their bodies, in such things as secondary sexual characteristics, skin color, and fashion accessories. While this is true, and of undeniable importance, each of these things remains a limited example from which to conjecture about the place of the body in group life.

To relate preexisting differences to predictable group outcomes is to bracket out the question of how the body becomes, is marked, or is maintained as a key term in social relationships. While it is possible to observe the behavior of individuals in the group, and to relate this to chosen categories, this does not help to explain how, for example, gender differences might eventually be overcome in the course of a group discussion. To observe differences in behavior among individuals of different classes is to presume to discover what it is that mediates both the status difference and the various outcomes e.g., the finding that women show more socio-emotional expressions than men do (Strodtbeck & Mann, 1956). This criticism applies even to studies that focus specifically upon the relationship between men and women. For example, Henley's (1977) review of the literature on nonverbal communication differences between the sexes shows that gestures and postures can be read as signals of patriarchy. While such a reading is possible, it implies a consistency in the relationship of men and women in all situations. This consistency is borne of every such relationship being primarily of a gender–power kind, so that the aim of communicating appears always to assert the primacy of men over women. The point here is not that Henley's claim is untrue; it is that it might well be more true in some situations than others. How the body bears these status differences, how they are amplified, modulated, or run together with other expressive forms may be constitutive of new group differences, not just recapitulations of old ones. There remains the likelihood that social groups do not attempt just to maintain social control through their bodies (such as in gender–power displays), but also to distinguish themselves with their bodies in expressive acts. Much of the remainder of this chapter is concerned with this latter possibility.

Style: The Expression of Inequality

In their report of the Hawthorne studies, Roethlisberger and Dickson (1939) described the men of the Bank Wiring Observation Room as forming two cliques. One of these adhered more closely to the norms of the group as a whole, being engaged in more technically advanced work and having a greater output. They regarded themselves as being superior to the men in the other clique and their conversations as being on a higher plane. In contrast, the men in the other clique, which was determined by their lower-skilled jobs, located at the back of the room, created a culture opposed to their colleagues. It was a culture of resistance and was expressed through noise, horseplay, and overindulgence in eating candy bought from the company store. In effect, the subordinate clique created a subgroup ethos that was expressed in a physical rather than in a verbal way; their style of behavior simultaneously expressed their resistance to their colleagues' ideals and also their inability to do anything about altering their subordinate relationship to them.

The idea that subordinate groups might express their disadvantage through some form of bodily behavior was mooted in Chapter 1 when discussing women, crowds, the sick, and the mentally ill as fringe groups for social psychological study. The argument has already been made that the dominant Western culture is a public–rational one, which, in key areas, relies upon and distances itself from the body in its strivings for higher and better things. To be identified with the labors of the body—with children and the household—has always been to be placed in a position of relative inequality. Where members of these groups have protested against these deprivations, they have often had to utilize the powers that they have been allowed to develop most fully, namely those involving the body in its passive mode. For example, women in nineteenth-century America were described as having adopted the role of hysteric in order to escape from the conflicts and tensions of their lives, only to purchase that escape at the cost of intensifying their traditional passivity and dependence relative to others in the household (Smith-Rosenberg, 1972). In this, we see again the use of the body as symptomatic of a group's social condition, displaying the contradictions that relationships of inequality can impose. These contradictions are not, however, wholly one-sided. The intransitivities involved in moving between verbal and bodily communication systems means that those in positions of power may well be temporarily placed in a difficult position by bodily outbursts, which their rational systems cannot readily accommodate or comment upon. At a simpler level, the child who farts in the classroom or the student who yawns in the seminar make a statement about the situation that the teacher or professor cannot easily handle within the terms of the educational exchange. The disruption to the household caused by the hysteric woman in the past was considerably greater, though the system of patriarchy usually ensured that, sooner or later, she would be subjected to powers that curtailed these perturbations to domestic life.

This argument identifies, once again, the body with subordinate groupings, who exist in a culture dominated by a rational logocentric perspective. This does not mean that cultivated people abhor the body, in spite of the controls that limit it for them as a legitimate medium of expression (Douglas, 1973). It does mean that its use as an expressive medium, being of a different form to that of discourse, is less understood and less controlled by the cultivated group. This allows for the possibility that subordinate groupings might use the body to gain space for themselves in a culture that denies them advancement in the terms it puts forward—that is, those of conventional education and capital. Such a movement is first a symptomatic expression of protest; however, once recognized outside of the group, it can also become a stylistic presentation of difference and distinction.

One example of this has been provided in a study of a group of "motorbike boys" (motorcycle-riding youths) living in an English town (Willis, 1975). As a minority group, it had forms of expression quite as varied as those of apparently more sophisticated cultures, but of a kind that made them opaque to verbally mediated inquiries. Willis makes the point that it is precisely because these forms of expression are passed over or are misinterpreted by the middle classes that they are allowed to become the vehicle for the elaboration of a group ethos. The motorbike boys in this study were not merely engaged in a functional skill that the middle classes would easily understand—that of riding a bike well. This normally involves maintaining the machine and the rider's accessories in a condition where, for example, they provide least resistance to the airflow while affording maximum protection to the rider. The bikers, in contrast, wore their clothes loosely, avoided helmets and goggles, preferred cattle-horn-shaped handlebars, and removed the baffles from the motor's silencer. These adaptations opened out the inherent characteristics of the motorbike so as to maximize the sensations of the ride, amplified by the wind resistance, which they sought to meet, not avoid. This provided a potential space for the form of expertise in terms of which the group members defined themselves; on the one hand, wrestling with and overcoming the demands of the machine at high speeds, and on the other appropriating the power of the bike through their physical accommodation to it.

This group expressed itself in its style of riding, portrayed in the way that its members handled their bikes on the public roads. Off the road, this desire for a physical mode of expression was continued. Willis describes their preference for rock music with its beat, its movement, and the potential for a style of dancing consistent with the form of rough bonhomie that portrayed their essentially masculine existence. This, however, was not to be confused with the masculinity associated with sport, a healthy team involvement. The bikers showed a disrespect for sport played with the niceties of rules and skills, preferring to mold games of football to their own need for movement and spontaneity. Central to their style was a rough and ready "matey-ness," displayed in mock fights, which celebrated the real fights that they had been in, and those that they would be in should the occasion demand.

From this piece of ethnographic research, one can see the importance of the physicality of the bikers' lives for the establishment of themselves as a group. To recapitulate on the point made previously; it was the difference between the physical world in which they lived (i.e., riding the bikes) and the world of words and texts that was vital to their identification of themselves as different. This not only is true for what might be regarded as a dissident group, but also applies to individuals who share interests in demanding or exciting pastimes. The worlds of mountaineers and skydivers are relatively closed to other people who have not experienced the sensations or acquired the skills pertaining to the physical situations that these individuals enjoy. In making this point, one must be careful not to suggest that this argument applies only to situations in which people engage in physical activities. On the contrary, it is argued that the body has a special role for many groups or subcultures who are defining themselves as different from the mainstream of society in which they live.

How then should be see the body, as given in the description of the motorbike gang? Although one accepts that there were particular activities concerning bike riding, it is not these alone that defined the group. Other people in society ride bikes too. What made the motorbike boys distinct was the way in which they rode, in particular the way in which they rode differently from conventional riders. They evoked what can only be called a "style," in that the gang members' deportment had features that were recognizable because of their stable contrasts with the norms of the day. As Willis pointed out, these were things that were effective because they were physically achieved and were expressed both in the ferocity and undeniable presence of the moving bike and in the physical manner that the gang members retained when they were away from their machines.

The preceding point makes it easier to see why the motorbike boys' behavior should not be seen as some kind of nonverbal code. Their bodily movements did not communicate some other abstract meaning but were a portrayal of the group's ethos; this ethos would not have been said better in *words*, the communication vehicle of the middle classes. Their style of life was simultaneously expressive of their similarity to one another and of their difference from others. Carried on together in riding the bikes, in dancing, and in their conversations in roadside cafes, their bodily conduct can be seen as a kind of ceremony, an ongoing celebration of a way of life that is distinctive. For members of the gang, this meant reaffirming with their bikes (i.e., in the act of riding) not just who they were as a group (i.e., some self-concept), but also the way of life to which they were committed. As was pointed out in the previous chapter, bodily communication aims not (at least, primarily) at making discrete propositions but in establishing a way of living in the world.

I have used Willis's study as an example because it highlights most clearly the use of the body, not merely as a vehicle of communication but, to use Douglas's (1971) words, as "the proper tender" of social life. In the course of this and subsequent chapters, I explore the possibilities and the limitations of this idea. First, there is the claim that this scenario is not attached to one kind of grouping only—the group of young male "tearaways" as seen by people from outside. Second, there is the need to see that even in groups where the body appears to play a very muted role, such as in academic life, it remains important for what it does not say, for the expressive control that the containment of the body communicates as people appear only to speak and to share thoughts with one another.

For the moment, it is worth noting that the use of the body in dissident groupings does not always mean machismo, or loud and violent display. The hippie counterculture of the 1960s and 1970s was evoked in gatherings of mainly young people whose appearance and demeanor announced, in a way clearer than some of them could articulate, a view of the world and of humankind. Perhaps the most common feature was hair, the length of which was a definite sign of the refusal of rules of order based upon clear-cut boundaries. Clothes also evoked a free and easy attitude, being loose, flowing, and encouraging of the juxtaposition of bright colors. Open and free communication meant a reinstatement of touch in a society where bodily contact is limited (Musgrove, 1974). This contact was indicative of an ideology that was based upon increased personal sensations, culminating in a search for awareness, the heightened consciousness of the "head" as locus and metaphor for a knowing person (Willis, 1978). This focus upon the sensual body as a way of knowing the world was put into practice in communities where rituals of dance, prayer, or encounter exercises were used to express the togetherness of the group (Kanter, 1972).

In both of the dissident groups mentioned (the working-class bikers and the middle-class counterculture), the body serves as the medium of expression. This is not to contrast it with some idea of mental life or ideology, but to affirm the opposite; that groups establish their (ideological) relationship to society through their appearance and actions, fused as style. The notion that clothing has some relationship to people's social attitudes is not a new one. People who subscribed to the counterculture that emerged in the United States and in other Western countries in the 1960s were identifiable in their mode of dress, the form of which was a homologue of their attitudes toward war and toward the world of business (Thomas, 1973). This was not just an alternative style of dress, but first and foremost a refusal of the norms of the majority, as expressed by individuals who acceded to the dominant style of the day. While there were oppositions to that style (long hair versus the "military" haircut), the counterculture attempted to disrupt the dominant image rather than merely to negate it.

Announcing oneself as part of a dissident group involves a heightened awareness that one's clothes express one's social attitudes (Buckley & Roach, 1974). The dress styles of dissident groups are often obviously fabricated, so that they display the difference from the surrounding culture openly. This is achieved by a repositioning and a recontextualization of items that serve other purposes in conventional contexts (Hebdige, 1979). For example, in Britain during the 1950s, the "Teddy Boys" clothes were borrowed from the styles of the Edwardian era (long jacket with velvet collar) and juxtaposed with modern footwear (the "brothel creeper" thick-soled shoes). In the 1970s, the "Punks" in Britain deliberately utilized cheap, and what are commonly regarded as vulgar, materials (e.g., lurex, [yarn with metallic sheen], PVC [polyvinyl chloride]) from which to make clothes. These matched their hair, which was partially shaved and garishly colored. In the Punks' case, the difference of the group from the dominant culture was virtually screamed in their clothes, bodily adornment (e.g., rings through the nostrils) and literally so in their musical taste. This difference was significant in what it affirmed and, perhaps more so, in what it denied— the desirability of the surrounding culture's values.

All this points to the body as being key in the establishment of certain social and political differences in modern life, made possible by the range and the availability of commodities to serve as markers of distinction in dress and presentation. How does this work? When applied to youth sub-cultures, particularly those drawn from disadvantaged sections of society, the answer may lie in the inversion of the relationship between what Douglas (1973) called the "physical" and the "social bodies." This explanation has already been mooted in the preceding description of the motorbike culture. The dominant culture is restricted in its use of bodily expression and gives priority to verbal analysis. By overturning this, the dissident group communicates (a) a difference between the group and the culture, (b) the refusal of the dominant culture's way of life, and (c) the legitimacy of the body as a way of knowing the world. The body of the dissident person can then become a focus of attention, a site of contradiction, and a field of ideological struggle. Whether this occurs depends upon other factors to do with the historical and political context in which the movement takes place. For example, clothing and hair styles have traditionally been a locus of continuing debate about what is acceptable, desirable, or offensive in the public presentation of men and women.

The points made so far seem to suggest that the body is treated as an open book, and as all of a piece by dissenting members of society. This is not necessarily the case and, in the light of proposals outlined next, may be seen to be too simple an idea. This can be illustrated by reference to people who choose to make their marks of social difference upon their body in a literal way, through being tattooed. Tattoos have been seen largely as a mark adopted by people who are already marginalized in some way within society. Therefore, they stand as a symbol of disaffiliation, directed at those who lead conventional lives (Sanders, 1988). Where youth subcultures see their dress as a public portrayal of their group identity, the tattooed person may not necessarily do so. Some individuals choose to have their tattoos on parts of their body where they can be hidden if preferred, to be displayed only on certain occasions or with people who are trusted. Women tend to see the tattoo as primarily intended for personal pleasure and for the enjoyment of those individuals with whom they are most intimate—hence, the choice of more private parts of the body where the decorations will only be seen by intimates. In contrast, men typically see the tattoo as a symbol of their dissociation from conventional society, a public display of their freedom to do what they want to do, and to "be a man." For this reason perhaps, men tend to choose large lurid images, sited on the forearm where they can be readily seen. In this emphasis upon difference, they are also distinguished from (some) women, who see the tattoo as a mark of affiliation. In this context, Sanders mentions a woman who was tattood in order that she be accepted by the group of bikers to which her husband and her friends belonged.

The use of the tattoo as a form of body adornment by subgroups is paralleled in its deployment by individuals who are rejecting the control of groups to which they have so far belonged. The tattoo, like the ritual marks made during rites of passage, symbolizes the person's transition from one status to another. One should not see this as being only another instance of portrayal for others, though it is this too. In one quotation, a tattoo artist reported that his clients came to find out once again who they were. The experience "pulls you back to a certain kind of reality about who you are as an individual" (Sanders, 1988), reminding us that the body is not only a site for the portrayal of identity but a field of experience too. As with the aforementioned bikers, the body serves as a vehicle for communicating ideas and feelings, and it establishes the mode within which those ideas will be expressed. By this, I mean that style is not just about how to show oneself to others; it is a way of living sensually and physically in a material world evoking pains and pleasures. Having been tattooed is itself an experience that binds tattooees as a group; wearing an effective stick-on tattoo could not be a substitute for this function.

Contrasting the use of the body as a site for display and as a medium for experience is a useful distinction to have made. In the world of youth and racial subcultures (and some might argue gender too), effective displays of difference serve to repel and to distance the surrounding society. As already mentioned, this wins space for these groupings—space to congregate, to pursue leisure activities such as dancing or other recreations (Clarke, Hall, Jefferson, & Roberts, 1976). Effectively, this means time to experience together the establishment and the celebration of such things as riding motorbikes or attending rock concerts. While the heterogeneity of the urban setting is likely to promote activities such as dancing (Hanna, 1979), the point to be emphasized is that these activities do not merely reflect group differences; they also embody them.

This discussion of the body styles of dissenting groups shows them to be responses within a culture, to that culture. Though youth groups, for example, have different focal concerns from the mainstream of society, they draw upon it (and remain members of it) to the extent that they are the sons, daughters, sisters, and brothers of people who live conventional lives (Clarke et al., 1976). As members of less privileged or working-class sectors of society, they draw upon these parent cultures in the ways that they borrow and modify objects and behaviors in the construction of a style. As young people, they react against their parents' generation in their interests and in their attitude toward life; as members of a disadvantaged section of society, they rebel against the values of a middle class in which they are not allowed to participate. Their bodily expressions can therefore be seen as a working out of this conjunction of these two dimensions of society, in which the articulate and refined interests of the privileged, together with the resignation and conventionality of the mature, are simultaneously rejected in physical and dramatic ways.

Marks of Distinction

The use of the body is not limited to subordinate groups who are trying to establish a separate identity, although the reasons why such groups might find physical expressions advantageous have been discussed previously. In a society that places high value upon verbal analysis and, in Douglas's terms, that seeks to place a distance between social interests and the body, there is scope for subcultures to arrange differences in their ways of achieving this. This cautions us against thinking of the dominant cultures in Western societies as being "wholly verbal," and dissident subordinate groupings as basing their identity upon physical expression (as if this were separate from their attitudes and values). Dominant cultures are also concerned with the use of the body, as they must be if they are to influence how the body should be thought of in society as a whole. That is to say, they too must work at defining their interests in the field of bodily expression, if only to set and maintain the relationship (or distance) that their members desire between the body and social concerns.

An analysis of such practices, considered as tastes, has been provided by Bourdieu (1984) who has argued that they derive from class culture turned into nature—that is, they embody the shape of society. In all of the practices pertaining to the maintenance of the body, in feeding, at work, or in leisure activities, it is revealed as the most indisputable materialization of class taste. The working-class ethos, with its strong theme of masculinity, means that in the selection of food, there will be avoidance of those items that are light or insufficiently filling. More important, foods will be avoided (such as fish) that require, in order for them to be ingested, that the working-class man must adopt a body attitude contradictory to the masculine style. Bourdieu pinpoints this as restraint, such as is required of the fish-eater, using small mouthfuls, chewing gently at the front of the mouth, with the tips of the teeth. Where the French working class see food as a material reality, a nourishing substance, the bourgeoisie forgo strength and substance in order to highlight the asceticism of form and good shape in their choice of foods. This is not a mere difference in food choice, but a reflection of a distinction between two ideologies of how life should be lived in its detail. This means that each grouping is aware of the other's style and assesses it accordingly. From the position of the bourgeoisie, the working class conduct themselves in a vulgar fashion, while from the alternative position, the middle classes are seen as doing things only for the sake of looks, for form's sake, consisting of fine words and empty gestures. There is here a difference between the classes in the emphasis upon substance and style, the working class seeing in the body its material needs and potentialities and the bourgeoisie attending to its stylistic possibilities.

Having made this broad distinction, we are in a position to use Bourdieu's analysis to see how members of the dominant section of society can deploy their bodies so as to forge boundaries that separate them from subordinate groups, as well as to determine the shape of the relationship between the body and society. By the latter I mean how they can, through their privileged position, set the standards of conduct for society in general, as part of which will be the scope of the body as a legitimate medium for communication. Bourdieu notes the choice of leisure activities of the bourgeoisie as relating to a concern for good appearances and health consciousness. Jogging and gymnastic exercises of all kinds are only meaningful in relation to a theoretical knowledge of the effects of exercise. Broken down into its parts and abstracted from the world, these individuals can concentrate upon the effects of the exercise upon, for example, their "abdominals" without reference to its real-world utility. (It is the health-giving aspect of these practices to which Bourdieu drew attention, rather than to their effects upon muscular development, which is the concern of body-builders). There are two points to be made here. One is that the dominant section of society chooses sports that enable them to be further distinguished from "the masses." This is partly achieved by the opportunities that they enjoy, in order to take up activities that demand investment of time and money. Golf, tennis, sailing, riding, gliding, and fencing are examples of sports that require facilities (many exclusive and expensive), training, and social connections if they are to be pursued seriously. It is easy to see why the less privileged groups in society are likely to find these activities closed to them; and yet, this is not the key point that Bourdieu makes, nor is it the one that bears directly upon the argument concerning the body.

While taking up physical exercise that the masses cannot enjoy serves to distinguish the bourgeoisie, to make them more distinct, it is the form of the exercise that Bourdieu considers to be particularly important. The working classes engage in team sports that rely upon physical competencies that are equally accessible to all, and that call for bodily contact as well as for qualities of strength and collective discipline. It is this immediacy of contact, the commitment to the team, the risk of physical and verbal violence (shouting, wild gestures) that the dominant class wishes to avoid. This is not because they fear pain or discomfort, but to avoid an offense to their dignity as people having a particular social standing.

What they seek in their sports is to regulate their use of the body, to aestheticize it further, through a distancing of their social practice from the body in its natural state. Members of the bourgeois class "treat [their] body as an end, make [their] body a sign of its own ease. Style is thus foregrounded" (Bourdieu, 1984, p. 218). As a consequence, they develop an assuredness of manner that passes back into their everyday dealings in the world, reinforcing what Bourdieu refers to as their "body schema," the embodiment of a whole world view by which they live.

Because Bourdieu's work relates to the French culture, his class-based analyses cannot be generalized to other societies without caution. Nevertheless, the thesis that the dominant sector of society distinguishes itself from the others by a particular use of the body, and one in which a sense of greater role distance is achieved, is consistent with Douglas's proposals discussed in the previous chapter. It also show that the use of the body is not confined to subordinate groups who wish to refuse the verbalizations and the sensibilities of the middle classes. However, in the case of the dominant groupings (or at least, those with capital to pay for them), this use of the body is quite distinct from that of the bikers considered in the previous section. Where the bikers consolidated their identity in their joint actions—they rode together, danced together, talked and fooled around together—the bourgoisie are also engaged in elaborating their identity through the refinement of individual skills. As pointed out previously, these are not merely mechanical skills, but are constitutive of a style that permeates their bearing and is identifiable as such. Having such a bearing, living out such a world view, this privileged grouping is the arbiter of values that other sections of society will seek to emulate but that groups such as the bikers will attack. What is conceived by social psychologists as "behavior," as if the actions of groupings in different locations in the social system were all much the same, is seen to be altogether more complex when the body is introduced into the analysis. One cannot presume that all groupings have a style of conduct, if by this is meant that such styles are equally available to all, or are equally visible to outsiders. The conventional working-class people described by Bourdieu abhor style as a bourgeois mannerism; the middle classes adopt leisure styles in their attempts to be distinct from the masses, while some youth groups, paradoxically, adopt expressive forms to undermine the normal conventions of style itself. In each case, these ways of living express and comment upon the distance between the body and the social self. It is this, the use of the body in the establishment of what is thought to be upright, cultivated, and desirable, that is presently underestimated in social psychology.

The Gendered Group

I want to move in this chapter to a consideration of gender in the establishment of group relations. Lest it be thought that gender is an arbitrary example, it should be pointed out that this is not the case. Gender relations are basic to social life and permeate all manner of distinctions that are drawn in what are sometimes thought to be neutral fields. A consideration of the gendered group is, therefore, an illustration of the wider cross-association of group interests drawn from different spheres; it is also (and more importantly so in this book) a revelation of the way that the body serves as a vital aspect of relationships that might seem to have passed beyond the sexual differences of physical existence.

In his description of the motorbike boys, Willis (1978) drew attention to their masculine style and bravado, which was at its clearest in relation to the women present. The men were rough and heavy-handed toward the women in the gang, who were outnumbered and dominated in virtually all matters. While they offered a form of protection toward "their women," this was done because females were believed to lack the wherewithal to do this for themselves. They lacked, as it were by definition, the essential qualities of maleness that characterized the ethos of the group. This was pointed up through a comparison of the men's treatment of women with that of a (male) dwarf, a member of the gang. The dwarf engaged in mock fights with gang members, which were such because he lacked the physical stature to be a real threat to anyone. However, his overdramatizing of the masculine role without its substantive potential meant that he symbolized the values of the group, and hence expressed in a distorted yet accurate way what mattered to its members. As Willis (1978) put it, "I never saw a woman's hair ruffled in quite the way in which Joe would end a mock fight sequence with the dwarf." This statement indicates, not that women lacked any symbolic status in the group, but that their status was covert and recessive. Understanding how gender relations contribute to the functioning of groups and how the body plays a key role in this is the task of the remainder of this chapter.

The motorbike gangs were mainly of working-class origin, and their attitudes toward women drew upon their class culture. In another study, looking at the transition from school to work of young people of a similar background, Willis (1977) noted similar social distinctions to those already mentioned in the previous section. In school, the counterculture was represented by a gang of boys who rebelled against the ideology of the teachers and differentiated themselves from pupils who were seen to accept the conventions of hard work and good behavior. Interestingly, Willis notes that the former group (called "the lads") labeled the latter pupils as "ear 'oles," a reference to their perceived passivity in listening to what they were told by the teachers. In contrast, "the lads" carried on a life of rebellion, which turned upon both physical disobedience and excursions into activities known to be disapproved of by the school authorities. Unlike the bikers, who adopted an alternative style, these pupils lived out a way of life directly opposed to that of their teachers. In common with the motorbike gang, however, the boys at the school who were "lads" expressed their superiority over girls and over ethnic minorities. Their sexism took the form of discussions among themselves about girls as sexual prey; it also meant that they engaged the girls in sexual banter designed to display the boys superiority and power in all of their social relationships.

The similarity between the bikers and "the lads" lay not only in their being from working-class backgrounds; also both groups were male dominated (the latter exclusively so) and had at the center of their ethos an exaggerated masculinity expressed in their bodily conduct. Girls, too, will form dissident groups, though in similar British school contexts, these have been shown to take a different form. Where the boys made up large gangs, which opposed the school culture directly, the girls formed smaller, more personal friendship groupings (Griffin, 1985). This raises the question as to how the relationship between men and women operates in group contexts. This goes beyond the question of how men and women act or speak differently in discussion groups (Aries, 1976), to the issue of the way in which gender differences are employed in the course of furthering other matters in the group.

The question of masculine style is one that has been addressed directly by Willis (1977) and offers us a purchase upon the question of gendered groupings. He has argued that the characteristic style of speech and movement of these youth gangs always holds something of a "masculine spectacle." The ability to take the initiative, to seek out a passive appreciative audience (particularly female), to do the unexpected, and to gain sexual experience are admired masculine qualities. That is to say, the attributes that serve these dissident groups well in their rebellion against convention are also those that are countersupported in the culture by the feminine role. In the school or in the café, this means women being compliant and laughing at the boys' jokes; in the home, it means filling the role of wife, sister, or mother. Therefore, the youth gangs develop their style in relation to the dominant culture and in relation to the opposite sex at the same time. The reaction to a culture within a culture (as framed previously) takes the form of the youths borrowing from their parent group the ideology embodied in the styles of their domestic setting. This means, effectively, the transposition of behaviors that, in the working-class situation, are divided according to gender. What the youths borrow is the ideology and the expressive manner of the working man who is supported by a domesticated wife.

Willis is more specific about the form that this development of style often takes among these young men. He argues that they borrow from their parent culture the ideology of gender differences, as well as beliefs concerning the distinction between manual versus mental work. In one of these structures, the youths are superior (gender); in the other, they are disadvantaged (mental/manual ability). The adoption of their eventual style is the result of the association of manual labor with the social superiority of masculinity and the concomitant association of mental work with socially inferior femininity. As a result, maleness is given a further external form of production and assertion, while manual work becomes a means of domination. Manual labor takes on certain "sensual overtones"; the toughness, the awkwardness, the fatigue-engendering aspects of the work setting take on symbolic sexual significance as "man's work." These aspects of the external situation are seen to call out bodily qualities of strength, determination, and hardness, which are expressed in the will to be a man and embodied in the style with which tasks are undertaken and completed. This suffusion of machismo into manual work is not limited to the workplace; as with the bikers considered earlier on, where the boys drew upon the power of the machines they rode, this transformation of masculinity extended to all areas of life in which being a "working man" required that they conducted themselves in such a manner.

The counterpoint to this transpostion in the lives of these youths is the association of mental work with femininity. Those who "push pens" for a living can be derided so long as femininity is regarded as socially inferior. In effect, the maintenance of the masculine style depends upon the restriction of women to the home, and of their opportunities in the world of work. Similarly, the way that the youths in these groups treated the women members is amplified by the ideological division of labor and its association with patriarchy. These matters issue in the bodily styles discussed in the previous section; we can see now that such styles are not mere embellishments or expressions of more basic attitudes or identities, but are constitutive of the relations between the parties concerned.

Style, therefore, is not a given; it is not an attribute of an individual that can be reduced to the movements of the body, nor does it belong to the group considered as a social entity. In this case, masculinity is given its particular form through the participation of maleness in laboring, and this is completed in the transposition of this form to other situations—that is, the masculine style can be brought to bear upon matters other than work or sexual relations. Underlying this is the fact that the two structures or spheres of action (male–female; mental–manual work) have their own existence as bodily potentialities. Productive acts and sexual acts can be carried on independently, but it is when they are brought together in the aforementioned way that the embodiment of masculine and feminine styles occurs. When that happens, the style then engendered is not just information; it is also a claim, a demand, an insistence on the legitimacy of treating the world in a particular way. Its establishment depends upon the effect it has upon others in and out of the group, and upon their position emerging (or being maintained) in stylistic form. The rough macho attitude of young working-class males in the preceding examples was complemented by the passive attitude of the girls in that setting. Yet, this should not be taken as a process, an inevitability.

We can gain a further perspective on the place of the body in the formation of group relations if we consider that the association of gender and work structures does indeed involve claim and counterclaim, some struggle between the sexes as to who is to define the situation and their place within it. While it may appear from the work cited in this chapter that men are wholly active, while women are passive, this falls short of the wider picture provided by other evidence. Where young children at play have been studied, it has been shown that girls can take control of the situation by converting it from a workplace setting (e.g., playing hospitals, where the nurses help the doctors) to a domestic one (where one nurse elevates tea-making and room tidying to being privileged activities, Walkerdine, 1981). Power does not inhere in the roles that men and women play but in the practices in which they signify as key figures. In the case of women, these practices belong to the domestic setting, and they can be employed wherever they appear in the public sphere (e.g., the secretary who bandages her boss's cut finger while telling him to be brave).

By the same token, men exercise power wherever they can introduce masculine practices (patriarchy) into a situation. Walkerdine (1981) provides a chilling example of the way in which two 4-year-old boys denigrate the authority of their female nursery school teacher by the use of sexually based insults. The boys resisted the authority of her teaching practice by drawing attention to her body, thereby signifying her as a member of the inferior and less powerful group, women. By this means, the boys become more than little boys and the teacher becomes less than their teacher. This suggests that the cross-valorization of Willis's two structures—male–female and mental–manual labor—begins at a much earlier stage than his analysis could have predicted.

Two points can be drawn from this work, which bear upon the place of the body in group life, and specifically upon the way in which gender relations are a central issue. One concerns the way in which, by instituting a particular style, a person can constitute the other as the powerless object of that practice. The other concerns the body as the site of such struggles, and as the focus of resistance. To grasp the first point, one must accept that we are dealing with power relations and with inequalities.

There is a difference in the bodily manner of the person (or group) whose style prevails and that of the person (or group) who is thereby objectified within it. We know it simply as the difference between confidence and ease on the one hand, and embarrassment and immobility on the other. Where economic and cultural capital is to one's advantage, then one may be capable of neutralizing the objectifying gaze of others and capable of "imposing the norms of apperception of one's own body . . . which, even when they reside in the body and apparently borrow its most specific weapons, such as 'presence' or charm, are essentially irreducible to it" (Bourdieu, 1984, p. 208). Whether man or woman, in public life or in the domestic setting, the claim that forms an integral part of the practice to be instituted is signified with the body, as well as in discourse. The embodiment of patriarchy is the masculine style that Henley (1977) catalogues in her political analysis of nonverbal communications; the nonverbal communications of women are the stylistic possibilities open to them as a consequence. The question then becomes how and in what ways is the body used to signify these group differences.

Although this chapter began by focusing upon groups who amplify the expressive possibilities of the body, this does not mean that, for those who contain the body's communicative potential, there is the implication that such power relations are muted in consequence. To refuse to acknowledge any protests from a subordinate group other than in verbal form is to deny its members the opportunity to signify their position, where that signification depends upon the exercise of practices other than discourse. The valuation of talk over action, of rationality over emotion can be aspects of a practice which, in rejecting the legitimacy of the body as a medium of expression, covertly recognizes its key place in signifying one's own position over that of others.

The second point concerns the body as the site of struggle and of affirmation. In their attempt to resist the authority of the school, many children wear clothes or makeup that are disapproved of by the teachers (Griffin, 1985; Willis, 1977). In Britain, where school uniform has been common, it is not surprising that clothes should be one way in which dissenters could show their disrespect for the authorities. In other ways too (for example, smoking), these children showed their disaffection. As seen with the motorbike boys, the adornment of the body, the hair length, and the physical manner become points at which people can locate their difference from the conventional culture. For example, teachers will attempt to define their subjects as pupils through regulating their appearance and their conduct ("don't run!, stand up when I speak to you"). At the same time, the children try to subvert this practice by borrowing objects and fashions from their parent culture, which is part of the adult world. Hence, smoking, drinking, and the use of makeup are sites of concern for teachers because (among other things) they indicate a refusal of the legitimacy of their authority. These borrowings should not be thought of as occurring only when groups wish to resist. Even young children will make use of the world of adult heterosexuality in their games. Walkerdine (1986) cites the example of a 6-year-old girl who leaves the classroom to sing a pop song with erotic content, miming and posing in front of the washroom mirror. It is clear that the bodily styles that people use draw upon their involvement in several groups at one time, something to which I return later on in this chapter.

Just as style is generated through what has been called a kind of *bricolage*, the reordering and recontextualization of objects to create new meanings (Clarke, 1976), so it is made to appear natural by making the ideology of the practice homomorphic with aspects of the body's appearance or with its dress. This is seen at its most extreme in the military inspection, where the soldier's turnout is subject to close scrutiny, and failures to comply with regulations present opportunities for superiors to apply sanctions and to shame the offender. The body of the person who is objectified in this way carries the markings of the social system upon it, so that the collective perception of others can locate, in its variations and alterations, any deviation from the norm. This shows that the style of a youth group is an expression, not just of difference, but of the freedom to be different. This freedom is limited by the experience of one's body as an inevitability, a condition fostered by the objective gaze of others, which identifies one's potentialities and limitations upon (or in) one's body. This is the situation that patriarchy creates for women, who feel themselves identified with a state of being (being a wife, being a mother). Around this state crystallizes the domestic setting into which they are cast as if naturally, and with respect to which they feel regulated through their (imputed) bodily qualities (e.g., of caring, of feeding, of supporting).

Taking these two points together, one can see how the imposition of one's own style over that of others involves a real difference in the way that each of the parties may use and will experience their bodily potentialities. For the dominant party, the body is a way of signifying the state of affairs; in knowing the world in this way (in an easy gesture, a confident pose), that ease remains elusive, as Bourdieu says, irreducible to the body from which it appears to emanate. For the subordinate party, the person who is objectified, the body matters in a different way, being the location of dissent about what should or should not be done. In extreme cases, this objectification might mean that the body is so identified with its positioning in the social structure (or discourse) that it seems to belong to, or to be a part of the setting in which the person is cast; it is overdetermined. Fleetingly, we know this in embarrassment and awkwardnss in the face of another; in the long term it is experienced as oppression.

These comments show why a study of gender relations in group life inevitably involves the body, and how this understanding might apply to all group settings where inequalities and power relations are at issue. It also underlines once again that disadvantaged groups who wish to assert their own independence often do this through forms of bodily dissent. For social psychology to ignore this, or to regard the body as inferior to the mind, is to refuse the terms in which the claims of these groupings can sometimes best be understood.

Women, Bodies, and Group Boundaries

In her study of ritual pollution and cleansing, Douglas (1966) proposed that the body's boundaries serve as symbols for the boundaries of the community. She cites the Coorgs of India, whose obsession with impurities entering their bodies is paralleled by their fear of penetration from members of humbler castes lower in the social system. Elaborate rituals governing entries to and exits from the body's orifices can be taken as expressive of anxieties about the political and cultural unity of the group. Functions to do with procreation are, especially, matters of ritual concern, for membership of a caste or group is determined by lineage. Douglas compares male and female physiology to vessels that must not pour away or dilute their vital fluids; females are the entry by which the pure content may be sullied, while males can be considered as the pores through which, by leakage, the whole system may be weakened. In the case of women in a patrilineal society, they act as the doors of entry to the group, for it is through their adultery that impure blood can enter the system. For this reason, Douglas suggests, "the symbolism of the imperfect vessel weighs more heavily on the women than on the men" (1966, p. 126). This proposal forms the basis of the discussion that follows.

The consequence of this difference in the valuation of the sexes is a moral double standard about sexual behavior, and one that can be seen to alter its form with changes in group relationships. In the case of the youths studied by Willis (1977), the boys' treatment of the girls as sexual prey was colored by their belief that once the girls had sexual experience, they became completely promiscuous. This meant that these youths, like those in the Norton Street Gang 40 years before them (Whyte, 1943), would not consider taking as a serious girlfriend (let alone wife) a girl who was known to be "easy". The reputation (i.e., the purity) of the group would then be tainted. During courtship, the girlfriend would be referred to by the boy as his "missus", a reference that points up the connotations of the woman in the home. She is dependable and domesticated and, above all, desexualized in relation to the group. Her honor must not be impugned by other boys referring to her previous sexual experience, and her worth as a partner is extolled in terms of virtues recognizable as those characteristic of "mum" at home.

For girls, courtship means a transition from the world of female friendships to the more limited role of preparing for the domestic setting, which is to be her world (Griffin, 1985). Indeed, in more traditional societies, such as those in some Mediterranean countries, this breaking off of the girl's female friendships is provoked by the families of the couple concerned. In Naples, for example, this takes the form of encouraging the girl to give up her work in the factory, for this is now considered a "dangerous" place for her (Goddard, 1987). The danger, which is only tacitly acknowledged by both men and women, is that should the girl remain working in the factory, she risks being thought a whore. Her transition from girl to intended wife points up the double standard of sexual behavior, and reveals that the concern about her virtue comes at a time when she takes on, symbolically, the role of gateway to the group. Rituals surround her body (where she may take it, how she should conduct herself, who must not enter it), setting clear boundaries to the family that she will join through her marriage.

Goddard argues that in these societies, women are both social boundary markers and carriers of group identity. It is for this reason that women's bodies and their sexuality are fundamental issues in understanding group relations. In the sphere of race relations, the motorbike boys in Willis's (1978) study were racist in the extreme, nothing being more threatening to them than the conquest of a white girl by a black man. In Douglas's terms, this can be explained as the fear of penetration of the group by someone regarded as socially inferior, manifested in the horror of the bodily act itself. Therefore, in these societies, women are both agents who mark social boundaries through the regulation of their lives, and also potential passive objects in the hands of others, strangers included. This dichotomy, of mother–whore, corresponds to the opposition of us–them (Goddard, 1987). The ambivalence that men feel about women lies in this duality, of the passive woman who can yet allocate her sexuality to other active men. The sexual-allocation potential is a latent one and therefore is less likely to be openly expressed or acknowledged by men in particular. It is externally manifested in the perception of women by men as dangerous and polluting, and internally formed in its countersupport for an aggressive, masculine role.

The expectation that the issue of women as pure–dangerous would be associated with extreme masculine conduct is confirmed in a study of the fantasies and the ideology of fascist *Freikorpsmen* in Germany between the two world wars (Theweleit, 1987). These men lived within a rarefied male ethos, in which discipline and demanding moral codes were matched by the expression of violent and destructive acts committed against other groups (e.g., communists, Jews) whom they treated as socially inferior yet threatening. Their military bearing and exaggerated masculine life-style was supported by a view of their women—wives, mothers and sisters—as desexualized beings. It was believed essential that the men marry a virgin, preferably the sister of a comrade-in-arms. Theweleit points to their image of what he terms "the white-nurse" as symbolic of this sister–mother desexualization and its embodiment in nurses on the battlefield who attend to the soldiers' wounds. She is called "sister," she wears a white apron, and she is disinfected. Theweleit sees the white nurse as "an emblem for the bourgeois woman's renunciation of her *female* body" (1987, p. 134, emphasis in original). In the ideology of these men, such women were virtue personified, and slurs upon their honor met with a violent response.

The opposite to the white nurse was what the *Freikorpsmen* called the *Flintenweiber* (riflewoman), the fantasized proletarian woman who was believed to carry a weapon and was often armored in other ways. Theweleit regards weapons as penis symbols, and the women were believed by the fascists to be sexually promiscuous by nature, servicing their men at one time and fighting with them in the streets at another. They are the embodiment of loose women, sexually experienced and potent, whose primary aim is to pollute and to corrupt. Where the white nurse might be tainted by a man from a "lesser" culture, the *Freikorpsmen* maintained a rigid defense against contact with the riflewomen—contact that would weaken and taint his body. In the fantasies of these men, such women, when caught, were not raped, but brutally exterminated.

This example reflects, in a more extreme way, several of the points already mentioned about the place of women as boundary markers, and about the relation of this practice to the adoption and maintenance of the masculine attitude. The ways in which the crisscrossing of gender (or, for that matter, race) with other group affiliation serves to amplify social categorization and identification remains an interesting question for social psychology. Interestingly, and consistent with Theweleit's description, there is evidence that such a juxtaposition (e.g., black men and white women) enhances rather than reduces differentiation (Brown, 1988), although the broader significance of that opposition escapes the paradigm that sees social life as synonymous with perceptuocognitive existence.

Gender and Organization

It was noted previously that women might also be bearers of the values of the group. These values are not the values of the group's public life, but those that derive from its private life, from the intimacies with which women are best acquainted. It has been suggested that, because of this role, it might be important in traditional cultures to separate them from the practices and ethics of the marketplace (Goddard, 1987). A woman's place is in the home, not only because she is wanted there but because she and the group are at risk while she is in a work setting. In such cultures, her continued involvement in a world where strangers mix freely is seen as a challenge to her capacities to act as a good wife–mother and, hence, to be a good woman. In bringing attitudes from the workplace into the home, there is a risk that she will be the carrier of something that will undermine its sanctity.

These attitudes have their correlate in the way that men and women behave toward each other in the workplace. In recent years, there has been a gradual movement of women into management positions. The work organization, as part of the public sphere, has traditionally been dominated by men, for whom the spirit of managerialism has been suffused with the masculine ethic (Kanter, 1975). This ethic emphasizes the need for successful managers to show tough-mindedness and to put aside personal and emotional concerns in order to benefit the rational interests of the firm. In its development, the organization became an extension of the male role, or rather it offered a structure (like that of manual work described in the previous section) through which masculinity could develop its particular form.

The models used in the past to understand and to promote the effectiveness of managers has emphasized the possibilities of, in Kanter's words, "engineering efficient structures, given specific measurable goals" (1975). This focus upon goals helped to legitimize the authority of managers as keepers of the goals and to make them visible in this role. By comparison, women workers in organizations tended to occupy maintenance functions, so that their contribution was relatively underexamined. This gender difference was, of course, predicated upon the wider division of labor between the sexes. This cross-association of gender with organizational position was underlined by the assumption, prevalent in the Harvard Business School perspective (Roethsliberger & Dickson, 1939), that workers were controlled by sentiments and by their informal ties with each other. This was supported by the complementary assumption that (successful) managers were relatively free of these influences, being able to control their emotions and to make controlled dicisions. Taken together, this meant that women were likely to be seen as being temperamentally unfit for management. It also meant that, "While organizations were being defined as sex-neutral machines, masculine principles were dominating their authority structures" (Kanter, 1975).

This can be interpreted as a development in which maleness entered into management in a way that provided an ethic and a style, a way of working and of *bearing oneself* in relation to one's colleagues and to the firm. Working through the managerial structure (in the abstract sense of the term), maleness was transposed from the body to the organizational activities, through which it signified as a mode, a way of living. This had the effect of placing a distance between the manager and the world of emotions (including bodily desires), which accounts for the previously noted point that organizations are sex-neutral machines.

This does not mean that organizations are devoid of sex; it means that they are *engendered* structures in which the roles of men and women are shaped by the masculine style that lies within the managerial ethic. However, where women are seen as embodying their sexuality in the workplace, men are seen as having transcended their bodily desires in their commitment to the job (Gutek, 1989). Sexuo-organizational behavior in which men do engage (e.g., sexual harassment) is therefore masked by it being seen either as a personal weakness (and nothing to do with the organizational hierarchy) or else as a natural part of the relationship between different positions in the hierarchy (boss and secretary). Women workers, on the other hand, carry their sexuality in their appearance and in their attention to the semi-private needs of the men whom they have traditionally supported in the firm. This makes their sexuality visible, and they are seen as being respon-sible for its deployment. The signifying power of masculinity is therefore further hidden by the visibility of women workers, who are posed by it to dress attractively, to behave enticingly, and to be held to account for any misdemeanors of a sexual kind (Gutek, 1989).

In management groups where women are in the minority (true for most organizations), they are likely to be judged by their male colleagues both as workers and as women. In one study examining sales personnel, Kanter (1977) noted that the "token women" were measured by the double yard-stick of how, as women, they carried out the sales function and how, as salesworkers, they lived up to the image of womanhood. These women found that their technical abilities were eclipsed by their physical appear-ance—that is, the visibility of their sexuality obscured their power to signify like a male manager. More to the point, this outcome was a resistance on the part of the men to acknowledging that women might act in this way. By a variety of devices that reasserted the inclusion within the sales role of masculine sexuality and that emphasized the women's feminine or domestic role, the men in the group made it difficult for the women to act in a man-agerial capacity. Kanter notes that women who successfully resisted being cast in the role of mother, seductress, or pet faced the prospect of being desexualized (and rejected) by their colleagues as an "iron maiden". This reference to the body as being cold, like a machine, indicates the splitting of the structures of management and female sexuality in the attitude of these men. The woman may be a woman or a manager, but she cannot be both; having tried to point up her traditional female qualities and to erode her attempts to adopt the managerial ethos, she is eventually refused that ethos by divesting it of its masculine spirit, until what remains are the purely technical functions that, the men presume, she performs in a machinelike way.

The important point to note here is that these relationships are not re-ducible to individual or to gender differences. They stem directly from an ethos, a style, a discourse that has its form within the organizational struc-ture itself. What these women must at times respond to on a personal level are overtures or resistances that deny that they have their basis in that structure. The extension of sexuality from the male body to the organization, and the localization of sexuality upon the female body are crucial to the way in which the dynamics of such groupings are worked out.

The Body at the Intersect of Group Relations

In the simplest sense, the body appears in group psychology as the index of external status characteristics—whether someone is a man or woman, black or white, of middle- or of working-class background. Simmel (1955) saw the intersect of people's group memberships as defining them uniquely, so that the body might be thought of as being crisscrossed by the multiplicity of social involvements concerned. This view, however, suggests that the body preexists as an entity that travels unchanged about the social world. While it may do so as a material thing, the psychological body, by which I mean the body as lived, is constituted by and helps to define the boundaries of the groups to which people belong. Simmel differentiated between what he termed "objective" and "natural" criteria, being the basis upon which people form groups. *Natural criteria* are those such as race, gender, and family; *objective criteria* are those based upon rational thought, such as the community of scholars, or a business organization. His suggestion that the latter form a superstructure over and above the former tends toward the proposition that natural criteria are overlayed and are rendered quiescent by rational interests (Durkheim argued similarly; see Gane, 1983). From what we have seen in this chapter, this is often not the case and cannot be the basis of theoretical speculation. The issue is not whether natural criteria can or cannot be overcome. Arguably, the body as a source of such criteria remains a potent source of signs for displaying and maintaining the boundaries of social groups. What challenges for explanation is the way in which these signs are used to point up or to obscure their relevance for the life of the group, as part of which certain aspects of social life are located on the body and become linked into natural criteria.

I want now to return to the question of the place of the body in the intersection of groups. While it implies a looser use of the word *group* than many social psychologists might prefer, Willis's (1977) claim that the two structures of maleness and manual labor formed a cross-association can be seen as just such an intersection of interests. While this can be seen at a level of discourse, it was in terms of bodily presentation and style of conduct that the youths simultaneously rebelled against the authority of the school and set norms for their own group. Why should this be? One answer, put forward in the early part of the chapter, is that the body provides a level or sphere of communication that the dominant culture finds difficult to control. While I would underline this for specific groupings, it cannot be true for all groups in social life. Yet, the body—in its appearance and its style of conduct—is always there in people's attempts to forge new groups or to leave old ones, and it is a key medium in both cases. I would argue that this is due to the fact that its mode of communication is, as was seen in the previous chapter, analogic, presentational, and synthetic. This means that it can convey, at one glance or in one movement, *the form* of the inter-sect (i.e., the relationships) of the structures concerned. In the case of the youths studied by Willis, this meant infusing into the modality of physical labor a disposition of sexuality that was evidenced in their style of conduct. The body displays this at a stroke; its semantic is powerful and undeniable. The presentational form allows for the contradictions and changes in modu-lation that tell whether one structure embraces another in complemen-tary fashion, or whether they are juxtaposed in an uneasy opposition. For example, as a woman member settles into one of the mock juries studied by Strodtbeck et al. (1957), she might change her manner from "female diffidence" to "participant juryperson". This change in manner (which might not happen all at once) is not merely a signal of change in her, but, in Simmel's terms, is also a portrayal of the establishment of a rational group out of people divided by apparently natural distinctions.

I return to the dissident group for one moment. The use of the body here is special. A surrounding culture that uses verbal means to further its interests (which would include hierarchical organizations) signifies away from the body, so that wild gestures, loudness, and emotional eruptions are declared not to be legitimate means of communication. The maintenance of this distance between the social and the physical body ensures that only people with access to verbal culture can participate fully. It is this that the youth groups reject and do so in a way that is particular to the body. For the body cannot negate (as language can); it can only refuse. It is in the simplest movements, but therefore across the broadest span of ordinary life, that such groupings can refuse the values of the dominant culture. The place of pop music in this is not accidental, albeit that there are other social and economic reasons why it should be important in this context. For pop music at once provides a homomorph of the style that is being portrayed and serves as a solvent in which the various strands of young people's interests can be, as it were, dissolved together. The dancing, moving, gyrating body expresses these interests in ways that a string of words cannot. More than this, the screaming of the fans and the broken cinema seats were (in their day) the expression of a substantive revolt that was transformed later on into a style, a manner without the threat of real refusal (Melly, 1989).

The body at the intersect of groups is one that introduces movements, borrows adornments, and reassembles expressions. To engage in one group while being a member of others is to deploy whatever capabilities, both substantive and ceremonial, are appropriate or pleasing in that context. These might be actions that are called for by the new group (such as mas-culine confidence), or they might be performances that serve to assert one's independence from the authority of others (such as a schoolchild who leaves the classroom to mime to a pop song). We can best view the body here as an assemblage of potentialities, which are brought together through the cross-association of structures such as those discussed previously. These potentialities are not wholly dictated by social structures because some are suffused with desire, with the pleasure that comes from their enactment. Where Simmel talked of individuals being subsumed under different general groupings, we can propose that the potentialities and capabilities of the body are differentially mobilized, are organized together, or issue in contradictions according to the social situation of the people concerned. For example, someone who has been married for many years and then divorces may feel a sensuous freedom (or threat) of sexual expression that colors her or his relationships in a variety of unexpected ways. Leaving or joining certain groups can be seen as a change in the scope for acting and for feeling with the body. Those capacities or practices that were formally bound together may now be practised independently; even simple things that could be invoked in a number of contexts (e.g., laughing out loud) may decline when the person joins a group in which such activities are constrained.

Finally, the idea of inequality in groups has been shown to involve the way that people live with their bodies, in the scope that they have for signifying with it or for being the subject of other people's objectifications. Using the prime social distinction of gender, it has been argued that men and women traditionally use their bodies in different ways. This is not a sex difference, in the sense of a characteristic that inheres in one class of beings but not in another. The point is that the relationship that binds and separates them, that of patriarchy, works crucially through the body to maintain other forms of social relationship as well. This is revealed in studies of sex-role spillover (Gutek, 1989) and in studies of the differences between the way men and women act in small groups (Bartol & Martin, 1986).

The styles that men and women use, when together or apart, consist of both substantive and ceremonial aspects. For the women trying to establish themselves as managers, their efforts, to which they may bring capacities drawn from the feminine world are indeed real and substantive. They may, on the other hand, be seen only as sexual style by male colleagues. Where does this perception come from? It can be seen as the invocation of an *imaginary* form, a way of being that answers to, and countersupports the men's perception of their own existence; this poses them as successful managers, as exemplifiers of an ethos that, similarly, has an imaginary aspect. These imaginary forms extend to the body as a sensible and sensitive entity; to the softness of women and to the hardness of men. The beliefs that each sex has about the other serves to support the virtual images that each creates for itself. Extending beyond the body, they engage with the objects, practices, and qualities that form the sensuous world. It is to this topic that I turn in the chapter that follows.

Chapter 6

Matter of Significance

The majority of social psychology's concern with the body, small as it is, has been framed in terms of conceptions, attitudes, and images. These terms render it an object of consciousness or of contemplation. The study of non-verbal behavior has shifted to examining its capacity to send information, to be a signaling system. Neither of these approaches has addressed the fact that the body is also living flesh; our bodies are, in a vital sense, ourselves. However, the obviousness of this fact must be set against psychology's working assumption that the task of scientific disciplines is to provide causal analyses where possible. This means that the ideas of a living body and an embodied self are not easily worked into a system of thought premised upon objectivity and the experimental method. We have already seen that the question of intention, as it applies to the sender of nonverbal communications, is one that investigators in the area have tended to avoid. The problem of the body as flesh is one psychology did not have to deal with once it relinquished all but mental life; this effectively became an issue for physiologists to think about. Where the self was concerned, its relationship to the body emerged, but remained within, the fringe area of illness, where such things as discrepancies between mental and physical experience partly defined the field. As outlined earlier, the relationship of the mind to the body was, and continued to be, a central issue for psychoanalysis. However, this relationship was often conceived in terms of the effect upon the body of a disturbed psyche. Recent concerns with stress-induced illness have tended to retain the body as a passive object, the endpoint on which failures of personal (mental) adjustment will leave their mark.

It is only in phenomenology that questions concerning the lived body have been of major concern, but it is fair to say that this approach has had little influence upon mainstream social psychology. All too often, the work of the phenomenologists has been seen (with some justification) as being subjectivist and concerned with individuals (Buytendijk, 1961). There is a double reason for this , which underlines the points made in the first chapter about social psychology's views of the body. In talking about feelings, there is a risk of being seen to be inquiring into the realm of sensation, which is all too easily assimilated to the realm of psychophysiology; this belongs to the world of substance, not to the social world of signification. The second aspect concerns the focus upon the individual; such feelings are, by definition, to do with persons in isolation, whose identities are established on the basis of their own experience rather than in terms of their membership of or attitudes toward groups of people. Therefore, from the perspective of social psychology, the phenomenological critique appears based upon an approach that is doubly faulted in its emphasis upon a thing/self entity. Put aside in this way, the body as thing and/or self is consigned to the social-psychological shadows to remain a nonquestion; this contributes to the attitude described in an earlier chapter, whereby this dismissal of the body serves to maintain a definition of what it means to be social.

The Ambiguity and Unity of the Body

Merleau-Ponty (1962) took up the question of what it means to call the body an object. He made the point that it has permanence like an object and can be subjected to partial scrutiny under one's gaze, but these do not provide the terms in which its permanence is known to us. Unlike external objects, which can be turned around and inspected in their various aspects, the body defies this kind of exploration and is always presented, as it were, from the same standpoint. It is never wholly in front of us but is always at the margins of our perceptions; it is *with* us. To observe the body as an object, one would need a second body from which to carry this out, and so on ad infinitum. The permanence of the body is unlike that of an external object. It does not appear and disappear but is the condition for the appearance and disappearance of other things. This happens as we move toward or away from them, as we reach to pick them up, stoop to enter a building, or enter the water for a swim. It provides a primordial presence within which the things of the world can be known. Merleau-Ponty argued that, in being the ground from which objects are known, the body can never be reduced to one thing among other things. It might have thinglike aspects, but these compose its subsidiary features, which cannot be appreciated without realizing first and foremost that the body is *sensible*. This condition of subjectivity also applies to its spatial movement and position and in this way distinguishes it from the positioning of objects in physical space. This is not to be confused with the declaration of "here" when someone asks you, "Are you there?" meaning "I am in the kitchen, rather than in the hall or some other place." Knowing where one is was compared by Merleau-Ponty to one's body having an attitude directed toward an existing or possible task. He gave the example of leaning with one's hands on the desk, so that one's back and shoulders, though on the margin of awareness, form the background or support for the specific action of leaning. It is this background aspect of the body, against which specific gestures or movements stand out, that constitutes the subjective coordinates that form the horizons of our spatial position.

This ground from which we act, the body as lived, is preobjective; hence, it cannot be described directly but only through its relationship with the world of things. In order that one can move one's body toward an object, the object must first exist for it. This means that we move intentionally, we aim toward the object in order, for example, to grasp it. The body is not so much *in* space, or *in* time as *inhabiting* space and time (Merleau-Ponty, 1962, p. 139). Here is the fundamental difference between the body and other material entities; it is not just something that I have, but it is also that I am. There is a sense of mineness about my body that is disclosed in every small movement that I make and in every event where something or someone impinges upon my physical being. It is my reaching that makes the glass available, my tiredness that makes the book by my bedside a welcoming escape from the work that I have yet to complete. Seen from this perspective, one's body is not an entity to be conceptualized, or imaged, or possessed, or used as something separable from oneself. It is that through which the world is knowable and one's potentialities made manifest.

From the point of view of the phenomenological critique, it is not just the intentionality of the body that marks it off from cognition as the basis for understanding how we know the world. The body's material aspect is crucial for our sense of its resistance to our efforts, its shape, solidity, or warmth. This is a very different position to that from which either a world of qualities stimulates the senses (a realist vision) or else a knowing subject discriminates and conceptualizes a world of things (cognitivism). Instead, through its specific aims and its material nature together, the body is able to gear into situations so that

> For instance, the figural quality of softness is perceived only inasmuch as a gentle resistance is *encountered by* a more or less perpendicular transgression of *touching movement*, which stands out from the rest of the body just as the softness does from the perceived background. There is no weight without the exertion peculiar to *lifting*, no odour without *inspiration*, no circularity without the regular *curving of the gaze*, and no hole without a *penetrating insertion*. (Wertz, 1987, p. 121 emphases in original)

The body is neither a passive recipient of sensations nor the handmaiden of a transcendent mind that conceptualizes its world. To anticipate the argument I make later in this chapter, the validity of this point regarding our commerce with the material world must have implications for the status of the body in social life. For the present, we need to press the point that we know the world, not merely through the distance senses as something to be viewed or inspected, but through our bodily engagements with it. This does not exclude the eye but emphasizes that the body is a unity of intention, not a compilation of sense organs. As Wertz (1987) has put it, in order to perceive "a handle," I must not be a pure consciousness but rather a *handler* with a *hand* that is substantial enough to itself grasp hold of the cup. In its turn, for it to be perceived as "a handle," the object must stand in relation to the bowl of the cup in such a way that it can support it and must be of such strength and form that it can withstand my grasp. The handle "asks" to be picked up as the chair "asks" to be sat upon. This makes sense once we accept that the body's capacities answer to forms in the world; similarly, objects in the world answer to the potentialities of the body, to its reaching out. This is true of settings as well as of specific things, so that "the body forms itself in anticipation of the aim it serves, it assumes a 'shape' . . . a shape for doing work, for fighting, for feeling," as well as a "shape for loving" (Van den Berg, 1952, p. 177).

This idea of a shape does not refer to the physical form of the body, although the form might be expressive of the intention that is inherent in it. To take an example, sexuality is not (from the phenomenological position) a type of corporeal function but a general power to orient oneself toward a certain structuration (Barral, 1963). It is an original form of intentionality that is cross-associated with other forms so that it suffuses all our social relationships. Therefore, the claim that men and women are sexed beings through and through is not an argument either for identifying this capacity in the physical body (e.g., in the genitals or the hormones) or for elevating it as a superordinate principle in psychological life. Instead, it underlines the general thesis that the subject matter of social psychology—people— would not be what it is were they not embodied. It also points up the more specific argument that the spatialization and fragmentation of the physical body, the skilled body, and the imaged body overrides an essential ambiguity in human life. To know individuals in any one of their manifestations is to know them in their totality but not to know precisely the motivation of any one act in particular (Barral, 1963).

The idea of objects resisting our efforts was integral with G. H. Mead's (1959) writings on sociality, both ideas being important to his development of a "philosophy of the act." Indeed, Mead's ideas are similar to those of the phenomenologists in this respect, and they serve to illustrate the relevance of Merleau-Ponty's work for social psychology. In his discussion of the social self, Mead drew a parallel between (a) the "conversation of gestures" in which we engage during social relationships and (b) the attitude that we have toward nature. The latter he saw as being equally a social attitude; he cites the engineer constructing a bridge as someone meeting stresses and strains by "taking the attitude of physical things. . . . in his thinking" (1934, p. 185). The physical thing (as representative of its environment) is not a separate preformed object, but "an abstraction which we make from the social response to nature" (1934, p. 184). If we do "take the attitude of the environment" (thing) toward ourselves, how is this possible? Mead's suggestion is similar to Merleau-Ponty's:

> To take hold of a hard object is to stimulate oneself to exert that inner effort. One arouses in himself an action which comes also from the inside of the thing. . . . The organism's object arouses in the organism the action of the object upon the organism, and so becomes endowed with that inner nature of pressure which constitutes the inside of the physical thing. It is only insofar as the organism thus takes the attitude of the thing that the thing acquires such an inside. (1959, p. 122)

Mead is here attempting to formulate, as Merleau-Ponty did after him, the way in which the world might be known by beings who are both sentient and material, and he puts forward a thesis that depends upon both of these features. Things are known through the body's engagement with the world, which depends upon its subjectivity and its materiality. This is the first order of its ambiguity, expressed in experience as the body that one both has and yet lives (is). Beneath this is the ambiguity that arises whenever one tries to treat the body as an assembly of separate organs, or as the expression of a particular function (e.g., sexuality). In this case, the body is always more than these things taken separately, or even alone; its unity is, as Merleau-Ponty says, always implicit and vague. We have no means of knowing our own body (and ultimately the body in general) other than by living it, by recovering from its engagements in the world some sense of its capacities, possibilities, and limitations.

This brief overview of the phenomenological critique marks out a different position from the one that covertly underlies most of social psychology. It indicates the possibility of envisaging how social relationships might be rethought once we acknowledge that individuals live in a world of objects, many of which they help to fashion. To take a simple example, the point made previously about this body being mine applies to those things that people use to extend or to ease their movement. The clothes that I wear are mine, so that if someone touches the sleeve of my jacket, they touch me. If someone runs into my car, I say that they ran into me. Neisser (1988) has used these and similar examples to argue that the embodied person is aware, through a coperception of self and environment, of what he terms the "ecological self." This sense of self (one among others such as "the interpersonal self," "the extended self," "the conceptual self") arises from a perception of ourselves as being embedded in the environment. He accepts that at this level, such perception is not reflective, for we know ourselves as we act. In this way, Neisser conceives of the relationship between the body and its accompanying artifacts in terms of movement; those things that are attracted to me or toward which I move come to be seen as part of my ecological self. However, while movement is clearly important—when I wear a pair of trousers, they are me in a way that they are not when hanging in the wardrobe—it is not the essential aspect to understanding this problem, as I show in a moment. Ultimately, this analysis stops short of the subjective, intentional body proposed by Merleau-Ponty; the ecological self is not primary as the body is for the phenomenologists.

The Body as an Instrument

What happens when we adopt something, such as a stick, to use as a probe? At first, it may feel rough and ungainly in the hand, and if using it in the dark or in an inaccessible place, the end of the stick might not usefully discern much at all. However, with practice, the sensations that one had at the palm of the hand are superseded by the discriminations that are located at its tip. The stick has become, like that in the hand of a blind person, an extension of oneself through which the physical contours of the world may be known. Polanyi (1967), using a similar example, speaks of the stick having become "interiorized," and of the person "dwelling in it." These terms point to the way in which it has changed from being a separate thing *toward which* the person attends, to becoming an extension of the arm *from which* the person attends to other things. The stick enters into what Polanyi terms the "tacit basis of knowing," subsidiary to the focal features discerned at its endpoint.

This example was also used by Merleau-Ponty (1962) as an illustration of the way that the body comprehends movement. With use, the stick ceases to be an object, felt in itself, and becomes an extension of the scope and active radius of touch. His point is that the stick is not used as a measure of objects, its length does not enter as a middle term; those things that it touches are not known through its objective features. Taking up the stick means taking it up "into the body," or using it as an extension of the body, which does not calculate itself in objective space. This is true of other things that we employ in this way—hats with brims or cars to be maneuvered through narrow spaces. Once the hat is on your head or the steering wheel is in your hands, these things cease to be objects related only to other objects and become instead "potentialities of volume" (Merleau-Ponty, 1962, p. 143). As such, they are adjuncts to our bodily capacities and limitations. We know them, like the stick, through the objects that they discern and the circumstances that they transform.

This example raises a number of questions, about the status of things, as well as about the embodied self. Bateson (1987) has argued that it calls into question the ontological status of the self presumed to be located in a mentality somewhere inside the body. He suggests that to ask the question where I begin and finish—at the top of the stick, at the end, somewhere in between?—is to make for unnecessary (and nonsensical) difficulties. Instead, he proposes that the way to delineate it as a system is to recognize that the stick is a pathway along which transformations of difference are being transmitted. This system, in which mind is immanent, includes the person, the stick, the environment, the person, the stick, the environment, and so on. The problem with this view is that, taken by itself, it collapses the body and the various physical objects into one ontological frame. (This is precisely the point of view adopted by Argyle, 1983, in his model for describing nonverbal behavior as a social skill.) It has been criticized by phenomenologists, who argue that it reduces the body to the status of an instrument, a "means by which" the goals presumed to be forged in our mental (i.e., cognitive) existence can be achieved. One can put down the stick but one cannot divest oneself of one's body. Their argument is that, while on occasions the body may be used instrumentally, this is not its primary mode; its primary mode is one that makes any instrument or "relation of having" possible (Zaner, 1966).

It is true, however, that the world always appears to us in terms of the objective possibilities that our instrumental engagements offer. The nail that must be driven refers both to the hammer that can do the driving and to the pieces of wood that are to be joined together. Sartre (1957) speaks of these instrumental complexes as giving the world that we apprehend its objective appearance, so that "step by step" across them, every means is referred to the center (the phenomenal body) as a favorable or adverse opportunity. For this reason, he says,

> This is why my body always extends across the tool which it utilizes; it is at the end of the cane on which I lean and against the earth; it is at the end of the telescope which shows me the stars; it is on the chair, in the whole house; for it is my adaptation to these tools. (p. 325)

Instead of assuming, as a cognitive psychology or one centering upon psychophysiology might do, that we first need to endow the body with fully fledged powers in order for individuals to know the social world, this position argues that it is these instrumental things that, in their appearance, indicate our body to us. As Sartre says, the body is not a screen between things and ourselves. By entering into the world of instrumental relations, our capacities and the thing like nature of the body are indicated to us. These properties of the body as one object in a world of things include such features as our strengths and weaknesses, our skills of manipulation or even of charm; yet these are given as the correlate of the things or situations that we have encountered through our engagements, in which the phenomenal body, of which we are subsidiarily aware, remains elusive.

The phenomenological critique offers a view of the body as at once both transcendent subjectivity and material form. These are not Cartesian alternatives, separable and locatable in different places; nor is one of these aspects possible without the other. In essence, our body provides us with an ambiguous mode of existing, a tension that is reflected in psychology's attempts to comprehend and to describe social life. In the main, this has meant the formulation of mind and behavior in terms of the sphere of inanimate objects. In its latest form, this is expressed in terms of systems theory and the computer as a model of mind. This reification of mental life has been rejected along the lines of the preceding critique, noting that no simulation of what people do is adequate to describing the experience of being a person (Buytendijk, 1974). In a paper entitled "Why computers must have bodies," Dreyfus (1967) has pointed out that the building up of skills through the assimilation of objects to the body is central to the way that people create and know the world. Once the role of the body is acknowledged, no amount of complex thought by a digital computer can be taken as a model of how people made of flesh and blood actually think in the course of acting. The objectification of mind through computer simulation cannot be complete in itself; this, too, is recognized by those who would, for whatever reason, have us credit computers with autonomous powers (Janlert, 1987).

It is important to note that this analysis of the body through experience does not lead to a concern with pure subjectivity or with individuals taken separately. Instead, our attention is directed away from studying the meeting of minds to the analysis of how people engage each other in the world. This phrase "in the world" is all too abstract, and it is the job of subsequent sections to examine how this can be made tangible within social psychology. I just note in passing that one direct line of investigation into the ambiguity of bodily existence is that of identifying the treatment of the body in the legal world, where moral issues are paramount (Harré, 1986a). Questions of the rights to alter or to dispose of parts of one's body, or to assume responsibility for the bodies of others pose moral dilemmas. These reveal, if only in part, the contradictions that stem from the indissolubility of the body's instrumentality and its subjectivity. It is not just a question of whether, taken in its material aspect (e.g., the blood or the kidney donated), it is subject to being seen as a thing, but also whether it is proper for bodies to be used like things (e.g., as in slavery). For a part of the body to be used as an instrument may be acceptable, where the remainder can be conceived as the habitus of the individual qua person, or yet for people to lend themselves temporarily as part of an instrumental action (e.g., holding up a pole to help someone else erect a tent). The treatment of a person as a mere thing is always morally reprehensible in a civilized society, which underlines the error of conceiving of the body (or the mind) as an object. The body as instrument is always figured against the elusive background of the embodied person as a phenomenal being, even if this demands, as it apparently did for the slave owners, giving up the souls of their charges in order that they could exploit their bodies (Harré, 1986a). This, however, raises the wider question of the acceptability of the treatment of the body as an instrument by social psychologists, working in the context of a society that requires it to be seen in this way. This is a topic that I leave for discussion in the following chapter.

The Body in a World of Objects

The phenomenological analysis summarized so far in this chapter is central to our consideration of the body in social psychology. Indeed, this school of thought is unique in having given thought to it as a psychological, rather than a physiological or material, phenomenon. Its conclusions, to which attention has been drawn, focus on the body as having a primordial relationship to the world, which cannot be reduced to objective characteristics. We are originally living, acting beings of flesh and blood, and only secondarily bodies that move and can be plotted in Cartesian space. Paradoxically, the reestablishment of the body's subjectivity has been shown to make objects matter more, not less, to individuals. In this section, I want to take up this point in order to sketch out a direction that a focus upon the body makes relevant and significant for social psychology. The division between a subjective mind and its physical environment (which includes the body as physiological entity) puts all material things outside of psychology's direct concern. There are very few psychological studies of artifacts (Graumann, 1974), of homes and possessions (Gauvain, Altman, & Fahim, 1984), in spite of there being studies of the general environment in which people establish their relationships. I am thinking here of the work in environmental psychology, which, in spite of the breadth of its concern, remains wedded to a philosophy of disembodied subjects who are affected by and respond to situations as they perceive them (Saegert & Winkel, 1990). Traditionally, this has meant that measures are made of the environment in geometric terms and correlated with measures of the subjects' behavior or cognitive maps. *Cognitive maps* expresses precisely the placing of subjective mind within objective space. Even recent attempts to establish the social scientific study of objects has tended to focus upon their symbolic value for reflective individuals (Csikzentmihalyi & Rochberg-Halton, 1981). The phenomenological critique undermines this by showing the material aspect of knowing (with the body), and the subjective aspect of objects and settings that appear qualitatively distinct in our experience.

The implications of this approach for social psychology have yet to be worked out. For Schutz (1967), the body was a ground of a working self "living in the vivid present," a basis from which individuals could observe each other and establish an intersubjectivity essential for communication and cooperation. This, however, leads us back to a concern with the body as a sign–vehicle, a medium for the expression of intentions and meanings through which individuals make sense of each other in face-to-face relationships. This suggests a view of social life as the meeting of individual minds clothed with bodies but still meeting in a psychological ether, as far as their objective setting is concerned. In its extreme (i.e., traditional social psychological) form, the inclusion of the body would be to envision two abstracted individuals. It becomes, as in Heider's (1958) theory, the mediation between the centers of the persons who are looking at each other and who, as a consequence, must be disembedded from their context in order to be perceived for themselves.

The point that was made in the previous section is that social life is not the meshing of minds, or even of embodied individuals, but the fashioning of a society that has a material form. Things matter to people, and how they matter makes for significance in the relationships of individuals. At a general level, this point converges with the idea that society, while a human product, is also an objective reality into which people are born. By comparison, its subjective aspect lies in the fact that objects are not merely encountered or perceived by people, but are fashioned and maintained by them as well. Bachelard (1969) gives the example of how, by carefully applying wax to a table "with the woollen cloth that lends warmth to everything it touches," a person "increases the object's human dignity" (p. 67). The subjectivity of objects lies in their being a resource for and a recipient of the human capacities by which people are distinguished in their being. That is why one phenomenologist, following Sartre, expressed what appears to be (until we understand its meaning) a heretical statement about the human sciences:

> Whoever wants to get to know a man should leave him as quickly as possible. He is in the last place there where he stands. All the time he silently moves away from himself by expressing himself in the world of things. (Van den Berg, 1952, p. 166)

To return to the objective aspect of society, this is more easily understood as being the institutional forms into which people are born, and the genesis of which they cannot reconstruct except at one remove, through historical study (Berger & Luckmann, 1971). The things of the world appear for what they are partly through this fact, that they are pregiven, and their completeness is therefore taken for granted. In the various institutions of society, the material aspect is one that in-forms our relationships and our knowledge of how things are; they are a testimony to the legitimacy of the cosmologies into which people of different cultures are socialized. This means that, just as there is no generalized body in the sense of one that is lived, so there is no objective space when considered in the light of people's way of life in their surroundings. How the world appears—the fields, the streets, the things for sale in the shop windows—is evidence of differences in the way that individuals are constituted in their being as people.

For example, a study of elderly people in Switzerland revealed differences among members of the social classes in their ways of relating to their environment. In their different capacities, and with their different opportunities to exercise these, the physical spaces in which they lived had quite distinct phenomenological appearances (Lalive d'Épinay, 1986). These were not images of entities with prescribed boundaries but descriptions of places that answered to particular ways of acting in the world. For working-class people, who do not own their homes but perhaps live in rented rooms, the neighborhood is adopted by them as their domicile. It is a place appropriated through everyday actions; the street is a way to the shops, a park for walking the dog, a corner for meeting friends for a chat. The neighborhood is felt to belong to them; and in turn, they belong to it through the history of their ancestors in the area. Unlike the middle classes, who peek out at the alien streets through their curtains, the working-class individuals in this study viewed the environment as a means of escape from the paucity of their domestic situation, in "making little journeys, and also by gazing at the pageant of life and history" (Lalive d'Épinay, 1986). This experience is one that is confirmed in cases where the authorities (the working classes, having little control, are always in fear of what they might do) relocate people in order to develop an area of the city. Deprived of their home neighborhood, such people may suffer grief reactions that are concrete symptoms of a dislocation that is experienced in the body. Fried (1963) reports individuals from the West End of Boston saying such things as, "I felt like my heart was taken out of me," and "I always felt I had to go home to the West End and even now I feel like crying when I pass by." While psychologists since Fried's study have studied people's perceptions of their neighborhoods, it is to its subjective nature, not its cognitive meaning, that I am drawing attention.

The last point can be clarified by a comparison of working and middle-class elderly in Lalive d'Épinay's study. For the latter, the home is defined by one's dwelling, the place of one's own, which, in a very real sense, constitutes one's whole life as the end, the summary of life's journey. It is a small kingdom, the Swiss equivalent of the Englishman's castle, to which one can retire and not be disturbed by others. In its contents, in its "did-it-myself" refurbishments, the middle-class home is overinvested with affection. This is revealed in the distrust of the outside world, whose dangers lurk beyond the garden gate in the public streets, which are "not me." As Sartre (1957) points out, I live my body in menacing machines as well as in manageable instruments; the danger that threatens my house and its contents threatens me. For the Swiss middle-class elderly, threats to their property and to their health and strength were often run together in their accounts of daily life.

This comparison shows that people are constituted differently in their relationships with objects; they do not respond differently to the same things, but they and their environments are distinguished in the forms of the relationships in which they stand. There is no pregiven common environment or set of objects with which all individuals are faced; differences in wealth and in property ownership make this obvious. Nor is there a common set of cognitions or capacities that all individuals bring to situations; there is no universal subject peering out at a ready-made world or having a universal set of needs to express in the world. Even when it comes to the North American middle class, the ways in which people furnish their homes, and the ways that they speak of and value their possessions show that there are different ways of being in relation to artifacts (Pratt, 1981). Objects are not, in essence, expressive of values and needs that are held to have existed prior to those objects; this assumption is itself a consequence of a more basic orientation toward consumer goods, which are geared to the elaboration of the individual subject. As I show in the next chapter, it is also part of this orientation to mask its own assumptions, while presenting itself as the natural state of affairs in the life of people and the things that they own.

The argument that individuals both *have* bodies and yet *are* their bodies has been linked to the claim that the relationship between the organism and the self is an *eccentric* one. Because of this, people's experience of themselves "always hovers between being and having a body, a balance that must be redressed again and again" (Berger & Luckmann, 1971, p. 68). This concept of eccentricity suggests that the relationship between the sense of oneself acting, or being and the grasp of oneself figured objectively will progress unevenly. This eccentric progression is entirely in accord with what we should expect in a world in which people's capacities, and their grasp of themselves as human, are objectified in the artifacts that form the material aspect of society.

At times of new inventions, or during epochs of agrarian or industrial change, new things appear in the world, which make demands upon people's capacities (ways of doing, of knowing, of feeling). These capacities are grounded in the bodies of individuals who are accustomed to a different life. The historian E. P. Thompson (1967) described just this kind of situation having occurred during the Industrial Revolution in Britain. The factory managers were faced with the problem of inculcating in their work force practices that were conducive to the efficient running of the plant. During this period, they were particularly concerned with establishing habits of good time-keeping among the work force. The work force was drawn from a population that was used to the life-style of a peasant culture, in which people attended to the necessities of the day or of the moment. This involved a way of living (not merely of knowing, or of talking about) space and time, which was at variance with the demands of the new factory discipline. Effectively, therefore, this was a time of overlapping epochs, an eccentricity in the relationships between the bodily capacities, desires, and needs of the people and the constraints and requirements for synchrony demanded by the newly organized machinery. This led to clashes and to contradictions between two modes of living, such that it was noted at the time that the workers' "restless and migratory spirit" meant that they "never sit at ease at the loom; it is like putting a deer in the plough" (Pollard, 1963). This image summarizes precisely the difference that can arise between the body that one is and the body that one has, when posed in certain new relationships to the world.

At times of social change, new artifacts with which people have to come to terms may actually appear to blur their intercourse with the world. This happens with the development of new machines and the experience of those who first use them. Early on, the machine is perceived as an object in itself, as a source of possibilities and problems, some of which might never be overcome. Once the machine is established in its near-final form and is usable by individuals who need know nothing of its development (e.g., myself writing this on a word processor), the artifact appears natural in its ease of assimilation to their intentions, so that it has become an instrument upon which they can rely. Speaking of the airplane in this context, the pilot and writer Antoine de Saint-Exupèry wrote,

> In the machine of today we forget that motors are whirring; the motor, finally, has come to fulfil its function, which is to whirr as a heart beats— and we give no thought to the beating of our heart. Thus precisely because it is perfect the machine dissembles its own existence instead of forcing itself upon our notice.
>
> And thus, also, the realities of nature resume their pride of place. It is not with metal that the pilot is in contact. Contrary to the vulgar illusion, it is thanks to the metal, and by virtue of it, that the pilot rediscovers nature. As I have already said, the machine does not isolate man from the great problems of nature but plunges him more deeply into them. (1954, p. 55)

When these changes occur suddenly, or more often with the erasure of the erratic line that the development of the artifact really took, people can be faced with things (be they buildings, cars, or airplanes) that appear to have sprung into being ready-made. While we know that this is not true, nevertheless, the way of being, the mode of action that we now take for granted as we drive to work or turn up the central heating comes to seem the essential, unchanging nature of our humanity. To understand that this is not the case is to make possible the recovery of different ways of seeing the world, of different ways of being for people who relied upon and attended toward different things than those we know today. The world is, of course, a psychologically different one in each case, as is the figure who feels, sees, and acts in an objectively different perspective. The material aspect of the social world is a vital clue to the standpoints that people can take about things in their commerce with each other.

We need, finally, to clarify the difference between this position and the idea that people as subjects live in a world of objective things. The point is that a world of sensuous, desirable, or dangerous objects is a psychological world, in which we touch and see the qualities ascribed to it. This is what was meant earlier in saying that the material environment is also a subjective one. The correlate of this is not only our own facticity, but the knowledge of ourselves as part of the world. To see a person within such a perspective is to recover that individual as a figure, a standpoint, or a way of seeing (Romanyshyn, 1982). To see the things, or to handle them in a different way is to be posed in relation to them as a different figure. Therefore, it is not an empirical self or a unitary subject that provides social psychology with its subject matter, but a person who is capable of being refigured in the shift from one mode of engagement with the world to another. (This can be compared with the idea of individuals being produced as a nexus of subjectivities [Walkerdine, 1981], as mentioned in the previous chapter). As pointed out previously, with respect to workers during the Industrial Revolution, this change is not a voluntary one, as would be a shift in perceptual perspective, but may involve the overlap of epochs, which involves transformations in the ways that individuals live in space and time.

The removal of the empirical subject also implies that we do not think of the social world as being unitary in its material aspect. Objects appear, in their different modes, to have functional, aesthetic, and moral characteristics. The aforementioned nexus of subjectivities is answered in the physical thing by the condensation of these qualities within it. However, in the realm of everyday things, it is often the functional aspect that dominates within instruments that allow us to achieve specific and often predetermined ends.

Artifacts define the contemporaneous aspect of social life. They do this by being simultaneously present, so that individuals assume attitudes and exercise capacities within their understanding of what their situation offers them. This does not mean that objects offer the same opportunities to or make the same demands upon different people. The bowl that contains the food means something different to the diner than it does to the waiter or to the person out back washing the dishes. The home demands things of the housewife that it does not demand of her working husband. The inequalities of social life are not merely symbolized by objects, though they are remarkable for doing this while seeming to be just trivial things (Miller, 1985); these inequalities are exercised through these things. We can come to know each other through the ways in which, together, we handle objects (Radley, 1979).

Take the example of two people carrying a large trunk upstairs, which, unbeknownst to either party, is unevenly loaded. The size and weight of the box, together with the angle and dimensions of the staircase provide the physical constraints within which this must be done. These, however, are not known geometrically (unless measurements are first taken) but through the efforts of the pair to maneuver the trunk upstairs. The person carrying the lighter end will have a different experience from the one holding the heavier end, although this difference in their relationship will also be discovered in the course of their joint anticipation of the project. That is to say, the nature of the trunk (its unequal weighting inside) is revealed simultaneously with the inequality in the relationship of the two individuals concerned. Furthermore, what each person discovers is not something about himself or herself as an isolated subject, but as part of a project with distinct social and physical constraints. While this example is about something explicitly involving physical effort, it does make the point that the world of artifacts is not merely one to be perceived. In their social relationships, people assume varying degrees of control of physical things. Through the maintenance, transformation, consumption, or conspicuous display of these things, the differing capacities that people exercise are either reestablished or brought into question.

Taking the body as a starting point, we have seen that this involves social psychology in an appreciation of the social world as having a material form.

These objects are not secondary to an understanding of social life but are constitutive of the practical relations through which social life is lived.

Objects and the Aging Body

The eccentric relationship between having and being a body, set out in the previous section, is one that applies to the situation of old age. In particular, the process of physical decline may not always be accompanied immediately by a sense of the loss of one's capacities, certainly not of one's preferences and desires. Nevertheless, it is a time when the body "as a hinge between nature of which we are a part and nature from which we are apart" (Eng, 1984) then becomes apparent. In this section, however, I do not want to discuss old age in general, but its relationship to the world of objects. This is not a movement away from a concern with the aging body, as I show subsequently, but a slant on the issue, which highlights the ambiguity that has been proposed as being at the center of our discussion of physical being. With increasing old age, the body's physical decline leads to a change in the body's appearance, as an object of contemplation; the slowing down and the loss of control in movement are reflected in such things as not reaching the telephone before it stops ringing, or spilling the milk as it is poured into the cup. This change in the body's capacities is revealed at first in the shortcomings in the things that the person wishes to influence; later, it may be sensed directly in the tremor of the hand or arm. For the elderly, the physical environment can take on radically different valences with regard to objects and places that are friendly or dangerous and, with that, they may have a changed sense of being in relation to the world of things.

Hazan (1986) described a center that provides weekday care to members of the elderly Jewish population in a borough of London. For these individuals, as for other elderly people, the problem was one of sustaining a way of life in the context of a physical body that no longer supported their customary claims to being. Attending the day center provided them with a secluded space, in which they could live with some autonomy. This gave them a sense of being independent of the outside world, of mastery over their everyday lives. The key problem identified by Hazan was that their appearance as aged, together with any lapses in physical control, always threatened the image that they wished to sustain of themselves as worthy citizens. One way in which they countered this was to refuse photographs of themselves, explicit evidence of their physical appearance and reminders of the decline that had taken place. Another was to dress in ways that made them unobtrusive, choosing clothes that expressed a kind of nonchalant dowdiness. Appearance was neither a subject for discussion nor a source of rivalry or competition. (In this, these individuals were different from a group of elderly people who lived in an American slum hotel [Stephens,

1976] and serves as a reminder that these issues are subject to relevant cultural and economic situations.)

However, it was in dancing that the members of the center spent most time. Hazan concludes that this was because, among other reasons, dancing created a unification of mind and body which, even if only temporarily, overcame the separation of what they could do and still wanted to be. Dancing can be seen as a mode of bodily conduct separated from the concerns of the outside world, which achieves a transcendental form by changing the drabness and the dangers of the environment into a space for communing together, a space for pleasure. At the same time, it envelops the dancer in a world of the present, away from the grief of a lost past and the anxieties of the future. Drawing upon both Merleau-Ponty's (1962) and Mead's (1959) analyses of time, Hazan suggests that this analysis of dance can be seen as standing for a more general orientation of the elderly in the center. Collapsing the past and the future into the present is a way of dealing with the decline of the body–object, which is inevitably pointed up by focusing upon what has gone before and how things have changed.

This study implies that space and time can be transformed through activities such as dance. It suggests that, with the onset of old age, and where individuals are removed from the demands of the outside world, the establishment of such a timeless present might be achieved through their modes of apprehending objects. Little research has been carried out in this area to date. What there is suggests that objects are used by the elderly as a means of coping with transition (McCracken, 1987). This can mean that, as people get older, they enhance identification with parents and ancestors through the valuation of family heirlooms, and they create a sense of timelessness, which expands the present to embrace the past and the future. A different form of this sense is perhaps achieved through the passing on of valued objects to children or grandchildren, objects that capture the affection and care of their original owner. In spite of these studies, there is much that could be discovered about the ways in which the elderly, who are isolated or who have retired from the outside world, transcend the linear progression of time in order to make their material situation comfortably respond to their diminished bodily capacities. I am not referring here to an ergonomic problem but to the acts of transcendence, of imagination, through which they establish a psychological world that figures them as being once again worthy and dignified individuals.

Sickness and the Adjustment to Illness

The symptoms of pain or of physical malformation are changes read as being signs of disease. It is at this time that the body, which is so easily surpassed (in Sartre's terms) in effortless action, makes itself known to the person who has up until then taken it for granted. Through its limitations, the sick body is an object of attention, but it still remains the ground of psycho-logical life. In many cases, these limitations are realized only when, as with the elderly, the world to which we attend fails to change in ways that our actions would command. The act of reaching for something cannot be achieved without straining the arm, or the words on the page only become legible if I bring the book closer to my eyes. I once interviewed a man diagnosed as having Huntington's chorea. As an editor on a major movie, he first knew something was wrong when he began to tread upon the film on the cutting room floor. Although we do wake up with palpable signs of sickness (the headache and aching limbs being a common example), even these are often only fully disclosed for what they are when we try to focus our eyes or to get out of bed. In sickness as in health, the body is not seen *in essence* as an object, but is disclosed through action; through our efforts in the world, the limitations of the sick body, like those of the healthy, are objectified for us.

The limitations that illness implies are taken up within a view that in-cludes, as it were, a biographical account of one's body. Individuals place feelings and pain within the context of an objectification that bears the mark of their past life.

> People have to inhabit their bodies, and their physical identity is part of themselves. Particularly as they grow older, they have a need to account for this identity, to draw together all that they have experienced. This body is their inheritance, it is the result of the events of their life, and it is their constraint. (Blaxter, 1983, p. 69)

This means that the apprehension of illness is subject to the body's use in everyday life. Those feelings to which one's constitution and one's role in society most often give rise have a naturalness that discourages their being interpreted as symptoms.

Once recognized as symptoms, signs of bodily change or of pain are no longer variations in the usual form of the body exercising its daily potential. A lump is not a temporary eruption, a pain is not the result of overexercise: instead, these are read as signs of disease, so that they are transformed from being weaknesses of the living body into indices of a bodily state that is separate from the person. This is another example of the condition in which we feel ourselves in relation to nature of which we are a part and apart. In Western cultures, to have a disease is experienced as having something wrong with one's objective body, not with oneself. Disease is an intrusive object, so that it is common for individuals to speak of the afflicted parts or region in impersonal terms (Cassell, 1976). This is particularly so when the diseased area is responsive to medical intervention, so that "it" can be surgically removed or attended to.

To become the object of the surgeon's attentions, the body had first to enter medical discourse deprived of its subjectivity. Medical language has played a large part in forming the modern Western way of conceiving the body, so that its parts are understood in everyday discourse in a way that owes much to how doctors speak of "it." This is not true in all societies, however, where (in primitive cultures particularly) the living body is the paradigm for deriving meanings of other significant objects. This is the opposite of the use, in Western cultures, of external objects to signify physical being (Manning & Fabrega, 1973). In spite of this, it is not true to say that the objectification of the body is an essentially negative thing. In medical examination, for example, part of the work of the episode is to displace the self from the body in order that the doctor's intrusions are seen as functional and limited. This does not mean that there is a strict demarcation between the embodied self and the objectified body; in the course of the doctor's physical examination of the patient are often inserted narratives about the person, which preserve his or her sense of self, the sense of a person with moral dignity (Young, 1989).

The ambiguity, the eccentric relationship that has been identified as describing the condition of people as embodied selves, is nowhere made more pronounced than in the situation of chronic illness. In this condition, individuals have to continue living life as best they can in spite of their illness. If they wish to remain active in society, then they must find ways of containing their symptoms, of bearing pain and discomfort in order that others accept them as normal. There is a kind of circularity here, for the degree to which sick individuals are successful at doing this has implications for the demands and opportunities that other people will make upon them and create for them. This balancing of the demands of symptoms against those of society is rarely easy to make and not always successful. For example, the rheumatoid arthritis sufferer has been described as being involved in "a nightmare race" in which the daily variation in the body's limitations are matched against the changing demands of keeping up a normal life (Wiener, 1975).

This need to try to keep going in spite of illness, to make more effort, to become engrossed in work in order to distract oneself from pain, places the person in the position of living out these attempts at normalization (Alonzo, 1979). The acts of covering, of overriding, of dissembling in order to contain symptoms are ways of *bearing illness*. In that sense, they are ways of living the body in order to adjust to the illness condition and, even if not consciously intended, may become part of the self-image of the person concerned. The balance is no longer something to be struck between a subjective body and an objectified one (the body one has versus the body one is), but between a sick self and a healthy one, both of which must coexist. This is not a movement that belongs to individuals and cannot be understood at this level alone. It also involves the individual's relationship to society. When feeling well, people perceive the body as the repository of good health; illness, as manifested in the dangers of pollution and disease, is seen to lie outside, in society (Herzlich, 1973). This unawareness of the healthy body, its inexpressible taken-for-grantedness, is consistent with what has been said already about its phenomenal location as the tacit ground of being. To know the body as ill requires that it be objectified for us in terms of the ends that we cannot reach, the work that we cannot do. For many people, being ill means just this: the inability to go to work or to otherwise fulfill one's daily duties. As long as one attends to the task and keeps going to work, the fuzzy head and feeling hot are sensed as deviations within a project in which the body retains (albeit with some difficulty) a shape for working. However, the minute one accepts, for example, that influenza has struck, these same feelings are transformed in experience into symptoms. Attending to them is itself the adoption of a bodily orientation. Sartre (1957) used the example of pain in the eyes to argue that "pain is *precisely the eyes* in so far as consciousness 'exists them.'" With the emergence of this new psychological world, objects too are different (e.g., putting away the squash racquet that was to have been used that evening). More significant, the person is refigured as a sick individual, for whom sickness and health no longer appear as separate spheres but have become incorporated as two poles of experience (Herzlich, 1973). For people with chronic diseases, this can mean the establishment of an opposition between their sick selves and their healthy selves. The different ways in which this uneasy balance is maintained are informative of how the body is used in social relationships.

Bodily Style and Adjustment to Chronic Illness

From what has been said so far, it is clear that adjustment to chronic illness is not merely adaptation to an outside intruder. For once people have begun to live with the disease, their own ways of adjusting begin to constitute the illness with which they must deal. The longer one lives with a disease and accepts and adapts to it, the more likely one is to see the illness refigured through one's efforts to maintain daily life. The illness might not be preferable (to health), but its contours may be known and its demands anticipated in the reshaping of one's body to accommodate it. The idea that illness is lived is illustrated in the descriptions of people who have suffered low back injury (Murphy & Fischer, 1983). Patients can be identified whose comportment is absolutely upright. They express, through this attitude, a position of moral rectitude, of needing to show that they cannot be blamed for any shortcomings in what they can carry out as a result of their injury. This example shows, in a direct way, that illness is not merely adjusted to "in the mind," or that it is coped with as a separable object, but that it is constituted in the way that people project themselves into the world. This use of the term *projection* implies anticipation and direction, as well as the idea that by being this kind of patient, the psychological world itself is apprehended in a particular way. It implies that people bear illness with a particular style or mode of adjustment—that is, with *their* bodies, in *their* real-life setting.

One response to illness, whether chronic or acute, is to attempt to minimize it as far as possible by maximizing normal life. For example, some men with coronary disease have been shown to deal with their symptoms through the assertion of good health in activity (Radley, 1988a). Taking on extra jobs at home, continuing with overtime at work, and conducting oneself in an upright fashion all attest to the fact that one is not really ill. These men dealt with objects in a way in which the resistance (the hardness, the heaviness) was objectified in their bodily efforts in terms of their own sense of permanence and invincibility. They tended to speak of their illness using the metaphor of the machine, so that heart surgery would become, in some cases, a matter of "fixing the plumbing" and hence distanced from themselves. Yet the disease was, as they had been informed by the doctor, part of their bodies. When placed in a position of being unable to deny this, it was not unknown for this style of assertion—"active-denial"—to take a reflexive form. One patient spoke of times when he went out for long walks, forcing the pace while muttering, under his breath, taunts to his heart to dare it to fail him then.

In terms of the living body, this mode of adjustment is one where, in simple terms, one can say that the ambiguity is resolved in favor of the demands of society and at the expense of the dictates of the disease. By trying harder, by keeping busy, any discomfort arising is sensed within this mode as being, if anything, evidence of the extra effort one has made. The world is grasped as something still manipulable, still conquerable, and the person is constituted as a figure of social worth, someone who "doesn't give up easily," who "doesn't complain." An example of this was given by a man who, in the early weeks of his recovery from heart surgery, spent time splitting logs in spite of his wife feeling that this was unwise. What was interesting was that this misdemeanor was reinterpreted by the wife later on as, "There's no holding him when he's alright" (Radley, 1988a, p. 129), suggesting an orientation to illness that was embedded in their social relationship, not just embodied in the man's actions.

An alternative response to the onset of chronic disease is one where the person collapses in the face of the consequences of illness. The response of resignation is typified by people who have had to give up work and who feel that the illness has invaded their whole lives. The loss of the means to demonstrate one's worth through the lack of opportunity to exercise one's bodily capacities is particularly damaging. Resignation as a mode of adjustment is shown both in bodily comportment and in the appearance of the patient's psychological world. The person reports sitting around, being dependent upon others; things appear to elude one's grasp, to be lost, to belong to others, to take on powers that the patient cannot contest. The retirement from active engagement in the social world means that there are fewer things in terms of which the person can realize his or her capacities. Emptied of their objects (no work, few social contacts, no household duties), bodily capacities are objectified only as evidence of loss of self-worth (Charmaz, 1983). Such people can take on a *phenomenal transparency* with respect to their inability to sustain a body fit for work (Radley, 1989).

These summary illustrations are meant to show that a study of illness necessitates an analysis of a phenomenological kind—by this, I mean some recognition that *being ill* is not primarily a cognitive or a physiological matter. It is an assertion of the key role of the living body in the way that illness is borne by patients and by significant others. What is expected of healthy people, or of patients who are recovering from an illness, are not just demands that are culturally formed but are also shaped by the social circumstances of those involved. The foregoing example of resignation is particularly striking among manual workers, for whom the use of their bodies as the direct means of earning their wages and of maintaining a mas-culine attitude (cf. Chapter 5) underlies their response to forced inactivity.

There is no universal body that is afflicted with illness; it is not only *what* people have to cope with that varies, but *the means* that they have of making these adjustments. What is called here an "adjustment style" is a summary term intended to convey the mode that a person adopts in the face of illness. This mode is not a coping style, as might be located in the psychological resources of the individual subject, but an orientation to the world, It is not located in the patient because it relies upon others for its legitimation and its opportunities for expression. What recovering patients ought to be feeling or doing are matters of social health beliefs, and of the relationships of the particular individuals concerned. When a man with heart disease will not desist from digging his garden in spite of the pleas from his wife, he is simultaneously making a statement about his relationship to the material world, to his wife, and to the illness that threatens his life; in his grasp upon the spade, that world and that figure are embodied. It is one person's resolution provoked by the ambiguity of being and of having a body, when this relationship takes the eccentric form posed by the onset of disease.

One final word can be said about the sick body and the physical environ-ment. When people are at home recovering from a serious illness, objects can often take on a significance that they did not have when the person was well. This is a common experience but interesting nonetheless. It might be said that this is due to the fact that sick people are cut off from the things of the outside world, allowing the body to become more salient. Alter-natively, it would seem that there is a very definite shift in the meaning of the home and its objects for the recovering patient. Places and objects once differentiated according to the manifold projects of the patient (things to work with, to relax with, to move out of the way) become related instead either to the outer world of health, which others enjoy, or to the patient's own circumscribed world. It is as if the objects map out the boundaries of health and sickness through their availability, their resistance, or their unattainability to the person concerned. In the sickroom, things reflect the course of recovery, just as they can help to shape it. When bedridden, the patient can be responsive to the weather, while when progressing each new obstacle surmounted restores the sense of ability vital to good health. With these small achievements comes a restoration of the ends that they make possible. "I can walk, climb or run" becomes "I can work, play and relax" (Radley, 1988a, p. 149). With the restoration of good health, ends are achieved unthinkingly, so that the body is constantly surpassed in the exercise of capacities that are known in terms of the changes that they make to the outside world.

These comments indicate a way of thinking about the sick and the healthy body that is unavailable to the developing field of health psychology (Stone, 1984). This field owes much to the emergence of clinical psychology as a profession related to medicine. However, one of the consequences of this relationship has been the acceptance of diagnostic categories and of biomedical symptoms as given. From this perspective, bodily symptoms have an a priori existence that justifies the interest or the intervention of the psychologist. One rationale for this research is the isolation of what, in the makeup of individuals or their social context, constitutes either risk factors or other pathogenic features leading to the onset of disease. The unintended outcome is to undermine psychology's potential contribution to understanding the sick body. This occurs through the acceptance of the body as essentially a physiological entity, its fragmentation and objectification as a system or process, and finally, the body's theoretical isolation from the social context by which it is presumed to be affected.

Things, Selves, and Social Psychology

Social psychology depends upon a more or less explicit view of the person as a thinking individual, someone who perceives the world and makes judgments about it. The idea that subjects know through social cognitions (Forgas, 1981), feel with social constructions (Harré, 1986b), engage in small-group decision making (Davis, 1973), and form attitudes in conceptual space (Osgood, Suci, & Tannenbaum, 1957) depends upon this basic assumption. It is not a view that embraces the person as someone with a body but as the owner of something to have an image of, or to speak about. There are two consequences that follow from this position. Both imply the retention of a broadly cognitivist perspective, in which subjects are assumed to look out upon a world of other subjects like themselves. The first is that individuals appear as universal subjects, having conceptual systems that are to be understood objectively. Paradoxically, the more thinglike the mind becomes, the less able does psychology seem to be to say anything about the world of material culture. If anything, the world of art and design has human elements that psychologists increasingly recognize but cannot study. Instead, all things that conceptual systems embrace are treated, through objectification, as "things," and appear on the same plane. Whether they are people's rooms, or their parents, or items from their shopping lists—all can be described in terms of theories of attitudes, or concepts, or linguistic devices. The disembodied subject looks upon a world in which he or she is one other object. The exclusion of the body is crucial to this perspective, in which abstract mind reflects upon things, the inner forms of which, as well as their qualitative differences, remain always opaque. Also, the body, as has already been noted, then remains at best a vehicle for conveying ideas or a screen behind which selves can dissemble; at worst, it is the locus of an animal nature, of biological eruptions that forever threaten to disturb social life from below.

The second consequence follows from the first. The adherence to a view that the social world consists essentially of a commune of minds means that subjects are presumed to look out upon a ready-made world. Even within a paradigm of cause-and-effect relationships, this assumes a state in which groups, classes, attitudes, and selves already exist. New ones may, of course, appear but how they do so, and as the consequence of what intentions, is not specifiable. The phenomena that are associated with time, with becoming, are foreign to a cognitivist approach that emphasizes the empirical subject in an objective environment. This is equally true of theories that allow for individuals to have their own constructions of events (Radley, 1977). The possibilities that follow from a recognition that the world is shaped by people's intentions, as well as by the constraints of artifacts and instruments, are closed to theories that accept the division of subject from object. The key to an appreciation of the genetic aspect of social life (and to the wider question of its temporality) is made up of precisely these two matters; the instrumentality of the body and the sociality of the physical thing.

The ambiguity of bodily existence need not be an embarrassment to social psychology but offers instead an entry into problems with which the discipline cannot presently deal. Issues that are normally kept on the fringe of the discipline (the body and the world of artifacts) could become incorporated into its basic assumptions. This was certainly Mead's belief:

> The mechanism of human society is that of bodily selves who assist or hinder each other in their cooperative acts by the manipulation of physical things . . . the bodily selves of members of the social group are as clearly implemental as the implements are social. Social beings are things as definitely as physical things are social. (1959, p. 169)

It follows from this that the phrase "social psychology of the body" should not conjure up the primary image of two (or more) physical bodies in some sort of abstract communion or dissent. This view fixes the body at one and the same time as being at the center of empirical attention and on the periphery of theoretical significance.

Chapter 7

Cultivated Attitudes

Social psychologists are used to thinking of *attitude* as something that people reveal in what they say about something. This is consistent with the idea that attitudes are somehow located in or are important aspects of the mental life of social individuals. There is an older usage of the word *attitude* that relates to the fitness or posture of the body; the phrase "to strike an attitude" conjures up this particular meaning. It is this meaning that is illuminated here, although the idea of images of body postures is not one that I wish to put forward. Instead, we can think of individuals expressing, in their conduct and in the deployment of their bodies, their orientation toward others and toward the social world. This is not an uncommon usage of the term *attitude*, though it presents problems for a psychology in which mind and body are separated. While people's actions might well be consistent with their stated beliefs, it is still in terms of the latter that, as social psychologists, we are likely to estimate the features of the attitude presumed to lie behind the behavior.

It is impossible for social psychology to conceive of attitudes as bodily expressions so long as the body is considered only the executor of individual behavior. What makes attitudes social, within traditional theory, is their objects. Individuals have attitudes about other people, about groups and societies, as well as about issues such as housing, racial discrimination, and environmental pollution. They also have attitudes about matters concerning the body—for example, whether babies should be conceived by artificial means, whether certain standards of dress should be maintained in public places, and whether abortion should be obtainable upon demand. Underlying this is a more fundamental attitude, expressed in the act of speaking about things at a distance. It is given in the relationship of the respondent to the questioner, and in that of the psychologist to the subject. There is an implicit understanding here that makes the whole inquiry possible. It extends to the assumptions made by both parties about the kind of social world in which they live and to the expressive features that are embodied in their orientation to each other. This understanding extends also to the ways that people know about events; it assumes certain kinds of commerce with everyday things, commonly held valuations of a range of outcomes and ideological commitments to the way that the world ought to be. In effect, attitude research depends, for its interpretation, upon a complex of ways of living in the world that can go without being stated because it is taken for granted.

In talking about the expression of social attitudes, I want to draw attention to some of these ways of living that traditional research sees, if at all, only in objectified form. As lived orientations, they might not be readily described in words or made available to consciousness. Bodily attitudes have often been seen in this way, as things that betray an unconscious commitment or a private belief (Deutsch, 1952). The orientation of individuals toward society is better seen in terms of the shaping of capacities and manners that answer to changes in the outside world. From this perspective, what makes an attitude social is not primarily its valuation function, but its form. In the previous chapter, it was argued that bodily capacities are "in-formed" by their intended objects; the world of artifacts and the sphere of intellect are mutually bound together. That argument was made in terms of a phenomenological position, one that elevates the experience of the individual in setting out its propositions. However, if one is to examine the social form of attitudes, seen as bodily capacities, it is necessary to look at the way in which these have been shaped in the course of social change. Only by recourse to an analysis of society is it possible to see the postures and the fitness of the body as constitutive of the attitudes of individuals toward their cultural milieu.

Before turning to this analysis, one important product of it should be pointed out. Once one sees attitudes in terms of social orientations, which give rise to particular forms of manners and skills, then it becomes possible to conceive of things such as needs and desires as social products. If we see attitudes as related to people's needs and desires, then the appreciation of these wants as being socially formed is important for understanding the role of the body in social life. Following from the previous chapter, individuals do not only have ideas about things, but they also want to own and consume objects, to shape them, and in so doing, to shape themselves. This idea of an attitude as an orientation toward the world can be seen in relation to political developments in society, in which the body has played a vital part.

Manners: The Civilizing of the Body

The forms of conduct referred to by social psychologists as social skills, and described by Mauss (1972) as techniques of the body were acquired over a lengthy period of time. What Elias (1978) has called "the civilizing process" embraced the full range of manners of daily life. Crucially, this process of change accompanied shifts in the distribution of power in European society at the end of the Middle Ages. More important for this discussion, it involved a change in the consciousness of people about their own individuality. The relationship of the individual to society changed at this time, and one medium of this change was the body, both in its scope and in how it was apprehended. Elias describes social life in the Middle Ages as having broad precepts of good and bad conduct, in spite of the appearance, to the modern eye, of a dirty and disheveled communal existence. People ate with their fingers, using a knife to cut meat from a shared joint; they drank, where necessary, from the same bowl and cup, at a table where the bones and scraps would be freely discarded onto the floor. (This was proper behavior compared to returning one's gnawed portion to the communal dish from whence it came.) The broad advice at table was never to fall upon the food like a pig, so as to appear a glutton; not to wipe one's nose with one's hand because one would seem a fool; to refrain from snorting or smacking one's lips while eating or else others will think you a yokel. In these broad recommendations are contained the linking of table manners with an awareness of social status as given in a courtly society having a hierarchical and segmented social structure.

Elias makes the point that the people of the Middle Ages stood in a different relationship to each other than we do today. This difference extended beyond a rational system of beliefs to an emotional complex in which their appetites and tastes were different from those of the modern individual. Sights, feels, and smells grasped a different world of likes and dislikes, of attraction and repulsion. In particular, the barriers that now exist between one human body and another in their natural functions were unknown to the people of the time. Many things that are likely to evoke shame or disgust today did not do so in that earlier epoch.

However, at the end of the Middle Ages, something began to happen, which suggests that society was in transition. Although Elias used the example of manners at table, he proposed that changes in conduct were reflected in all areas of society during the sixteenth century. People begin to see things with more differentiation, as multiple interests rendered the simple opposition of good versus wicked inadequate to the valuation of social behavior. Elias stressed that it was not so much the rules themselves that changed; the old ones were not simply supplanted by the new. He gave the example of people still eating without cutlery, even though by this time they had been taught that it was good manners to eat with three fingers only. The important difference is that where previously the rules of good conduct were more in the form of directives couched in folklore, tradition upon tradition, the advice now reflected a new way of seeing. Using the writings of Erasmus, Elias proposed that this accent upon seeing arose out of a critical eye brought to bear upon daily life, a gaze from which the people at court were not immune. There was no longer an acceptable and a vulgar (good versus bad) way to act at table, but recommended manners based upon the recording of individual differences in what people actually did. Advice progressed from, "Never pick up food with unwashed hands" (fifteenth century, quoted in Elias, 1978, p. 88), to "To lick greasy fingers or to wipe them on your coat is impolite. It is better to use the tablecloth or the serviette" (sixteenth century, p. 90).

To be a courteous person was bound up with this manner of seeing, which went along with the exercise of good conduct. One should look about oneself and pay attention to people and to their spiritual (i.e., eventually psychological) condition. As part of this exercise of observation, one should keep an eye upon one's own behavior. Extended to everybody, this engendered a sense of mutual control over conduct. This control was not between equals, however, but took the form of those who were socially superior advising their fellows upon how to behave. In place of the rule of force, there emerged a form of friendly, gentle correction by which one person could assist another to improve his or her social manners.

What are we to make of this change in the manners of people at the end of the Middle Ages? Also what does it have to do with the body, apart from the obvious control of behavior? To take the second question first, it has already been pointed out that in medieval society, people had different sensibilities about the body. It was not merely a matter of what one did but how it was done. This was reflected both in people's views of the body itself, as part of human nature, and in their sense of what the world offered, through their sensibilities and appetites. To take an example, one can compare the reaction of the average person of today, who sees meat being butchered, with that of the medieval diner sitting at a table where a boar's head is to be carved and served. The revulsion of the former person and the anticipated delight of the latter show that people's tastes, and the objects of their appetites, reflect real changes in the form of their relationships to each other and to their surroundings.

There is a second strand to this question of the body's significance, which concerns the social changes that were to occur in the redistribution of production following the growth of trade and its organization during the seventeenth and eighteenth centuries. The removal from the household of small-scale activities such as spinning, weaving, and slaughtering meant that its members were to become increasingly concerned with consumption. The labor, the conditions, and the uses of the body that some of these production activities had demanded would gradually be found to be less and less in keeping with the sensibilities of bodies engaged in domestic life.

The question of the relevance of a treatise upon the history of manners is that it shows how the use of the body, and all of the constraints, taboos, and sanctions that surround it cannot be divorced from the issue of the relationship of the individual to society. To take Elias's position, one would need to turn this around and to say that any understanding of the relationship of the individual to society (a central aim of social psychology) is incomplete without an awareness of the role that the body has played as a medium in the civilizing process. External restraint has been replaced by self-restraint, so that the need to eat properly at table stems not from an awareness of other people's offense, but from one's own need to maintain some inner standard of good behavior.

The idea of civilization as self-restraint is not wholly consistent with the modern idea of there being a multiplicity of pleasures that can be enjoyed; we do not live in a society that inexorably is more delicate about everything than its predecessor. The example of sexual behavior is one that springs immediately to mind. To unhitch ourselves from what would be a mistaken assumption, we need to be reminded that the transition from a medieval to a modern society involved the growth of trade and the establishment of the city as the place where commerce could flourish. These trade links, and the emergence of the free-moving craftspersons and merchants who worked them, meant that the body also had its boundaries extended (Theweleit, 1987). New trade routes offered novel pleasures; new objects (e.g., pepper, silk) held out new tastes and feelings. The establishment of the cities led to the emergence of what Simmel (1950) called "the metropolitan outlook." Previously, the towns and cities of the Middle Ages set barriers against movement and contact with the outside. This was paralleled by constraints upon independence and differentiation within the individual self. Later on, with the growth of trade and the differentiation of work activities, the modern city offered the individual a freedom under the law to specialize in his or her particular line of occupation, and thereby in himself or herself. There appeared, with the growth of the metropolis, what Simmel (1950) called "the differentiation, refinement, and the enrichment of needs," so that the sensibilities of people were expanded in some areas as well as being standardized in others. Standardization is perhaps too rigid a term to describe the civilizing process, but it is meaningful in relation to one important aspect of modern life to which Simmel drew attention. He said that the modern city dweller is pressed by time and circumstances to have to be brief and "to the point." There is a transience about many of the social relationships in the city, as compared to the leisurely engagements of the small town. In these brief meetings, there is a need for an economy of manners, which reflects the money economy that dominates the life of the people of the city. The double meaning of the word *economy* expresses precisely the point being made. Manners (the word is almost an anachronism in the modern city) are better understood today as the elements of a street-wise culture, in which the use of the body to make and to end social intercourse has been honed to a minimum (Goffman, 1972). However, alongside this brevity of public etiquette exists an expanded menu of individual tastes and needs, recognized upon the body and met through its diverse practices.

The Emergence of Shame and the Need for Privacy

In France, as late as the seventeenth century, kings and noblemen received inferiors in their bedroom while they were getting dressed, or even when going to bed (Elias, 1978). This is a mark of a hierarchical society in which shame was felt before one's peers and those socially superior, but not before those who rank far below. (That this feature is not restricted just to monarchs and their courtiers, but also characterizes certain classes is illustrated by Winston Churchill's wartime practice of calling a secretary into the bathroom to take dictation while he was in the tub.) The democratization of society meant that, eventually, it became an offense against good manners to expose one's body to others except under special circumstances.

In medieval society, it was quite normal for many people to spend the night in one room. Special nightclothes were rare if they existed at all, so that individuals went to bed naked or else fully clothed. From what has been observed about the behavior of the rich and powerful, this unconcern about showing the naked body cannot be explained by the house being too small or having an inadequate number of rooms. In contrast, it can be argued that the evolution of the house, with its separate divisions into private and public areas, is a reflection of the transition in consciousness about the body in social life. The introduction of a special nightdress can be seen as yet another mark of the peculiar sensitivity that had arisen about the body, and alongside this the division of the house into daytime and nightime areas. The bedroom becomes the site of activities that are held increasingly private—dressing, washing, going to the lavatory and engaging in sexual behavior. There was a growing separation of sleeping—the body in retirement—from the activities of waking life. Elias has argued that it was the sharpness of this separation that led to nightclothes being so formless, because they were designed to occlude the gaze, not to tempt it. Only with the increased mobility of modern life do nightclothes take on more functional forms (pajamas) so that they can be worn without shame on occasions where people's private activities must be carried out more openly (e.g., in hotels, in sleeping cars).

Putting bodily functions behind closed doors meant that there arose a sociogenetic shame and embarrassment about them. Increasingly, people kept these things within their private lives, within the family. Even in that context, at the height of the feeling that bodily functions and the sight of the body were shameful, the Victorian family created a host of rituals within the household to maintain the barrier between what was right and proper and what was wrong and blameworthy (Kern, 1975). In spite of this, the rearrangement of the house and the reform of manners made more room for private life, and for the establishment of what came to be the modern nuclear family. Privacy became something not only to be sought for oneself but, as a need, something to respect in others. As Ariès (1962) has put it, the modern family satisfied a desire for privacy and also a craving for identity. This was a movement pressed mainly by the middle classes, for whom the need to isolate themselves from the crowds fueled the morality with which they furnished their family lives.

European middle-class morality of the eighteenth and nineteenth centuries accorded legitimacy and sanctity to heterosexual relations between husbands and wives, so long as these were carried out in the privacy of their bedroom. It had, as its corollary, a social code that proscribed other forms of sexuality for people of each particular class. From the perspective of the upper classes, they had the freedom and the power to do what they pleased, while the lower classes, though held to account for their behavior, need not necessarily be shamed by it. By comparison, the strengthening of views about sexuality among the middle classes was managed through an increasing interest in defining its boundaries (Foucault, 1979). This meant that, rather than confining it within a narrower and narrower arena, what Foucault called a "discourse upon sexuality" had the effect of extending its limits. This is revealed in the growing interest in matters of sexuality (particularly in the nineteenth and twentieth centuries) as a different way of life, and in the various forms attaching to different kinds of marginal types of individuals. The product of this interest was sexuality as a mode of specification of individuals, a result of the working out of relationships of power and pleasure (Smart, 1985). How this relates to the process of individualization is considered in the next section.

The Sphere of the Individual Body

The distinguishing feature of the modern age, as far as social psychologists are concerned, is the emergence of the individual as the social being. This was the result of a complex of changes concerning the movement away from a hierarchical society to one energized by trade and bourgeois needs. The world of the Middle Ages bounded people into relatively stable groupings, fixed by birth and by geographical position. Such a world involved regular daily contacts between individuals concerning all aspects of everyday life. Therefore, it was more important to maintain social relationships than, for example, to become rich in a world where what was paramount was to improve one's honorable standing within the group into which one had been born (Ariès, 1962).

The decline of the need for *honorable standing* was prompted by just those things that undermined this stability, this taken-for-grantedness of people's existence. Trade, and the mobility it required, the specialization of occupations, the growth of cities in which this took place, and the loosening of the hierarchical structure of society itself were the main moving forces.

From the perspective of the social psychologist, equally important were the changes that have been discussed previously—the elaboration of manners that led to a code of etiquette for everyday behavior. With this came the emergence of what Elias called a "tone" in such directives of action, expressed as a new way of seeing. Where previously, people had relied upon tradition and external authority to guide their actions, there was emerging a sense of inner direction based upon the legitimacy of the point of view of the individual. What should not be done or should not be seen became matters of privacy, something to be carried out away from the sight of others. Elias claims that what began with the motive of not offending others ended with the sense that these actions were important to the person's self. That is to say, the individual's *sense of dignity* emerged as the reason for maintaining standards, replacing the requirement that it be done for the convenience or pleasure of one's betters.

In the movement from the old to the modern world was created the individual who no longer belonged to a particular group, but who was a cosmopolitan person. An allegiance to the cosmos meant that a learned man or woman could, metaphorically speaking, claim citizenship of the whole world (Tuan, 1982). With this claim went the sense that everything could be questioned, so that the pride of the individual flowered alongside a sense of uncertainty about life and fortune. The emergence of the modern self was furthered by these two visions, which, as I show subsequently, are crucial to an understanding of how the body is conceived and maintained in present-day society.

The modern person is someone who can (ideally) fill, take on, or step out of roles according to ability and circumstance. It is this individual whose body concerns social psychology, inasmuch as he or she has needs and capacities that can be developed or exploited. The attitude of the modern body—how it is represented in images and borne by people every day—is a product of this movement. Berger et al. (1974) have drawn precisely this distinction between the concepts of honor and of dignity. Both concepts bridge self and society. In the first case, *honor* relates to a world in which people are defined by and belong to their social groupings. The body serves as a reminder of this stability and, in its actions, as an endorsement of the group's traditions. In contrast, *dignity* relates to modern individuals who are conscious of their inalienable human rights as beings, who attempt either to adopt or to disengage from roles of their choosing. The body might endorse this role or that one, but its clothing and its material instruments should not be mistaken for the real self. Berger et al. argue that these things (as aspects of social roles) essentially hide the true self, conceived as the individual alone. The nearest a person will come to seeing the true self is to view the naked person, the body unclothed, stripped of its coverings. Yet, for a psychology built upon the idea of the person as agent and as image, the self is still thought of as hiding behind the body, which is considered merely a screen.

This distinction is one that has been anticipated at several points in the preceding pages. It is important to state it here because otherwise there can be no critical discussion of the attitude of the body in modern life. Without examining the changes that have occurred in the way that the body is lived in society, no purchase can be gained upon the question of the part it now plays in people's views of themselves and of others. The special reason for this is that the idea of the individual as the social being tends toward a peculiar ahistoricity in thinking (Berger et al., 1974). Selves and social roles confront one another in a timeless space; the body becomes one more thing with which to feel either more or less identified, toward which to have either this or that attitude.

The preceding section linked the privatization of the body (the sense of shame) with changes in the structure of the living space and with the emergence of the nuclear family as household. These things did not happen all at once, and they must be seen in the context of the wider changes that have been set out already in this discussion. The aspect to which I now want to pay particular attention is the movement of the boundary between the public and the private realms, and the change between these two spheres as a result. To recap briefly, the transition from the old to the modern world involved a gradual removal of the aspects of the body from the sight of others. This included the natural functions, washing, and getting dressed and undressed. Alongside this, the specialization of rooms (among the nobility and the middle class at first) satisfied the new desire for isolation (Ariès, 1962). One can see from these two changes how the body was a focal point of concern in the articulation of the boundaries between self and others, self and society.

The home of the emerging middle class expressed the new need for privacy, but it also began to serve as the vehicle for establishing the family's identity. This was achieved in part by the house becoming a place for the controlled admittance of others. Its division into private and public areas meant that the family could choose to retire into special rooms (e.g., for sleeping); it also meant that, in order to receive members of the extended family and others, the home became the place for the family to represent itself to the outside world. Effectively, "the house must be breached in order to have one's private identity affirmed" (Duncan, 1981).

This ambiguity in the attempt at isolation is important, not only for understanding the home but also for comprehending the body. As individuals withdrew from each other, this placed a burden upon them with regard to how they could establish their identity. The withdrawal of aspects of the body into privacy and the increase in people's sensibilities about its natural functions meant that there emerged an equal concern about its public aspect as an arena for establishing one's identity. Rules of etiquette, which proliferated in the seventeenth and eighteenth centuries, were designed to carry out just this function (Wildeblood, 1973). The body became a canvas upon which individuals could paint their claims to social status. Seen in this way, it has a front and a back region, a formal and informal aspect, with the scope for private and public displays. Indeed, just as a stranger can be invited into one's home or a friend allowed into the bedroom, so the body can be used to intimate closeness in the cause of trying to establish a particular identity.

The key point of this argument, however, is that the privatized body did not escape society, but achieved this privacy at the cost of needing to open other aspects of itself to the look of others. This was not all. In a world of growing *embourgeoisement*, the body in its public aspect became a field upon which the various forms of identity establishment would compete. The worlds of fashion and of material possessions grew up around a notion of the body as a key vehicle for the self to make its claims in the modern world. The ambiguity of the body as more private and yet more public can thus be recognized and appreciated in this context. It set up a tension that ensured that the body, though unavailable to psychology, became of central importance in a world of consumption and of image production.

The Pursuit of Health and Pleasure

The body in present-day Western society is intended as a repository of health and a source of pleasure. This is possible because individuals strive to control their bodies and because they are part of a culture that aims to stimulate and to satisfy people's desires. Though seeming to be opposites, both of these features work together toward producing a style of life that is consistent with the capitalist values of a consumer-oriented society. The control of the body has various aspects. One, that of diet, has been described by Turner (1982, 1984) as being linked at various points in history with religious asceticism and with political control. It was the rich English gentry who were seen, by Robert Burton in the seventeenth century and by George Cheyne 100 years later, as being idle through the overconsumption of food and drink. For these commentators, it was the rarity, the richness, and the quantity of the food that led the gentry into idleness and illness. In order to mitigate the spread of this disease of affluence, foods were classified and substances identified that were more likely to engender a healthy disposition. There was a strong moral element to these dietary regimens, in that obesity was not only a sign of deviance from the physiological norm, but also of moral degeneracy. Once incorporated into the Methodist code of ascetic behavior, the dietary regulation of the body was extended into the homes of ordinary people. Finally, with the extension of medical inquiry through the measurement of populations, the dietary regime eventually became a vehicle for the rationalization of food consumption of each and every individual.

Turner's analysis is based upon Foucault's (1977) argument that the disciplining of the body was an integral part of the growth of social institutions of all kinds. In the army, in the schools, power was exercised through "docile bodies," or rather bodies that were required to assume a docile form. The emergence of a science of anthropomentrics, through which individuals could be assessed and judged in relation to a norm, provided a view of an objectified body, the movements of which could be rationalized. In the nineteenth century, this led to the creation of systems for gymnastics (Broekhoff, 1972), which were justified in terms of the benefits that they granted to discipline and to good health. In more recent times, the application of the techniques of physiology have made possible a sports science, which subjects the body still further to inscription, and which amplifies the authority of the requirement that it be properly maintained. This process of objectification was transformed, however, in the course of attempting to make individuals follow the detailed regimen set for them. As Foucault pointed out, in trying to apply these schemes, the limitations and possibilities of the body as a living thing were further revealed. This opposition took the form of "showing the conditions of functioning proper to an organism" (1977, p. 156), so that behavior supplemented mechanical working as a guide to proper movement.

The coupling of the study of behavior—psychology—with the discourse on exercise is reaffirmed under the rubric of the claim that "the contribution of physical activity to health enhancement is potentially significant" (Biddle & Fox, 1989). This claim has been made for some time, but the argument now is that the exclusive focus upon physiology, as the arbiter of fitness, fails to comprehend that health benefits are contingent upon the process of regular exercise behavior. The implementation of psychological techniques into the domain of physical exercise opens up the possibility of assessing the relationship between performance and such things as anxiety, self-esteem, reactivity to stress, and motivation.

The introduction of psychology into the discourse on exercise and health brings this discussion back to the issue of self-control. For psychology as a discipline offers precisely those concepts and measures that allow comparison of individuals in terms of the degree to which they meet the goals that they set for themselves and that others set for them. The creation of norms against which people should assess their physical condition can be seen as a parallel to the norms of etiquette considered earlier when discussing the process of civilizing the body. The relationship of individuals to society poses them as beings with self-control, for whom the conditions of right living and correct exercise are obligations couched in terms of their own self-esteem, their own dignity. One should avoid eating too much or the wrong kinds of foods, maintain one's appearance, take regular exercise, stop smoking. These beliefs are not shared equally by all in Western societies, but coupled with the idea of health-preservation, they become moral obligations to conduct oneself as a good citizen. The problem is that the conditions of society are such as to make it very difficult, if not impossible, for all individuals to sustain these requirements for healthy living. Freund (1982) gives the example of advice given to managers to fire their secretaries if they have a personality style likely to promote aggression and hard driving, features believed to lead to the development of coronary heart disease. As he points out, this not only presumes that the reader is in a position to carry this out (or to want to), but it overlooks entirely the conditions under which the secretary works in her boss's interests.

This style of life, which is believed to encourage heart disease (Type A behavior pattern), is interesting because it aligns so closely with characteristics often associated with effective work (Friedman & Rosenman, 1974). Working long hours, being aggressive in the cause of one's employer, meeting deadlines, and taking on more than one can really cope with are things that many executives would not be ashamed of. That these are the very qualities that are believed to predispose people to have a heart attack points up contradictions arising within the social system. In one context, the individual is required to act in particular ways; in another, he or she is counseled to free himself or herself from precisely those actions. Heart-attack victims are caught in a bind in which the controls that they apply to their lives (which includes the body in its mode of working harder), are later judged to be the very aspects of themselves that they need to alter. The victim is effectively blamed for his or her own demise. The focus upon individuals alone keeps attention from the social conditions in which they live. The body in its various modes of working, which are part of the social world, is comprehended only as the endpoint of a series of changes presumed to follow from its pathological use at the behest of the self who inhabits it. In the broader arena of illness, this leads to debates about the styles of life that individuals should impose upon themselves in the name of health-prevention, as well as enabling a moral scrutiny of those who refuse to comply, and hence will "make themselves sick." For those who have serious illnesses, such as cancer, the ideology of the autonomous individual places upon them not only the opprobrium that comes with having the disease (i.e., relating to their personality, which predisposed them to get it), but the burden of having to wrestle with the disease in order to overcome it (Sontag, 1979).

The more obvious demands that individuals make upon their body concern appearance and condition. Diet and exercise are the means that are most often employed by people wanting to achieve these ends. Yet over-indulging in these things has been noted to lead to anorexia on the one hand, and to compulsive running on the other. These two conditions have been compared with regard to the elements of overcontrol present in each, to the presence of strong cultural ideals surrounding them, to the guilt experienced when the self-imposed regime is broken, and to the lack of an objective view of their condition by those concerned (Yates, Leehay, & Shisslak, 1983). The anorexic and the compulsive runner are different in that the former is usually a young woman and the latter a man in his early middle age. They are similar, however, in embodying contradictions that are engendered within a society that promotes self-control but erects barriers to those who would challenge its institutions (Turner, 1984). The rewards of overcontrol of one's body are double, though they contradict each other at different levels. On the one hand (at a surface level), the dieter and the runner create a body presentation that is in accord with the ideals of society; in the one case slim, and in the other, fit. However, at another (and deeper) level, both may be seen as engaging in a dialogue with significant others (family, friends, colleagues), conducted through their bodily conduct. This is acknowledged in the thesis that the anorexic girl uses food to break the control of an overindulgent family (Bruch, 1978). In a parallel fashion, there is the possibility that the (male) runner demonstrates in his demanding schedule those things of which he is capable at a time when his vocational or sexual performance is put in question (Yates et al., 1983). The contradiction lies in the overextension of the activity, which renders the body, through other changes, counter to the accepted view of normal life. The anorexic woman is desexualized with the loss of menses; the compulsive runner might have little time or energy for other socially valued activities. (About the latter, there is scant evidence.) The benefits to the individuals concerned may well lie, if not in the control over others, then in the establishment of a world that answers to their particular efforts, in spite of making its own demands. The conduct of a dialogue *with* the body produces a world of things and events that can be, if not sensuously enjoyed (as both dieting and exercise can be), then at least demonstrable of one's relationship to others. Freedom is gained at the expense of submitting oneself to control; indulging the social ideal is taken to lengths that undermine the authority that it espouses.

The key to understanding this relationship is to recognize that it is a paradox, the form of which is displayed but not articulated (i.e., it is realized with the body). A similar thesis may be proposed for the heart attack as a form of response to cultural conditions (Radley, 1984). The hard-working executive (to use what is only a stereotype) engages more and more in activities that are designed to demonstrate (*not* to articulate), the bind in which his work and family situations place him. What appears as hard work is, in fact, a mode of working, a style of use of the body integral with the person's orientation toward the world. By placing her- or himself increasingly at the behest of cultural/orgainzational demands, incorporated as goals or needs of the self, such a person embodies at the same time the contradictory relationships of mastery and of passive dependence. The point of this exercise—never voiced, hardly acknowledged—is to show through action the logical outcome of making excessive demands upon unsatisfied desires. The dictum "I'll work till I drop" expresses this orientation only half as well as the heart attack, which indicates the sacrifice made by the individual and signifies precisely the form of social control exercised. This is not so much a causal analysis of how people have heart attacks, taken as a symptom with which doctors must deal; it is more a reading of the coronary attack as a sign, something that allows us to conceive of the body as a location for the exercise of social and individual powers.

Desire and the Cultivation of the Body

Diet and exercise are not only means of controlling the body and of achieving an alignment of oneself with the norms that govern appearance and form. They are also ways of increasing the range of pleasures that the body can enjoy and of extending the connections that the senses have with the various aspects of life. This point has already been made at a theoretical level by reference to Foucault's writings on sexuality. However, in this section, I want to consider the body as the location of both asceticism and pleasure. In the modern world, such regimes are associated with a consumer culture that employs the discipline of the individual in order that desire is extended, not curtailed. The body plays an important role in this, in part because it has been the site of the division into private and public realms. As argued herein, this means that appeals can be made with reference to the observable aspects of ourselves and to the more intimate aspects of our lives.

The modern condition has been well described as one where,

> Consumer culture latches onto the prevalent self-preservationist conception of the body, which encourages the individual to adopt instrumental strategies to combat deterioration and decay . . . and combines it with the notion that the body is a vehicle of pleasure and self-expression. . . . Discipline and hedonism are no longer seen as incompatible. (Featherstone, 1982, p. 18)

Perhaps the best illustration of this is jogging. In this increasingly common form of exercise in Western culture, individuals can carry it out on their own, following a program of organized exertion. Distance, time, and pulse rate are the measures by which each person can evaluate his or her performance and monitor achievement. It requires commitment and a little sacrifice; it might be uncomfortable and temporarily tiring. However, jogging is more than socially acceptable, having become in some quarters a highly desirable form of activity. This is shown by the extent to which it is made visible to others, in part through the wearing of particular clothing. Trainers, tracksuits, and sweatshirts have become fashionable things in which to be seen. All this makes jogging both a form of display and a form of asceticism. The social cachet lies not just in one or the other, but in their particular combination. Jogging can stand for the modern association of hedonism through self-discipline.

The focus upon the healthy body extends to all forms of exercise, although some forms of recreation are more socially desirable than others. This means that there is a class bias surrounding sport (Bourdieu, 1984), though in an individualistic society, there is more equality between the sexes. "Working out" has become popular for city workers, who spend time in health and leisure clubs, which have sprung up to service and to develop their needs. While the expressed motives for this form of exercise will be varied, it is clear that one of the reasons for attending is to "mill" with similar people (Redican & Hadley, 1988). Not only is there an inner body to be maintained in physical shape, but an outer body to be validated in the eyes of others. In the case of working women, such a facility can serve a similar purpose to that of a gentlemen's club, in providing a place where people of similar background and interests can meet together. The positioning of the gym and the cost of membership help to provide an air of exclusivity in which the attentions to the body are carried out by individuals with a similar outlook and intention. Equally important is the affirmation of a commitment to working out, not just as a routine but as a style of life, as something suffusing one's general outlook. This affirmation is made with the body in the course of doing the exercise in the club, either in the sight of others or jointly with them.

There are important points concerning consumer culture and the body, which I pick up later on and discuss in a broader context. First, it is important to note again that society is not monolithic. Economic and educational differences, as well as gender differences, provide people with different opportunities to engage in leisure activities of different kinds. This is not just a matter of external constraint, but of the habitual and preferred mode of using the body, which attach to the different social classes. In previous chapters, it has been shown both that the bodily style of manual workers is incorporated in the context of a life geared to working close to material things and that the experience of illness relates to the kinds of loss of activity that enforced passivity brings. In a study of the health beliefs of a large sample of people in France, d'Houtaud and Field (1984) showed that there are important differences in how individuals of different social backgrounds think about their health. Working-class people see health instrumentally, as the maintenance of a body fit for work—that is, a body that can satisfy the demands of those who control their contribution to society. In this perspective, health has a utilitarian function, in being the means to reach other ends. For the middle classes, health can appear also as a value, a quality permitting each individual ego greater self-realization through the body's expressive use. This contrast of utilitarian with expressive function is entirely in accord with Bourdieu's (1984) claim that the idea of style is a bourgeois phenomenon. It is the difference between running in a race and jogging to improve one's general condition. The crucial point, which is worth stating once again, is that there is no universal body. What people in different locations in society work on, and work with, is a psychologically different phenomenon. That is to say, the body which they apprehend is different because they are distinguished *in their being*.

The values that are implied by the term *consumer culture* are those of a capitalist society. Its evolution has involved a proliferation of goods and services designed to answer to the needs of the body. However, these needs should not be taken to be natural to our physical existence, as if they are essential features of an unchanging human condition. As has been seen already, people's apprehension of their body was transformed in the course of social change; the body was not altered by society but served as an important channel through which the change could be brought about. Its use is expressive of the form of social relationships dominant in society at any given time. In a consumer society, there is an important linking of commodities with the body's needs or with its potential. The best examples of this are to be found in the world of advertising, where particular products are linked either directly or indirectly to the body. Examples of the former include the ranges of beauty products, tonics, and foodstuffs that we are told will improve our appearance and health. Such things as toiletries are sold with the claim that they will add to our appearance, promising the retention of a youthful, beautiful exterior attractive to the opposite sex. Tonics and foodstuffs are intended to make us fitter, leaner, and healthier in a world where these qualities attach to success in life.

The body has therefore become, in this kind of society, a field upon which the cross-valorization of products and needs is made in the cause of promoting desire. It is the discovery of new connections between goods and needs that offers the promise of new and different pleasures; these the individual incorporates as a furtherance of desire. There is no better example of this elaboration than the use of sexuality as the vehicle for the association of commodities and needs. For example, bath oils are sold to meet the needs of cleanliness and sensuality, using visual images that forge this connection in the picture of a naked woman who anticipates a sexual liaison after bathing. Cars are advertised explicitly as engines of desire, promoting needs that are energized by the linking of practical possibilities and technical developments within the body shape of sexual anticipation.

The multiplying of links between products and needs is aided by bringing together the various discourses upon health, fitness, sexual attractiveness, and work capability. This is nowhere more obvious than in the exercise industry, where clothes, foods, and equipment are sold with the manufacturer's promise that they will contribute to one or more of these areas of need, and thereby improve one's standing with respect to the others. We are told that to be fit is to be healthy; and to be fit and healthy is to be attractive. In societies that are based upon a cosmology that values the individual over the group, and boundary arbitration over segregation (what Douglas (1978) calls "low-group/low-grid culture"), harsh principles of selection will be in operation. This is the kind of competitive society in which consumerism flourishes. It is also the type of culture in which, because people must make their own way in the world and must be valued for their individual efforts, there is no refuge in old age as a place of wisdom and authority. In such a society, youth will be valued, both for its innovations and for its catalytic properties in establishing effective relationships with others in the marketplace. To grow old is to lose one's looks and to become infirm. In an individualistic society, little is to be gained from taking up the sick role, and it is better to try and keep fit lest "the judgement 'He doesn't look after himself' or 'She doesn't worry about her looks' is said in a rebuking tone . . . to the person concerned" (Douglas, 1978, p. 31). Therefore, the health and fitness industry will progress in any culture that is committed both to consumption and to a view of the life course in which aging is seen to bring no special advantage.

The consumer society thrives upon change, upon the proliferation of pleasures that might be obtained through the use of this commodity or the satisfaction of that need. This is aided by the use of body images that sharpen the difference between the individual's appearance and those of ideal forms pictured in advertisements. Our bodies require constant work from us if we are to keep them in the shape that we are told we should attain and should try to maintain. This exhortation draws upon the self-control that emerged as fundamental to the modern outlook. There is a moral obligation upon individuals to look after their bodies, to keep their eyes open for any fall from public standards, and to try out new things that could improve health and fitness. Rather than being fixed standards upon which one can rely, the plethora of information available about what one should eat, or how much one should exercise means that the individual must be ever-attentive to the body's needs and open to its pleasures. The mixing of asceticism and pleasure further expands the possibilities that individuals should explore, in what should be "a wide-awake, energetic, calculating, maximising approach to life [which] has no place for the settled, the habitual or the humdrum" (Featherstone, 1982, p. 20).

From this perspective, the consumer goods associated with maintenance of the body are not what they appear to be; they are more than mere objects of use (to clean the skin, to wear while running), having become revalued in the cross-association with other discourses of social life. A particular jogging top "says something about you" (so a label told me recently), when others see you wearing it. To wear this piece of clothing is therefore to attempt to realize, in the act of running, the figuration of oneself implied in the manufacturer's claim. Commodities such as this are not mere things, but commitments to the institutions of society in which we engage daily, "from the monent we rise from our beds and start eating on their behalf, seeing, feeling, moving around, in settings, fabrics, colors, and so on" (O'Neill, 1978, p. 228). Some are aimed at the most intimate and private aspects of our lives because the constant comparison of self with others is only possible once that privacy is breached by a democratic eye, which objectifies and renders things qualitatively the same. The activities of the bedroom and the bathroom are precisely the spaces about which the discourses of the body weave their imagery. As a result, the apprehension of the body as naturally embedded in its activities (e.g., the sweat of the laborer) is replaced by the sense of it transformed to become an acceptable tender, exchangeable with any other body. Once a product has been applied, a diet taken, or an item of clothing worn, then our physical being, even in the privacy of our homes, is revalued in terms of a vivacity, smoothness, and confidence available to all; and by implication, we are more available to the democratic eye through which we, too, see our bodies as more publicly appealing. It is interesting that the refusal of this democratic vision, which flattens qualitative differences, can involve just those body practices regarded as most intimate (e.g., the refusal of some supporters of the Women's Movement to shave their armpits or to use certain toiletries).

The promise of the consumer society is that the use of commodities will lead to pleasures. These are represented to us in the form of vignettes of the rich and famous. In these presentations, the body of the person concerned is dramatized for us through the intertwining of the various discourses; appearance, fitness, sexuality, worldly success, and the enjoyment of pleasures available only to the few. In one British newspaper report of a successful New York businesswoman, the article told the reader that,

> Pumped up, on permanent overdrive, she charges across the crowded lounge with her strawberry-blonde head bent forward. She is instantly recognized. Her short plaid skirt exposes more leg than is ordinarily flashed in corporate governance. She is lugging an oversized briefcase which looks heavy enough to dislocate her heavily padded shoulder. She rides competitively at an exclusive club [and is married to a company chariman who] gets up at 5.40, knocks off 900 sit-ups, or works out with an aerobics instructor . . . or lifts weights in his "muscle room." (*The Sunday Correspondent*, July 1990)

What Foucault (1980) has called "control by stimulation" involves the deployment of sexuality as a modality that is no longer tied exclusively to the physical body. Today, exercise has become "sexy," even work has become "sexy," as these practices are woven together in the special conjunction of asceticism and desire. These contribute to a modern view of the body as being central to the achievement of a happy, efficient life-style. It almost goes without saying that such a view was inconceivable to people of earlier centuries, whose attitudes to things and to the body were therefore fundamentally different from those that social psychologists might study today.

Points of Resistance

The concept that emerges from the previous section is that of a politicized body (Levin, 1985). The use of this summary term reflects the ways in which people's tastes, desires, and practices are subject to economic and social currents that flow through them: the lifeblood of the commodity culture. The image expressive of the computer age (not necessarily subscribed to by the majority) is that of the technocrat, be it man or woman. The body of this person is latent in the office setting, where surveillance of terminal screens and the use of mobile telephones show that geographical location is of secondary consideration. The mobility of individuals and the maintenance of the body in leisure so that this can be achieved, serve to stabilize

the social system. For this reason, it has been said that social well-being
and the regulated body are synonymous (Lewis, 1986). The threat of social
upheaval or decay has often been expressed in terms of body metaphors,
so that one can ask the question, what is it that is implicitly rejected in the
adoption of the dominant body style of a particular culture? I do not intend
to try to speculate upon this in this book, though it has been suggested that
the ideal man of the conservative utopia is one with a machinelike periphery, whose interior has lost its meaning (Theweleit, 1989). This mechanized body does not derive from the development of the industrial means
of production, but from the refusal of other human powers (or "shapes,"
to use a term from phenomenology). That is, the maintenance of the body
in its dominant social mode can be read as the denial of other capacities,
other orientations toward the world.

One way of getting a grasp on what is being denied is to look at particular
points of resistance to the dominant image, to that way of being. One
example of this is the bodybuilder. This might seem an odd example to
take, given the association in many people's minds of musclemen with
supermen, vestiges of a time when all men were urged to take programs
to build their bodies so that nobody would ever kick sand in their faces
again. With changes in the images of men, and an awareness of what women
find attractive in them, the idea of bodybuilding being just a vehicle of
power and phallocentrism is harder to sustain. Indeed, the sport is not
limited to men alone, as a glance at any of the magazines that serve its
adherents will show. Nevertheless, there is a lack of understanding as to
why individuals engage in bodybuilding.

> Their codes are undeciphered; one does not understand the programming,
> or the decision processes that assigns them their hours in cellars full of
> iron millstones and rudimentary machines. The process that elaborates,
> selects, and distributes the programming is not in the control rooms of
> culture nor even in the science of coaches and trainers. (Lingis, 1986,
> p. 125)

The acceptable image of the male body is one in which it is either gearing
into a tool in the cause of work, sleeves rolled up or shirt taken off, or else
standing its ground in the face of attack. Musculature gained in the cause
of manual work, or as a means to winning in rule-governed contests is seen
as virile and virtuous. Lingis argues that, in contrast to this, the unathletic,
nonmilitary male body, once unclothed, is often found to be faintly ridiculous. For women, in their turn, nudity has its place in pornography, but
the muscled body of the female bodybuilder is repulsive to the gaze of the
patriarchal stare. It is the maleness expressed in the spheres of commerce
and war and the femaleness of the world of glamour that are, perhaps,
tested by the bodybuilder's art: "There is then perhaps in our resentment
of them a dim sense that the cult of the body builders desecrates the ritual
structure with which we maintain dignity in and conjure ridicule from our
physical nature" (Lingis, 1986, p. 130).

Is this dignity perhaps that of the modern individual, pinpointed by Berger et al. (1974) in the "naked man expressing his sexuality"? Contrary to the idea of the working body, or the body as displayed to entice sexual interest, these individuals present their muscles as organs-to-be-seen, as a splendor, a vision of oiled and lustered surfaces. With this, there is what Lingis terms a displacement of the self, which extends itself across contours. As a result, the bodybuilder loses the perspective of an eye permanently fixed in a point of view and takes on the "impersonal gaze of a species in evolution."

In what sense then is bodybuilding a point of resistance? The clues lie in the difficulties that the public has of assimilating this explicit and focused attention upon the body into their own scheme of things. It offends generally held ideas about sexuality; it challenges the assumption that the body needs to be fit for something else, not merely its own narcissistic ends; and it contradicts the idea that the body should always be clothed with something else, even when stripped of all clothing. For example, the sunbather wears a tan, part of the holiday code of attractiveness and of belonging— that is, of having been there long enough to gain it. The female nude is known through the clothing that she has disposed of. The bodybuilder, however, invites the contemplation of his or her body directly, not for something else. That it is often read as not sexually attractive or as potentially dangerous in its strength is evidence of a refusal of this invitation. One might say that bodybuilding offers a silent commentary upon our embodied existence and that the resistance lies instead in society's response to it.

If the foregoing topic can be said to be concerned with the outer body, then vegetarianism is concerned with the inner body. As a subordinate position in a meat-eating society, being a vegetarian is to make a critical comment upon the social structure as it is known through food practices. The connection of meat-eating with patriarchy has been put forward as one reason why the vegetarian promotes criticism from others when meat is excluded from the diet (Adams, 1990). The division drawn between human beings and animals allows us to eat the latter, but not each other. Ethical vegetarianism (there are several kinds) rests upon the drawing of parallels between animals and oppressed groups. Adams draws a comparison between the language by which women are subjugated and animals objectified, and more precisely the appearance in literature of a discourse through which women are treated as "meat" for consumption by men. She proposes that the vegetarian—and particularly the female vegetarian—expresses her dissent, not in words (for the dominant culture holds a hegemony over the language) but through food choice. This is not just a series of conscious choices, but an existential act, in which one's body is committed to a specific relationship to the world.

The election of the ethical vegetarian not to eat meat because animals, like certain human groups, are oppressed means that wider comparisons are drawn between one's own body and those of animals. In recent research, it has been shown that some vegetarians have a strong sense of the potential dismemberment of their own bodies, a sense that they find disturbing in the prospect of their own fleshiness (Beardsworth & Keil, 1991). This leads to a need to distance themselves still further from matters of the physical body, which they find distasteful. Lest this idea of the fragility of the boundary between the eater and the eaten be pushed aside, it seems that children acquire these conceptual divisions only gradually. An experience of my own can illustrate the point. The young son of some friends was reading a book about dinosaurs, and asked me the question "Are we meat?" Not understanding him at first, I glanced at the book to see a picture of a large dinosaur chasing a cave man in full flight. The answer to the question was, to dinosaurs—yes; to each other in this society, certainly not! The conjunction of the issues of what it is to be human, and what is and is not eatable, can be seen as one of the foundations upon which our sense of the body is established. The loosening of this conjunction, through the (paradoxical) extension of the democratic view to embrace animal species, then becomes a point of instability in the way that the body is conceived. As a result, this loosening offers to the vegetarian a means of redefinition of other social relationships with which this life-style is associated, while also creating a threat to the embodiment of these relations in the meat-eating majority.

These two topics, bodybuilding and vegetarianism, are chosen as illustrations of the way in which the body (conceived as a physical entity) becomes figured in everyday life as a site of innovation and resistance. In spite of their considerable differences, both are examples that provoke contrasting feelings and rationalizations concerning the benefits and practical consequences of individuals pursuing one practice or another. Of course, there are many more examples that could be taken of how the body has become a point of deviation or protest for some, and simultaneously a marker of control or resistance for others. In Chapter 5, it was argued that it could serve as a vehicle for establishing group identity in a surrounding culture dominated by language. In the present chapter, it has been pointed out that the middle classes were in the vanguard of change, which brought about the modern view of the self as individual agent. The relationships of dominant and subordinate groupings, of traditional and innovative social movements, are premised upon differences in the way that they are distinguished in their being. The abstract term *being* is intended to embrace the different kinds of distinctions that people make with their bodies in the world, as well as those that are sensed upon their bodies in their own and other people's experience.

The Cultivated Body

The purpose of this chapter has been to show that the body has been and continues to be, of crucial importance in the constitution of the human subject. The idea of the self-controlling individual, of a subjectivity that invites study, is not essential or given; it emerged in the course of history. A key feature of this process has been the transformations in the use of the body, in its mode of objectification, in its deployment in the proliferation of a consumer culture with its commodity relationships. In a society of people with different interests, opportunities, and resources, the objective perspectives (Mead, 1959) in which they stand in relation to each other are engaged by their bodies. In general, the subjectivity that social psychologists seek to study is a figuration, a way of being, which depends for its essential properties upon forms of bodily engagement with the world (such as those discussed in this chapter). In particular, the standpoints or orientations that specific individuals have toward issues or things are distinct loci that are premised upon their embodied relationships in a world of inequalities and contradictions. The study of attitudes in the traditional sense of recording beliefs, feelings, or opinions about various items in the social world reflects these differences. However, in accepting uncritically the individual mind and human subjectivity as defining the sphere of inquiry, attitude research cannot speak about the lineaments of its subject matter. The qualitative differences upon which social psychology could comment, and the practical engagements that are people's attitudes in action, are closed to it. Is this because social psychology is stubbornly refusing to look at the place of the body in social life? More to the point is that the modern view of "self" demands a particular kind of orientation toward the body. The commoditized body underlines, supports, and at the same time excludes itself from the accepted image of the self as social being. Social psychology does not escape this predication; its commitment to individual experience debars it from grasping the practical assumptions that make this epistemology legitimate and the ideas that flow from it tenable.

Chapter 8
Revelation and Recovery

This chapter reviews some of the points made in the preceding analyses of specific topics and then goes on to consider the implications for approaching social psychology "with the body in mind." Its purpose is not to put forward a theory of the body or a framework for an embodied social psychology, whatever these might be. Instead, I want to make explicit some of the issues that have surfaced in the course of this book's specific discussions and to use these to explain more clearly the relationship between this book's treatment of physical existence and the discipline in general. At its simplest, we can say that acknowledging, denying, resisting, or endorsing the body in one's theory and practice makes a difference to the kind of social psychology in which one engages. We can add to this that these differences bear upon our awareness of the assumptions that we make about the subject matter of social psychology. Perhaps that is why the mere presence of the body as a term in the literature guarantees little about our becoming aware of these differences:

> The first difficulty to be faced is that the type of corporealism which has grown up since the 1970's has brought with it an excessive use of the term "body". The body would appear to be everywhere [in spite of the fact that] researchers who . . . don't deal with the topic in their work refer to it on every page. The basic approach has not, however, fundamentally changed even though the body is now exposed whereas before it was hidden and is referred to in various fields which have acquired scientific status such as diet, sexuality, beauty care, etc. The attention currently accorded to the body then is perhaps indicative of a fashion or even an intellectual movement which does not necessarily involve a step forward in knowledge. (Berthelot, 1986, p. 155)

Simply pointing to the body as a focus of interest in social life takes us no further in appreciating what this movement could mean to the study of social psychology. At base, this is why this book is about the relationship of the body to social psychology and not about physical existence itself. In the

177

end, we are interested in the implications of this refiguring of our subject matter for a deepening of our understanding of it. The purpose cannot be to open up a new topic that, by any admission, is every day revealed to each and every person. There is something faintly ridiculous in the idea of social psychologists now discovering that people live and move and have their being in a sensuous and material world. On the other hand, there can be few things more ridiculous than what amounts to the studied ignorance of the fact that attitudes, perceptions, groups, morals, and social classes relate to people who both have and are bodies. Perhaps the problem lies in the feeling that to record the mundane doings of the body is to add little to the corpus of psychological knowledge; one risks being seen to be trifling with the commonplace, the everyday. Far better to leave such things to the physiologists and doctors who know the body as the complex machine that it appears to be; then, from a lay position, this knowledge can be accepted (say, from one's doctor), while from a social perspective it can be excluded as inadequate to the task of explaining human action and experience.

Throughout this book, I have had to refer to *the body* as if there was one entity under consideration. At the outset, I warned that this was not the case and that the use of the single term might make for confusion. This is particularly so because the word is so often opposed to the term *mind* in the literature of psychology. The mind/body problem continues to be addressed within psychology as a philosophical issue as if, were it to be resolved, many of psychology's conceptual difficulties would be sorted out along with it. It is clear from the preceding chapters that further discussion about the relationship of a transcendent mind to a material body, each taken as a separate entity, is of little use to social psychology. Even a cursory examination of the evidence is enough to tell us that. We need to understand bodily existence in the context of real-life experience, across settings and over time. The problem is that this has to be done within a universe of discourse that separates mind and body and that has specific fields of study based upon this separation. This leads to the situation where it becomes very difficult for social psychologists to talk about the body and to be understood as *not* referring to a physical entity. In the course of this discussion, this has meant that references to the body have had to be qualified so that they are not taken as referring to a biological substrate common to everyone. The problem is to sustain a different meaning, a way of looking at things, when the accepted usage of key terms tends, inevitably, to reinstate boundaries that one has been trying to suspend. As with any new development, or emerging topic, one has to make do with existing terminology, or rather with refashioning it to make signs indicating different relationships than the ones to which people are accustomed. This is what we have had to make do with in this book, in the cause of throwing light upon a relationship that today still goes without being questioned by the mainstream of the discipline.

Revelations of the Body

The previous chapters have dealt with discrete topics: contemporary psychology, the emergence of the modern notion of the physical body, images of people, nonverbal communication, groups, the material world, and consumer culture. Taken together, the arguments surrounding them do not add up to a comprehensive view, let alone a theory of the body in social life. They should be seen instead as excursions into the problem of how the body is conceived by social psychologists. By this, I mean that they are intended as different reflections upon the question, each in turn raising distinct and yet related issues for consideration. By then reflecting these excursions back upon one another, one can attempt to discern more clearly how social psychology has proceeded with a particular view of people as subjects who are, at best, cloaked in bodies.

The notion of the body as a stable entity, a material form, has been shown to be the product of movements in scientific thought and in the wider society. The emergence of psychology as a discipline depended upon mind being discerned as a proper and legitimate object of scientific study. We have seen that part of this process involved the dislocation of the subject in the cause of objectifying behavior and experience. This objectifying view constituted a single plane within which mind and body became oppositions, at once held to be different but also subject to repeated attempts to link them together. The mind and the body became abstracted as essences that needed to be analyzed, each in terms of specialized disciplines. The development of psychology, and of social psychology within it, was premised upon this specialization.

For experimental and individual psychologists, the body has remained an ambiguous entity. On the one hand, it is the locus of mind, the medium of action, and therefore something with which mental life should join, if only in some ideal scientific world in the future. On the other, the material nature of the body, its tangibility, is a constant reminder of the difference between it and mental life. This contradiction stems from the opposition of these terms within a common perspective, where both are different kinds of things.

For social psychology, the issue is somewhat different. Partly because of the influence of sociological ideas, its subject matter is sometimes said to be "the individual in society." It is the group, the social representation, the attitude toward others, or the use of language that is held to mark out social psychology as distinct. Yet, in the light of this analysis, we can see that social psychology is not so different after all. By claiming that mind is not an individual affair but rather a social construction, social psychology has engaged in the conquest of the spaces between thinking (i.e., disembodied) individuals. Where experimental research locates its subject matter in the behavior and cognitions of individuals, social psychology directs its attentions to words and actions as they arise and are maintained in the relationships among persons, in groups, classes, and cultures. The establishment of a viable social psychology has meant that its practitioners have needed to make fewer references to the difference between the social and the biological. The more one accepts that the human subject is constituted by the social process, taken as a linguistic culture, the less one need be concerned with questions of the embodiment of the individual. In effect, the individual has become the social being and the mind transcendent; the body is reduced to being a vehicle that enables this to happen.

The inadequacy of this position has been pointed out at the beginning of this book. The truth is that, in terms of a broadly cognitivist approach, the individual as social being carries all of the marks made by the separation of mind from body. What is different is that these are disguised by the distance created by the movement of the social from the biological. The hidden assumptions about the body as a physiological entity are the countersupport for the promotion of a psychology of the social individual. Keeping these assumptions hidden is vital; this is not only to stave off difficult questions about the place of fleshy beings in a world of thought and language, but also to preserve the image of the subject matter of the discipline—the perceiving, judging, speaking, impression-managing person. When mention was made, at the outset, of the body being in the shadows, it was this process of subordination that was being indicated.

Lest it be thought that I am suggesting some sort of conspiracy among social psychologists to suppress all talk of the body, the argument needs to be made clear. The analysis has shown that psychology rests upon a division of mind from body; it has also revealed that the social psychological subject was constituted within a way of seeing that made it very difficult to conceive of the person across this divide. Posited as "the body," a generalized entity, it is rendered unknowable by social psychology except as the object of perception or as a commonly held signaling system. In that sense, the body of the medical textbooks is no threat to social psychology. It is amenable to people's constructions about its workings, and to their powers of socialization; its arousal is something I can interpret and reinterpret to make sense of my social situation, or else I can arrange that it promotes a chosen image of myself for others. Within mainstream social psychology, there need be no concern for the body because it remains an object; it simply does not signify.

This is not true at the periphery of the discipline, where the grasp of the subject figured by the psychological perspective (the healthy, male, middle-class, middle-aged or young adult, looking upon other people) is loosened. The introduction of groups such as women, the sick, the elderly, make the body signify in ways that challenge the dominant view. It is through the study of these groupings that the body is reintroduced into psychology: not as the neutral, objectified container of mind, but as an index of social distinctions now made legible where they were previously unseen. The threat to mainstream social psychology lies in this signification; the body ushered out of the shadows is an emissary of a subject matter, which, if known long ago or in other contexts, is now forgotten.

I now briefly review some of the main points that emerged from the separate excursions in the text. Looking and gazing are not abstract activities but are grounded in the relationships in which people stand together. The differences and inequalities of men and women are revealed through their different ways of looking, their being subject to the gaze of others. The body is both the ground of perception—the standpoint from which one sees—and appears differently within the context of distinct positions. That is to say, instead of there being a common perceptual apparatus available to each individual, looking is marked so that how men and women see, and what they experience as lookers and the scrutinized, is both expressive and constitutive of gender relations in society. It is not merely the body that appears, nor is it merely the eye that sees. In traditional psychology, the person is perceived as a subject, an individual personality. However, the person figured within a gaze need not be that of a subject but may be constituted in different relationships to surroundings, to other people, to possessions. What are commonly termed "looking at," "looking on," and "looking through" are indicative of qualitative differences in the figuring of the other. It is not merely the eye that sees, because the looker disposes of himself or herself according to the position taken vis-à-vis the perceived. Who looks, at whom, in what context, and for what purpose are matters that have forged the embodiment of inequalities, not merely recorded them once established. The idea that different people (e.g., the sexes) make themselves visible in different ways and exercise varying powers of surveillance is beyond the grasp of a psychology of generalized perceptual mechanisms.

The study of nonverbal behavior has treated the body as a means of communicating individual messages or as a medium for the regulation of interaction. While both of these possibilities exist, the emphasis upon them has reinforced what has been termed the *logocentric position*. This has had the effect of obscuring the body's primary mode, that of displaying, in a nondiscursive way, aspects of people's relationships to each other and to their world. In their disposition, their attitude, people can invoke relationships that are not self-expressive (the utterance of inner meaning) but that produce expressive forms. As virtual images, these allow us to conceive forms that spoken language is hard put to articulate. These are known through the languages of art, of feeling, and of suffering. They cannot be assimilated within the social psychology of coded meanings sought in body movements or in the arrangement of signals for interpersonal control.

The recognition of the body as portraying the relationship of individuals to the world opens up more than the logging of the rules and conventions that structure where and how this might happen. It also invites an examination of the settings, situations, and relationships in which such communications are valued, or disallowed, or reinterpreted by those who see them.

This relates to the issue of the legitimacy of these communications and to the different valuation placed upon the body by groups in society. Differences in power between social groups are exercised through the controls that are placed upon bodily conduct, and resistance to the word of dominant groups may be expressed through the breaching of thresholds of physical display. Most important, groups define themselves through the appropriation of powers that are marked in conduct, as style. These are not single but multiple relationships, whereby the different engagements of people in the world are, so to speak, condensed in the cross-association of their bodily potentialities. Gender, in particular, can be seen as such a potentiality, which becomes differently figured against the background of other group activities (e.g., work) in which men and women engage. Rather than considering the body as a single entity, it might be viewed as the site of associations, contradictions, and oppositions defined within different social practices and discourses.

In conduct and deportment, people make, maintain, and undo social boundaries. The body is no mere carrier of style; it makes style possible in its capacity to portray several things all at once. In expressing relationships to the world, it also defines place; it is a locus from which one acts, and in its uniqueness, it is not just *a* body, but *my* body, or *her* body. The phenomenological critique reveals these as grounds of action, tacit bases from which the world is known. *The body* (meaning any particular person's body) is both tacitly and objectively known. However, the objective knowledge is secondary, in being the recovery of aspects of our capacities from our engagements in the world. There is, therefore, a fundamental ambiguity about the body that can be expressed in the fact that it is both living and of material form. Its capacities and potentialities can be considered "shapes," which answer to the physiognomies of the world in its material aspects. People do not form relationships in a psychological ether but in the real world of working, playing, and loving. Bodily experience is a crucial reflection of the social world as praxis, in which people commit themselves to engagements in which they will subsequently discern more about their own and others' purposes. The outside world becomes a transform of differences in which certain aspects appear as things, others appear as personalities; the individual recovers aspects of "self" that answer to these changes, in terms of capacities, powers, or weaknesses to make some things happen or to render other things possible. These are ways of being figured, of being a kind of player, having a particular locus or a place in a discourse. We can say that it is a way of being distinguished in one's being, so that qualitative differences appear in oneself (as feelings), may be endorsed by others, and also appear in the world of artifacts as distinctly valued things.

This idea of being figured differently, and of the world appearing to be psychologically different in its turn, should not be read as applying only to individuals, although the phenomenological approach tends to cast the analysis in this form. We can think of these "figurations" (Elias, 1978) as referring to perspectives shared by classes of people who adopt similar attitudes *in* a common psychological world. The notion of a person being figured in one way at this time, and in another way at another time, tends to leave the impression of a constant subject who takes up these perspectives. Historical analysis shows, however, that this is not true. The emergence of the sovereign individual was the result of a social process that involved the transformation of power relations in society, the growth of trade and associated mobility, and the privatization of the home. In all of this, there was a civilizing of bodily conduct that should not be read as the honing of a preexisting subjectivity. To take that view would be once more to place the self behind the body, making the latter a screen, where instead the argument invites us to see social consciousness as an emergent feature in a world transformed through praxis. The refiguring of people extended to their notion of their own individuality; it did not start from it. Rather than underlining the presence of the individual subject as a single entity, this analysis reveals a multiplicity of practical engagements, and overlap of epochs, in which capacities and features of the psychological world have been subject to transformation.

Having set out briefly some of the points raised by the discussion of specific topics, the question is raised as to what kind of inquiry is possible by attending to the body in this way. In effect, one is not attending *to* the body, so much as attending *from* it toward those other matters that are signified within this approach. To underline an important point, one is not attending from an object, an entity, but from an idea of the body transformed through those things that it makes possible for our consideration. My intention here is not to outline the kinds of projects that might be carried out with increased awareness of the body's role. Instead, I want to point up those aspects of social life that become significant, and through this to indicate the potential of the body in psychological theory.

All of social life, not just the body, has a tacit aspect. When discussing the use of a probe, it was suggested that this could only be understood as attending *from* one position *toward* another. This is not just a facet of movement but has also been set out in terms of action (Polanyi, 1967). People act, in the social world, from positions, from grounds that they cannot make explicit as they depend upon them. Mead's (1934) concept of the "I," located inside individual experience and in consequence so often misunderstood, is an attempt to capture this idea. The introduction of the embodied person into psychology undermines the notion of total objectivity, of being able to fix, in a single gaze, all of the features of mind (social or individual) at one time. People act, as Mead said, *within* perspectives of which they can know only aspects; on the one hand, these aspects are objectified in the world, and on the other, they are figured in their own sense of themselves as agents. This ambiguity in social life has been revealed in theories that have drawn attention to the indeterminacy of action. Mead's is foremost among them, but one can include here Goffman's theory of the self as well as those that draw upon the body's capacity to be expressive as well as controlling. One way of dealing with this ambiguity is to identify the tacit aspect as some element of indeterminacy arising from the body as organism. This enables the other term—attitudes, behaviors—to appear as objective and hence measurable. There is a double error here which lies, first, in attempting to deny that action is ambiguous and, second, in trying to achieve this by reifying thought and action as processes or events.

By accepting the tacit aspect that is revealed by the body, one can see that it is not a property of "the body" at all, but of social life itself. The grounds of action lie in the perspectives (to borrow Mead's term) that relate people to their world and to each other. We depend upon relationships with others in a material world of our own making. The form of these relationships, like the movement of our limbs, is not given to us objectively, but through the progression of our intentions. These intentions, also, are not necessarily free choices, but are the constraints in which we find ourselves in a world of developed forms. Put simply, people act from positions that they know both objectively and tacitly, and the balance, movement between, and trans-formation of these terms is important to a full understanding of social life.

The preceding statements are very abstract indeed. In concrete terms, they indicate that the structure or form of the social world is lived, as well as seen. To appreciate this is to move to a position from which the forms of relationships in which people live become important to describe, for one can no longer assume that a relationship is an entity that can be comprehended from the outside. The differences in these forms are crucial, for they signify different experiences and mark movement in the transformation of relation-ships. To know, for example, that men and women participate in different ways of looking is to make such a distinction. Yet, this is not a distinction merely drawn between or upon the individuals concerned; it indicates a way in which, in their dealings with one another, men and women are differently distinguished *in their being*. The looker and the scrutinized live in different *psychological worlds*, which appear distinct on the horizons of their positions vis-à-vis each other. This particular difference cannot be reduced to one of variations in the physiology of the sexes; to imagine this is to miss the point entirely (Caplan, 1987). The bodies of men and women are taken up by ways of seeing that distinguish them, so that they become the tangible aspects of a psychological difference that is expressed through them. Such differences also reveal social life in its qualitative complexity, in which the consideration of inequalities then becomes possible.

If the body is the more tangible form of the ground of social life, then it is also the site of associations and contradictions between the various relation-ships in which people engage. Rather than thinking of individuals as subjects who belong to separate groups, an appreciation of display and of style reveals these as dependent upon the person being simultaneously in two or more perspectives. The example of the resistance of youth groups drew attention to the body as the crucible of innovative action, which depended for its effect upon capacities drawn from one context being deployed in another. In effect, the message of this resistance lay in the simultaneous refusal of one culture and the affirmation of an alternative. The power of the body in this case lay in the use of nondiscursive communication, which expressed a new relationship among the people concerned. More than this, it set out style, not as a mere marker, but as a way of seeing—in effect, a perspective within the world against which that world could be reflected.

The point made here is that we communicate nondiscursively with our bodies. Again, this is not to argue something about the essential nature of organisms, but to highlight the way in which relationships are displayed, marked, and transformed. It implies a social world of multiple perspectives, which are not just extant but are emergent through the praxis of people together. The body is important because it indicates the ways in which the manifold capacities it bears can be worked out afresh, or cross-related in the course of movements among groups, or in the establishment of new sub-groupings. It is this simultaneity of expression, capturing the old and the new, the group affirmed and the group denied, that offers a view of social life as involving the interpretation of perspectives. While we traditionally think of the body as being the substrate of a single self with an identity, this analysis suggests that it reflects a condition in which sociality lies in the emergent and conflicting relationships among groupings, among different "ways of seeing."

This way of thinking turns our attention outward, *from* the body, *to* the different forms of relationship in which it is but one field. To describe these forms requires that recognition is given to qualitative differences, which may appear not only on the body, or in its disposal in action, but also in the concrete settings of people's lives, in their intentions, and among the groups to which they belong. In addition, it draws attention to the transformation of relationships, obliging us to see social life as having, in the overlap of epochs, a historical mode. The tacit basis from which people act does not lie inside their bodies, still less inside their minds, but in the subjectivity of their joint intentions in the world. What have been called, at various places in this book, "perspectives," "relationships," "projects," "styles," "discourses," and "virtual images" each point, from their different positions, to this important conclusion. The condition of objectivity–subjectivity is not peculiar to the body, in spite of being apprehanded through it.

What does this imply for social psychological studies of the body? It underlines the point made already that *the body* as an abstract or ready-made entity is an inadequate psychological concept. It is always gendered, identified with, marked by social distinctions, reflected in the gaze of others, and grounded in concrete settings and relationships. To study these features of embodiment is to study the differences and transformations of the social world, to investigate not only what it is that signifies but also how it does so. Seeing, communicating (nonverbally), and acting then cease to be essential qualities of an abstract person and become capacities, the forms (qualitative differences) of which are understood in the context of the tacit basis referred to previously.

This argument is not intended to mystify the body or to pretend that the maturational changes to which it is subject are not important. The point is that these changes appear to be of a physical or biological body because that is how they are construed and how they are borne. This does not make them either less or more significant. The "natural" body is exigent, but its nature is already taken up within our divisions into the social and the biological, the inevitable and the constructed. Rather than trying to escape the constraints of our biological "nature," a social psychology that attended to embodied persons would investigate the ways in which these aspects of life are woven into and out of other social distinctions, say in the study of aging, of food choices, and of illness. The "aged body," the "meat-refusing" body, or the "sick body" can then be regarded as metonymic devices to cover the practices, relationships, settings, and figurations that each in its turn signifies. *The body*, as a single, universal, natural entity that ages, eats, and falls sick loses its claim to being on the psychological agenda—a claim that, in any case, has never been pressed very hard at all.

It is significant that the *psychological body*—if one can use that term—enters the discipline through the door marked "social." The history of psychology would surely have suggested otherwise—that it would be through the study of perhaps emotion or topics in psychophysiology that the body would be seen as most relevant. (Of course, some would hold this view as being a description of the status quo). The arguments in this book have been aimed at showing just the opposite; it is the elaboration of the social individual, the universal subject whose associations and differences make up the research agenda, that has subordinated the body in ways that have naturalized its capacities. The body as biological substrate is kept in place by a way of thinking, a discourse that actively promotes one kind of subject as universal, while recognizing that it is distinguished in its group affiliations and separated by its physical differences. The study of relationships between "men" and "women," the "sophisticated" and the "gauche," the "beautiful" and the "ugly" has depended upon the uncritical alignment of such affiliations and differences. The story that social psychology has for years been telling itself—that it is repelled by a determinate biologism of the body that it rejects—is but a comforting fiction. The truth is that the discipline has subscribed to an approach that has been active in naturalizing and somatizing psychological distinctions in order that a study of the individual as social being could proceed. The simple conclusion to this critique is to endorse the thesis that the body is thoroughly social and psychological, but it is equally one that claims that the social world is embodied through and through.

Symptomatology and Recovery

Earlier in the book, it was argued that the body makes its appearance only on the fringes of social psychology. I suggested that these fringe topics—women, the sick, the mad, crowds—are all evidence of a way that the body comes to matter in relationships of inequality. The association of the body and subordinate groupings is not, therefore, a matter of chance. However, the work of Foucault suggests that the body is not merely apparent among these fringe groups but is a locus of struggle in their exclusion and subordination. With this in mind, we could say that the body is not so much revealed through the analysis of these topics, as it is recovered by their being studied. Berthelot (1986) has described the introduction of the body into sociological discourse as being part of a "social symptomatology." By this, he meant the use of an ideographic rather than a nomothetic approach, so that the marked element is analyzed in preference to the unmarked (i.e., defining) category. Berthelot used the example of studying the marginal person rather than marginality, or the suicidal individual rather than suicide as a social outcome. This approach is one often associated with the ethnomethodological and phenomenological schools. The emphasis upon the bodily experience of fringe groups in social psychology can be seen in just this light. The question then arises as to whether this is an adequate approach for the discipline to take.

One view is that the symptomatic approach is a phase in which the body first becomes established as a site of interest for investigators in the field. The remarks made in the previous paragraph reemphasize that this is not accidental or just a matter of the predilections of researchers for using one research approach rather than another. There is a real significance in the emergence of the body as a key term in the experience of groups in subordinate positions, and this has been acknowledged as material to our thinking about the problem. It might be that the topic of "the body in social psychology" can only emerge further through more research of just this kind. This will tend to portray physical existence as if it were a mirror to be inserted into social life, so that it can reflect differences not otherwise discernable by social or cognitive theory. Indeed, this is just the kind of work on which this book has often relied in order to make its points. At the time of writing, one could only wish for more of this work to form a base from which one might elaborate theory of the kind referred to herein.

The limitation of this approach, however, is that it leaves the body as symptomatic of particular situations but does not allow us to conceive it as a sign of social action, of praxis. This involves first the recognition that the symptomatic body can only be understood in relation to the form of subjectivity taken up by the dominant culture. We have discussed this in two contexts: first, the generalization of the universal subject as male, rational, individual, and healthy, and second, the hegemony of spoken language, the logocentrism of psychology. Appreciating this difference allows one to see why the body should have taken so long to reappear at the boundaries of the discipline, and why its challenge to "the subject" is likely to provoke resistance. It is not just that notions of the living body or of multiple engagements or intentions are outside the comprehension of positivistic psychology, but that the removal of the organic, biological substrate as a countersupport to the social self undermines the Cartesian divide on which mainstream social psychology rests. Effectively, social psychology needs the biological body to be a legitimate entity, so that the living body will not come out of the epistemological shadows, dragging its inequalities, its ambiguities, and its unsayable features in its wake.

I have tried to indicate that this book does not seek to establish a theory of "the social body," in the sense of it being a "social thing" as much as a "physical thing." To do this would be to replace one reification with another. Instead, it has conceived the body as a field of investigation, a locus for us to discern qualitative differences of form in social life. To adapt a comment once made by George Homans about the group, bodies are not what we study so much as places where we go to study what we are interested in. This, however, should not be read as an invitation to leave off studying other aspects of people's relationships. It is the concrete setting, with all that that implies, which requires that bodily experience be situated, both with respect to the material world and to the discourses in which people find themselves variously positioned.

The recent status of the body, as far as social psychology is concerned, is that of an organism whose perceived naturalness and ordinariness allowed it to frame issues in a way that displaced attention away from its own form. As a result of the feminist critique in general, and of studies in such areas as illness in particular, there is a heightening of consciousness of the body's significance in social life. This book reflects this new interest, as well as the attention being focused upon the body in the other social sciences, as well as in the outside world. Far from taking us further into the abstracted individual, the body as a salient feature of social psychological research promises a renewed engagement with real-world settings.

The conclusion of this book is that attention to the body as both a conveyor and product of form implies a rethinking of social psychological theory, not just a rejigging of our ideas on selected topics, such as nonverbal behavior. As a plane of inquiry, the body offers a line of thought and research that is at present closed to those who see it only as a repository of emotion or else as a rather ornate signaling system.

References

Abercrombie, D. (1968). Paralanguage. *British Journal of Disorders of Communication, 3*, 55–59.

Adams, C. J. (1990). *The sexual politics of meat*. Cambridge, England. Polity Press.

Allen, D. E., Guy, R. F., & Edgley, C. K. (1980). *Social psychology as social process*. Belmont, CA: Wadsworth.

Allport, G. W. (1968). The historical background of modern social psychology. In G. Lindzey & E. Aronson (Eds.), *Handbook of social psychology* (Vol. 1, 2nd ed.). Reading, MA: Addison-Wesley.

Allport, G. W., & Postman, L. J. (1945). The basic psychology of rumor. *Transactions of the New York Academy of Sciences 8* (Series II), 61–81.

Alonzo, A. A. (1979). Everyday illness behavior: A situational approach to health status deviations. *Social Science and Medicine, 13A*, 397–404.

Alpers, S. (1983). *The art of describing: Dutch art in the seventeenth century*. Chicago: University of Chicago Press.

Anderson, R., & Bury, M. (Eds.). (1988). *Living with chronic illness: The experience of patients and their families*. London: Unwin Hyman.

Arendt, H. (1959). *The human condition*. New York: Doubleday Anchor.

Argyle, M. (1969). *Social interaction*. London: Methuen.

Argyle, M. (1975). The syntaxes of bodily communication. In J. Bentall & T. Polhemus (Eds.), *The body as a medium of expression*. London: Allen Lane.

Argyle, M. (1983). *The psychology of interpersonal behaviour* (4th ed.). London: Penguin.

Argyle, M. (1984). Some new developments in social skills training. *Bulletin of the British Psychological Society, 37*, 405–410.

Argyle, M., & Dean, J. (1965). Eye-contact, distance and affiliation. *Sociometry, 28*, 289–304.

Argyle, M., & Kendon, A. (1967). The experimental analysis of social performance. *Advances in experimental social psychology, 3*, 55–98.

Argyle, M., Lalljee, M., & Cook, M. (1968). The effects of visibility on interaction in a dyad. *Human Relations, 21*, 3–17.

Argyle, M., Salter, V., Nicholson, H., Williams, M., & Burgess, P. (1970). The communication of inferior and superior attitudes by verbal and non-verbal signals. *British Journal of Social and Clinical Psychology, 9*, 222–231.

Aries, E. (1976). Interaction patterns and themes of male, female and mixed groups. *Small Group Behavior, 7*, 7–18.

Ariès, P. (1962). *Centuries of childhood*. New York: Vintage Books.

Armon-Jones, C. (1986). The thesis of constructionism. In R. Harré (Ed.), *The social construction of emotions*. Oxford: Blackwell.

Armstrong, D. (1983). *Political anatomy of the body*. Cambridge, England: Cambridge University Press.

Armstrong, D. (1984). The patient's view. *Social Science and Medicine, 18*, 737–744.

Armstrong, D. (1987). Bodies of knowledge: Foucault and the problem of human anatomy. In G. Scambler (Ed.), *Sociological theory and medical sociology*, London: Tavistock.

Asch, S.E. (1952). *Social psychology*. Englewood Cliffs, NJ: Prentice-Hall.

Bachelard, G. (1969). *The poetics of space*. Boston: Beacon Press.

Bales, R. F. (1958). Task roles and social roles in problem solving groups. In E. E. Maccoby, T. M. Newcomb, & E. L. Hartley (Eds.), *Readings in social psychology* (3rd ed.). New York: Holt, Rinehart and Winston.

Bannister, D. (1968). The myth of physiological psychology. *Bulletin of the British Psychological Society, 21*, 229–231.

Barkan, L. (1975). *Nature's work of art: The human body as image of the world*. New Haven, CN: Yale University Press.

Barral, M. R. (1963). *Merleau-Ponty: The role of the body in interpersonal relations*. Unpublished doctoral dissertation, Fordham University.

Barthes, R. (1972). *Mythologies*. London: Jonathan Cape.

Bartol, K. M. & Martin, D. C. (1986). Women and men in task groups. In R. D. Ashmore & F. K. Del Boca (Eds.), *The social psychology of female–male relations*. New York: Academic Press.

Bartlett, F. C. (1932). *Remembering: A study in experimental and social psychology*. Cambridge, England: Cambridge University Press.

Bateson, G. (1958). *Naven: A survey of the problems suggested by a composite picture of the culture of a New Guinea tribe drawn from three points of view* (2nd ed.). Stanford: Stanford University Press.

Bateson, G. (1987). *Steps to an ecology of mind*. Northvale, NJ: Jason Aronson.

Bateson, G., & Mead, M. (1942). *Balinese character: A photographic analysis* (Vol. 2). New York: Special Publications of the New York Academy of Sciences.

Baumrind, D. (1964). Some thoughts on ethics of research: After reading Milgram's "Behavioral Study of Obedience." *American Psychologist, 19*, 421–423.

Beardsworth, A., & Keil, T. (1991). Health-related beliefs and dietary practices among vegetarians and vegans: A qualitative study. *Health Education Journal, 50*, 38–42.

Beattie, G. W. (1983). *Talk: An analysis of speech and non-verbal behaviour in conversation*. Milton Keynes: Open University Press.

Becker, H. (1963). *Outsiders: Studies in the sociology of deviance*. New York: Free Press.

Beloff, H. (1985). *Camera culture*. Oxford: Blackwell.

Bem, D. J. (1972). Self-perception theory. In L. Berkowitz (Ed.), *Advances in experimental social psychology* (Vol. 6). New York: Academic Press.

Benthall, J. (1975). Prospectus. In J. Benthall & T. Polhemus (Eds.), *The body as a medium of expression*. London: Allen Lane.

Berger, J. (1972). *Ways of seeing*. London: British Broadcasting Corporation/ Penguin Books.

Berger, P. L., Berger, B., & Kellner, H. (1974). *The homeless mind: Modernization and consciousness*. Harmondsworth, England: Penguin.

Berger, P. L., & Luckmann, T. (1971). *The social construction of reality*. Harmondsworth, England: Penguin.

Bernstein, B. (1971). *Class, codes and control: Vol. 1. Theoretical studies towards a sociology of language*. London: Routledge and Kegan Paul.

Berscheid, E. (1981). An overview of the psychological effects of physical attractiveness. In G. Lucker, K. Ribbens, & J. McNamara (Eds.), *Psychological aspects of facial form*. Ann Arbor: University of Michigan Press.

Berthelot, J. M. (1986). Sociological discourse and the body. *Theory, Culture and Society, 3*, 155–164.

Biddle, S. J. H., & Fox, K. R. (1989). Exercise and health psychology: Emerging relationships. *British Journal of Medical Psychology, 62*, 205–216.

Birdwhistell, R. L. (1952). *Introduction to kinesics*. Louisville, KY: University of Louisville Press.

Birdwhistell, R. L. (1961). Paralanguage twenty-five years after Sapir. In H. G. Brosin (Ed.), *Lectures in experimental psychiatry*. Pittsburgh: Pittsburgh University Press.

Birdwhistell, R. L. (1968). Kinesics. In *International encyclopedia of the social sciences* (Vol. 8, pp. 379–385).

Blaxter, M. (1983). The causes of disease: Women talking. *Social Science and Medicine, 17*, 59–69.

Bloch, C. (1987). Everyday life, sensuality and body culture. *Women's Studies International Forum, 10*, 433–442.

Bourdieu, P. (1984). *Distinction: A social critique of the judgement of taste*. London: Routledge and Kegan Paul.

Broekhoff, J. (1972). Physical education and the reification of the human body. *Gymnasion, 9*, 4–11.

Brown, R. (1965). *Social psychology*. New York: Free Press.

Brown, R. (1988). *Group processes: Dynamics within and between groups*. Oxford, England: Blackwell.

Bruch, H. (1978). *The golden cage: The enigma of anorexia nervosa*. London: Open Books.

Bruner, J. S., & Taguiri, R. (1954). Person perception. In G. Lindzey (Ed.), *Handbook of social psychology* (Vol. 2). Reading, MA: Addison-Wesley.

Buckley, H. M., & Roach, M. E. (1974). Clothing as a nonverbal communicator of social and political attitudes. *Home Economics Research Journal, 3*, 94–102.

Bull, R., & Rumsey, N. (1988). *The social psychology of facial appearance*. New York: Springer-Verlag.

Buss, A. R. (1978). Causes and reasons in attribution theory: A conceptual critique. *Journal of Personality and Social Psychology, 36*, 1311–1321.

Buytendijk, F. (1961). The body in existential psychology. *Review of Existential Psychology, 1*, 149–172.

Buytendijk, F. (1974). *Prolegomena to an anthropological physiology*. Pittsburgh: Duquesne University Press.

Caplan, P. (Ed.). (1987). *The cultural construction of sexuality*. London: Tavistock.

Cardwell, J. D. (1971). *Social psychology: A symbolic interactionist perspective*. Philadelphia: F. A. Davis.

Cassell, E. J. (1976). Disease as an "it": Concepts of disease revealed by patients' presentation of symptoms. *Social Science and Medicine, 10*, 143–146.

Charmaz, K. (1983). Loss of self: A fundamental form of suffering in the chronically ill. *Sociology of Health and Illness, 5*, 168–195.

Clarke, J. (1976). The creation of style. In S. Hall & T. Jefferson (Eds.), *Resistance through rituals: Youth subcultures in post-war Britain*. London: Hutchinson.

Clarke, J., Hall, S., Jefferson, T., & Roberts, B. (1976). Subcultures, cultures and class. In S. Hall & T. Jefferson (Eds.), *Resistance through rituals: Youth subcultures in post-war Britain*. London: Hutchinson.

Coghill, G. E. (1929). *Anatomy and the problem of behaviour*. London: Macmillan.

Collins, J. K. (1986). The objective measurement of body image using a video technique: Reliability and validity studies. *British Journal of Psychology, 77*, 199–205.

Cotton, J. (1981). A review of research on Schachter's theory of emotion and the misattribution of arousal. *European Journal of Social Psychology, 11*, 365–397.

Crutchfield, R. S. (1955). Conformity and character. *American Psychologist, 10*, 191–198.

Csikzentmihalyi, M., & Rochberg-Halton, E. (1981). *The meaning of things: Domestic symbols and the self*. New York: Cambridge University Press.

Davies, R. (1989). *How to read faces*. Wellingborough, Northants, England: Aquarian Press.

Davis, F. (1963). *Passage through crisis: Polio victims and their families*. Indianapolis: Bobbs-Merrill.

Davis, J. H. (1973). Group decision and social interaction: A theory of social decision schemes. *Psychological Review, 80*, 97–125.

De Beauvoir, S. (1972). *The second sex*. Harmondsworth, England: Penguin.

de Mause, L. (1974). The evolution of childhood. In L. de Mause (Ed.), *The history of childhood*. New York: Psychohistory Press.

de Saint-Exupèry, A. (1954). *Wind, sand and stars*. London: Heinemann.

Deutsch, F. (1952). Analytic posturology. *Psychoanalytic Quarterly, 21*, 196–214.

Devisch, R. (1985). Approaches to symbol and symptom in bodily space–time. *International Journal of Psychology, 20*, 389–415.

d'Houtaud, A., & Field, M. G. (1984). The image of health: Variations in perception by social class in a French population. *Sociology of Health and Illness, 6*, 30–60.

Dion, K., Berscheid, E., & Walster, E. (1972). What is beautiful is good. *Journal of Personality and Social Psychology, 24*, 285–290.

Doise, W. (1978). *Groups and individuals: Explanations in social psychology*. Cambridge, England: Cambridge University Press.

Douglas, M. (1966). *Purity and danger: An analysis of concepts of pollution and taboo*. London: Routledge and Kegan Paul.

Douglas, M. (1971). Do dogs laugh? A cross-cultural approach to body symbolism. *Journal of Psychosomatic Research, 15*, 387–390.

Douglas, M. (1973). *Natural symbols: Explorations in cosmology*. Harmondsworth, England: Penguin.

Douglas, M. (1978). *Cultural bias* (Occasional Paper No. 35). Royal Anthropological Institute of Great Britain and Ireland, London.

Dreyfus, H. L. (1967). Why computers must have bodies in order to be intelligent. *Review of Metaphysics, 21*, 13–32.

Duden, B. (1985). Historical concepts of the body. *Resurgence, 112*, 24–26.

Duncan, J. S. (1981). From container of women to status symbol: The impact of social structure on the meaning of the house. In J. S. Duncan (Ed.), *Housing and identity: Cross-cultural perspectives*. London: Croom Helm.

Duncan, S. (1969). Nonverbal communication. *Psychological Bulletin, 72*, 118–137.

Duncan, S., & Fiske, D. W. (1977). *Face-to-face interaction: Research methods and theory*. Hillsdale, NJ: Erlbaum.

Durkheim, E. (1952). *Suicide: A study in sociology*. London: Routledge and Kegan Paul.

Edinger, J. A., & Patterson, M. L. (1983). Nonverbal involvement and social control. *Psychological Bulletin, 93*, 30–56.

Efron, D. (1942). *Gesture and environment*. New York: King's Crown Press.

Eibl-Eibesfeldt, I. (1972). Similarities and differences between cultures in expressive movements. In R. A. Hinde (Ed.), *Non-verbal communication*. Cambridge, England: Cambridge University Press.

Ekman, P. (1972). Universals and cultural differences in facial expressions of emotion. In J. Cole (Ed.), *Nebraska Symposium on Motivation, 1971* (Vol. 19). Lincoln: University of Nebraska Press.

Ekman, P. (1977). Biological and cultural contributions to body and facial movement. In J. Blacking (Ed.), *The anthropology of the body*. London: Academic Press.

Ekman, P., & Friesen, W. V. (1969a). Nonverbal leakage and clues to deception. *Psychiatry, 32,* 88–105.

Ekman, P., & Friesen, W. V. (1969b). The repertoire of nonverbal behavior: Categories, origins, usage and coding. *Semiotica, 1,* 49–98.

Ekman, P., & Friesen, W. V. (1971). Constants across cultures in the face and emotion. *Journal of Personality and Social Psychology, 17,* 124–129.

Ekman, P., & Friesen, W. V. (1975). *Unmasking the face: A guide to recognizing emotions from facial clues*. Englewood Cliffs, NJ: Prentice-Hall.

Elias, N. (1978). *The civilizing process: The history of manners*. Oxford, England: Blackwell.

Eng, E. (1984). World and self in ageing and psychosis. *Journal of Phenomenological Psychology, 15,* 21–31.

Faust, B. (1980). *Women, sex and pornography*. London: Melbourne House.

Featherstone, M. (1982). The body in consumer culture. *Theory, Culture and Society, 1,* 18–33.

Feldman, M. M. (1975). The body image and object relations: Exploration of a method utilizing repertory grid techniques. *British Journal of Medical Psychology, 48,* 317–332.

Ferguson, M. (1978). Imagery and ideology: The cover photographs of traditional women's magazines. In G. Tuckman, A. K. Daniels, & J. Benet (Eds.), *Hearth and home: Images of women in the mass media*. New York: Oxford University Press.

Figlio, K. (1982). How does illness mediate social relations? In P. Wright & A. Treacher, (Eds.), *The problem of medical knowledge*. Edinburgh: Edinburgh University Press.

Firth, R. (1978). Postures and gestures of respect. In T. Polhemus (Ed.), *Social aspects of the human body*. Harmondsworth, England: Penguin.

Fischer, H. T. (1964). The clothes of the naked Nuer. *International Archives of Ethnography, 50,* 60–71.

Fisher, J. D., Rytting, M., & Heslin, J. (1976). Hands touching hands: Affective and evaluative effects of interpersonal touch. *Sociometry, 39,* 416–421.

Forgas, J. P. (1981). *Social cognition: Perspectives on everyday understanding*. London: Academic Press.

Forgas, J. P. (1983). What is social about social cognition? *British Journal of Social Psychology, 22,* 129–144.

Foucault, M. (1973). *The birth of the clinic: An archaeology of medical perception*. London: Tavistock.

Foucault, M. (1977). *Discipline and punish: The birth of the prison*. London: Allen Lane.

Foucault, M. (1979). *The history of sexuality* (Vol. 1). London: Allen Lane.

Foucault, M. (1980). In Colin Gordon (Ed.), *Power/knowledge: Selected interviews and other writings 1972–1977*. New York: Pantheon.

Freud, S. (1955). *The complete psychological works of Sigmund Freud* (Vol. 2). J. Strachey (Ed.), London: Hogarth Press.

Freud, S. (1957). *The complete psychological works of Sigmund Freud* (Vol. 14). J. Strachey (Ed.), London: Hogarth Press.

Freud, S. (1966). *The complete psychological works of Sigmund Freud* (Vol. 1). J. Strachey (Ed.), London: Hogarth Press.

Freund, P. E. S. (1982). *The civilized body: Social domination, control and health.* Philadelphia: Temple University Press.

Fried, M. (1963). Grieving for a lost home. In L. J. Duhl (Ed.), *The urban condition: People and policy in the metropolis.* New York: Basic Books.

Friedman, M., & Rosenman, R. (1974). *Type A behavior and your heart.* New York: Alfred Knopf.

Gane, M. (1983). Durkheim: Woman as outsider. *Economy and Society, 12,* 227–270.

Gardner, H. (1972). *The metaphysical poets* (rev. ed.), Harmondsworth, England: Penguin.

Garner, D. M., Garfinkel, P. E., Stancer, H. C., & Moldofsky, H. (1976). Body image disturbances in anorexia nervosa and obesity. *Psychosomatic Medicine, 38,* 327–336.

Gauvain, M., Altman, I., & Fahim, H. (1984). Homes and social change: A case study of the impact of resettlement. In K. J. Gergen & M. M. Gergen (Eds.), *Historical social psychology.* Hillsdale, NJ: Erlbaum.

Geertz, C. (1972). Deep play: Notes on the Balinese cockfight. *Daedalus, 101,* 1–37.

Gilman, S. L. (1982). *Seeing the insane.* New York: Wiley.

Gilman, S. L. (1985). *Difference and pathology: Stereotypes of sexuality, race and madness.* London: Cornell University Press.

Goddard, V. (1987). Honour and shame: The control of women's sexuality and group identity in Naples. In P. Caplan (Ed.), *The cultural construction of sexuality.* London: Tavistock.

Goffman, E. (1959). *The presentation of self in everyday life.* New York: Doubleday.

Goffman, E. (1961). *Encounters: Two studies in the sociology of interaction.* Indianapolis: Bobbs-Merrill.

Goffman, E. (1963). *Stigma: Notes on the management of spoiled identity.* Englewood Cliffs, NJ: Prentice-Hall.

Goffman, E. (1972). *Interaction ritual.* Harmondsworth, England: Penguin.

Goffman, E. (1976). Gender advertisements. *Studies in the Anthropology of Visual communication, 3*(Whole No. 2).

Gollin, E. S. (1954). Forming impressions of personality. *Journal of Personality, 23,* 65–76.

Gordon, C. (Ed.). (1980). *Michel Foucault: Power/knowledge.* Brighton, England: Harvester.

Gordon, C., & Gergen, K. J. (1968). *The self in social interaction: Vol. 1. Classic and contemporary perspectives.* New York: Wiley.

Graumann, C. F. (1974). Psychology and the world of things. *Journal of Phenomenological Psychology, 4,* 389–404.

Greenberg, J. H. (1966). *Language universals.* The Hague: Mouton.

Griffin, C. (1985). *Typical girls? Young women from school to the job market.* London: Routledge and Kegan Paul.

Griffin, S. (1981). *Pornography and silence.* New York: Harper & Row.

Gutek, D. A. (1989). Sexuality in the workplace: Key issues in social research and organizational practice. In J. Hearn, D. L. Sheppard, P. Tancred-Sheriff, & G. Burrell (Eds.), *The sexuality of organization.* London: Sage.

Hall, C. S., & Lindzey, G. (1957). *Theories of personality.* New York: Wiley.

Hall, E. T. (1963). A system for the notation of proxemic behavior. *American Anthropologist, 65,* 1003–1026.

Hanna, J. L. (1979). *To dance is human: A theory of nonverbal communication.* Austin, TX: University of Texas Press.

Harré, R. (1986a). Is the body a thing? *International Journal of Moral and Social Studies, 1,* 189–203.

Harré, R. (1986b). An outline of the social constructionist viewpoint. In R. Harré (Ed.), *The social construction of emotions*. Oxford, England: Blackwell.

Harré, R., & Secord, P. F. (1972). *The explanation of social behaviour*. Oxford, England: Blackwell.

Harris, C. C. (1977). Changing conceptions of the relation between family and societal form in Western society. In R. Scase (Ed.), *Industrial society: Class, cleavage and control*. London: Allen and Unwin.

Hazan, H. (1986). Body image and temporality among the aged: A case study of an ambivalent symbol. *Studies in Symbolic Interaction, 7*, 305–329.

Hebdige, D. (1979). *Subculture: The meaning of style*. London: Methuen.

Heider, F. (1958). *The psychology of interpersonal relations*. New York: Wiley.

Henley, N. (1977). *Body politics: Power, sex and nonverbal communication*. Englewood Cliffs, NJ: Prentice-Hall.

Herzlich, C. (1973). *Health and illness: A social psychological analysis*. London: Academic Press.

Herzlich, C., & Pierret, J. (1987). *Illness and self in society*. Baltimore, MD: The Johns Hopkins University Press.

Heslin, R., & Patterson, M. L. (1982). *Nonverbal behavior and social psychology*. New York: Plenum.

Hewes, G. W. (1955). World distribution of certain postural habits. *American Anthropologist, 57*, 231–244.

Hinde, R. A. (Ed.). (1972). *Non-verbal communication*. Cambridge, England: Cambridge University Press.

Hinde, R. A. (1982). *Ethology*. Oxford, England: Oxford University Press.

Hinde, R. A. (1987). *Individuals, relationships and culture: Links between ethology and the social sciences*. Cambridge, England: Cambridge University Press.

Hochschild, A. R. (1979). Emotion work, feeling rules and social structure. *American Journal of Sociology, 85*, 551–75.

Holland, R. (1977). *Self and social context*. London: Macmillan.

Homans, G. C. (1961). *Social behavior: Its elementary forms*. New York: Harcourt Brace Jovanovich.

Ichheiser, G. (1949). Misunderstandings in human relations. *American Journal of Sociology, 55*(Whole No. 2).

Jacoby, R. (1975). *Social amnesia: A critique of conformist psychology from Adler to Laing*. Boston, MA: Beacon Press.

Jahoda, M. (1972). Social psychology and psychoanalysis: A mutual challenge. *Bulletin of the British Psychological Society, 25*, 269–274.

Jahoda, M. (1977). *Freud and the dilemmas of psychology*. London: Hogarth Press.

Janlert, L. E. (1987). The computer as a person. *Journal for the Theory of Social Behaviour, 17*, 321–341.

Jersild, A. (1952). *In search of self*. New York: Bureau of Publications, Teachers College, Columbia University.

Jewson, N. D. (1976). The disappearance of the sick-man from medical cosmology, 1770–1870. *Sociology, 10*, 225–244.

Jones, E. E., and Nisbett, R. E. (1972). The actor and the observer: Divergent perceptions of the causes of behavior. In E. E. Jones, D. Kanouse, H. H. Kelley, R. E. Nisbett, S. Valins, & B. Weiner (Eds.), *Attribution: Perceiving the causes of behavior*. (pp. 79–94) Morristown, NJ: General Learning Press.

Kalick, S. M. (1988). Physical attractiveness as a status cue. *Journal of Experimental Social Psychology, 24*, 469–489.

Kanter, R. M. (1972). Getting it all together: Some group issues in communes. *American Journal of Orthopsychiatry, 42*, 632–643.

Kanter, R. M. (1975). Women and the structure of organizations: Explorations in theory and behavior. *Sociological Inquiry, 45*, 34–74.

Kanter, R. M. (1977). Some effects of proportions on group life: Skewed sex ratios and responses to token women. *American Journal of Sociology, 82*, 965–990.

Kelley, H. H. (1967). Attribution theory in social psychology. *Nebraska Symposium on Motivation, 15*, 192–238.

Kelly, G. A. (1955). *The psychology of personal constructs* (Vols. 1–2). New York: Norton.

Kendon, A. (1967). Some functions of gaze-direction in social interaction. *Acta Psychologica, 26*, 22–47.

Kendon, A. (1975). Some functions of the face in a kissing round. *Semiotica, 15*, 299–334.

Kern, S. (1975). *Anatomy and destiny: A cultural history of the human body*. Indianapolis: Bobbs-Merrill.

Kiritz, S., & Moos, R. H. (1974). Physiological effects of social environments. *Psychosomatic Medicine, 36*, 96–114.

Kleeblatt, N. L. (1987). *The Dreyfus affair: Art, truth and justice*. Berkeley: University of California Press.

Kleinke, C. L. (1986). Gaze and eye-contact: A research review. *Psychological Bulletin, 100*, 78–100.

Koestler, A. (1964). *The act of creation*. London: Hutchinson.

Kopytoff, I. (1982). Slavery. *Annual Review of Anthropology, 11*, 207–230.

Krech, D., Crutchfield, R. S., & Ballachey, E. L. (1962). *Individual in society: A textbook of social psychology*. New York: McGraw-Hill.

Kunzle, D. (1982). *Fashion and fetishism: A social history of the corset, tight-lacing and other forms of body-sculpture in the West*. Totowa, NJ: Rowman and Littlefield.

Lalive d'Épinay, C. (1986). Time, space and socio-cultural identity: The ethos of the proletariat, small owners and peasantry in an aged population. *International Social Sciences Journal, 107*, 89–104.

Lamb, W., & Watson, E. (1979). *Body code: The meaning in movement*. London: Routledge and Kegan Paul.

Langer, S. K. (1951). *Philosophy in a new key: A study in the symbolism of reason, rite and art*. London: Oxford University Press.

Langer, S. K. (1953). *Feeling and form*. London: Routledge and Kegan Paul.

La Piere, R. T. (1934). Attitudes versus actions. *Social Forces, 13*, 230–237.

Leach, E. (1972). The influence of cultural context on non-verbal communication in man. In R. A. Hinde (Ed.), *Non-verbal communication*. Cambridge, England: Cambridge University Press.

Leach, E. (1982). *Social Anthropology*. London: Fontana.

Le Bon, G. (1896). *The crowd*. London: Ernest Benn.

Levin, D. M. (1985). The body politic: Political economy and the human body. *Human Studies, 8*, 235–278.

Levy, R. (1984). Emotion, knowing and culture. In R. Shweder & R. LeVine (Eds.), *Culture theory: Essays on mind, self and emotion*. Cambridge, England: Cambridge University Press.

Lewin, K., Lippitt, R., & White, R. K. (1939). Patterns of aggressive behavior in experimentally created "social climates". *Journal of Social Psychology, 10*, 271–299.

Lewis, W. F. (1986). A perspective on the symbolization of the body. *Humanity and Society, 10*, 277–296.

Lindesmith, A. R. & Strauss, A. L. (1968). *Social psychology* (3rd ed.). New York: Holt, Rinehart and Winston.

Lingis, A. (1986). Orchids and muscles. *Journal of the Philosophy of Sport, 13*, 15–28.

Mackay, D. M. (1972). Formal analysis of communicative processes. In R. A. Hinde (Ed.), *Non-verbal communication*. Cambridge, England: Cambridge University Press.

Maier, R. A., & Lavrakas, P. J. (1984). Attitudes toward women, personality rigidity, and idealized physique preferences in males. *Sex Roles, 11*, 425–433.

Manning, P. K., & Fabrega, H. (1973). The experience of self and body: Health and illness in the Chiapas Highlands. In G. Psathas (Ed.), *Phenomenological sociology: Issues and applications*. New York: Wiley.

Marsh, P., Rosser, E., & Harré, R. (1978). *The rules of disorder*. London: Routledge and Kegan Paul.

Martin, E. (1989). *The woman in the body: A cultural analysis of reproduction*. Milton Keynes: Open University Press.

Marx, K. (1977). *Economic and philosophic manuscripts of 1844*. Moscow: Progress Publishers.

Mauss, M. (1972). Techniques of the body. *Economy and Society, 2*, 70–88.

McArthur, L. (1982). Judging a book by its cover: A cognitive analysis of the relationship between physical appearance and stereotyping. In A. Hastorf & A. Isen (Eds.), *Cognitive social psychology*. New York: Elsevier.

McCracken, G. (1987). Culture and consumption among the elderly: Three research objectives in an emerging field. *Ageing and Society, 7*, 203–224.

McLuhan, M. (1962). *The Gutenberg Galaxy: The making of typographic man*. London: Routledge and Kegan Paul.

McNeill, D. (1985). So you think gestures are non-verbal? *Psychological Review, 92*, 350–371.

Mead, G. H. (1934). *Mind, self and society*. Chicago: University of Chicago Press.

Mead, G. H. (1959). *The philosophy of the present*. La Salle, IL: Open Court.

Mehrabian, A. (1968a). Inference of attitudes from the posture, orientation, and distance of a communicator. *Journal of Consulting and Clinical Psychology, 32*, 296–308.

Mehrabian, A. (1968b). Relationship of attitude to seated posture, orientation, and distance. *Journal of Personality and Social Psychology, 10*, 26–30.

Melly, G. (1989). *Revolt into style: The pop arts*. Oxford, England: Oxford University Press.

Merleau-Ponty, M. (1962). *Phenomenology of perception*. London: Routledge and Kegan Paul.

Milgram, S. (1963). Behavioral study of obedience, *Journal of Abnormal and Social Psychology, 67*, 371–378.

Milgram, S. (1974). *Obedience to authority*. New York: Harper and Row.

Miller, D. (1985). *Artefacts as categories: A study of ceramic variability in central India*. Cambridge, England: Cambridge University Press.

Mischel, W. (1968). *Personality and assessment*. New York: Wiley.

Mitchell, J. (1974). *Psychoanalysis and feminism*. London: Allen Lane.

Mixon, D. (1974). If you won't deceive, what can you do? In N. Armistead (Ed.), *Reconstructing social psychology*. Harmondsworth, England: Penguin.

Moscovici, S. (1984). The phenomenon of social representations. In R. M. Farr & S. Moscovici (Eds.), *Social representations*. Cambridge, England: Cambridge University Press.

Moscovici, S. (1985). *The age of the crowd: A historical treatise on mass psychology*. Cambridge, England: Cambridge University Press.

Murphy, M. A., & Fischer, C. T. (1983). Styles of living with low back injury: The continuity dimension. *Social Science and Medicine, 17*, 291–297.

Musgrove, F. (1974). *Ecstasy and holiness: Counter culture and the open society*. London: Methuen.

Nead, L. (1988). *Myths of sexuality: Representations of women in Victorian Britain.* Oxford, England: Blackwell.

Neisser, U. (1967). *Cognitive psychology.* New York: Appleton-Century-Crofts.

Neisser, U. (1988). Five kinds of self-knowledge. *Philosophical Psychology, 1,* 35–59.

O'Neill, J. (1978). The productive body: An essay on the work of consumption. *Queen's Quarterly, 85,* 221–230.

Orbach, S. (1978). *Fat is a feminist issue.* London: Paddington Press.

Ornstein, R. E. (1977). *The psychology of consciousness* (2nd ed.). New York: Harcourt Brace Jovanovich.

Osgood, C. E., Suci, G. J., & Tannenbaum, P. H. (1957). *The measurement of meaning.* Urbana; IL: University of Illinois Press.

Patterson, M. L. (1982). A sequential functional model of nonverbal exchange. *Psychological Review, 89,* 231–249.

Polanyi, M. (1967). *The tacit dimension.* London: Routledge and Kegan Paul.

Pollard, S. (1963). Factory discipline in the Industrial Revolution. *Economic History Review, 16,* 254–271.

Pratt, G. (1981). The house as an expression of social worlds. In J. S. Duncan (Ed.), *Housing and identity: Cross-cultural perspectives.* London: Croom Helm.

Radley, A. (1977). Living on the horizon. In D. Bannister (Ed.), *New perspectives in personal construct theory.* London: Academic Press.

Radley, A. (1979). Construing as praxis. In P. Stringer & D. Bannister (Eds.), *Constructs of sociality and individuality.* London: Academic Press.

Radley, A. (1984). The embodiment of social relations in coronary heart disease. *Social Science and Medicine, 19,* 1227–1234.

Radley, A. (1985). From courtesy to strategy: Some old developments in social skills training. *Bulletin of the British Psychological Society, 38,* 209–211.

Radley, A. (1988a). *Prospects of heart surgery: Psychological adjustment to coronary bypass grafting.* New York: Springer-Verlag.

Radley, A. (1988b). The social form of feeling. *British Journal of Social Psychology, 27,* 5–18.

Radley, A. (1989). Style, discourse and constraint in adjustment to chronic illness. *Sociology of Health and Illness, 11,* 230–252.

Redican, B., & Hadley, D. S. (1988). A field studies project in a city health and leisure club. *Sociology of Sport Journal, 5,* 50–62.

Richards, M. P. M. (1974). The biological and the social. In N. Armistead (Ed.), *Reconstructing social psychology.* Harmondsworth, England: Penguin.

Roethlisberger, F. J., & Dickson, W. J. (1939). *Management and the worker.* Cambridge, MA: Harvard University Press.

Romanyshyn, R. D. (1982). *Psychological life: From science to metaphor.* Milton Keynes: Open University Press.

Romanyshyn, R. D. (1989). *Technology as symptom and dream.* London: Routledge.

Rose, N. (1988). Calculable minds and manageable individuals. *History of the Human Sciences, 1,* 179–200.

Rose, N. (1989). Psychology as a "social" science. In I. Parker & J. Shotter (Eds.), *Deconstructing social psychology.* London: Routledge.

Rudé, G. (1964). *The crowd in history, 1730–1848.* London: Wiley.

Saegart, S., & Winkel, G. H. (1990). Environmental psychology. *Annual Review of Psychology, 41,* 441–77.

Sanders, C. R. (1988). Marks of mischief: Becoming and being tattooed. *Journal of Contemporary Ethnography, 16,* 395–432.

Sartre, J. P. (1957). *Being and nothingness.* London: Methuen.

Sartre, J. P. (1971). *Sketch for a theory of the emotions*. London: Methuen.

Scarry, E. (1985). *The body in pain: The making and unmaking of the world*. Oxford, England: Oxford University Press.

Schachter, S., & Singer, J. (1962). Cognitive, social, and physiological determinants of emotion. *Psychological Review, 69*, 379–399.

Scheff, T. J. (1966). *Being mentally ill: A sociological theory*. Chicago: Aldine.

Scheflen, A. E. (1964). The significance of posture in communication systems. *Psychiatry, 27*, 316–331.

Schellenberg, J. A. (1970). *An introduction to social psychology*. New York: Random House.

Scheper-Hughes, N., & Lock, M. M. (1987). The mindful body: A prolegomenon to future work in medical anthropology. *Medical Anthropology Quarterly, 1*, 6–41.

Schneider, D. J., Hastorf, A. H., & Ellsworth, P. C. (1979). *Person perception* (2nd ed.). Reading, MA: Addison-Wesley.

Schutz, A. (1967). *The phenomenology of the social world*. Evanston, IL: Northwestern University Press.

Schwartz, B., & Miller, E. F. (1986). The icon and the word: A study in the visual depiction of moral character *Semiotica, 61*, 69–99.

Scott, R. A. (1969). *The making of blind men: A study of adult socialization*. New York: Russell Sage Foundation.

Secord, P. F., Dukes, W. F., & Bevan, W. (1954). Personalities in faces: I. An experiment in social perceiving. *Genetic Psychology Monographs, 49*, 231–279.

Shaw, M. E. (1976). *Group dynamics: The psychology of small group behavior* (2nd ed.). New York: McGraw-Hill.

Sheldon, W. H. (1940). *The varieties of human physique: An introduction to constitutional psychology*. New York: Harper

Shorter, E. (1984). *A history of women's bodies*. Harmondsworth, England: Penguin.

Shortland, M. (1985). Skindeep: Barthes, Lavater and the legible body. *Economy and Society, 14*, 273–312.

Sigall, H., & Ostrove, N. (1975). Beautiful but dangerous: Effects of offender attractiveness and nature of crime on juridic judgement. *Journal of Personality and Social Psychology, 31*, 410–414.

Simmel, G. (1950). The metropolis and mental life. In K. Wolff (Ed.), *The sociology of Georg Simmel*. New York: Free Press.

Simmel, G. (1955). *Conflict and the web of group-affiliations*. New York: Free Press.

Skinner, B. F. (1938). *The behavior of organisms: An experimental analysis*. New York: Appleton-Century-Crofts.

Smart, B. (1985). *Michel Foucault*. Chichester, England: Ellis Horwood.

Smith-Rosenberg, C. (1972). The hysterical woman: Sex roles and role conflict in 19th century America. *Social Research, 39*, 652–678.

Soltis, J. F. (1966). *Seeing, knowing and believing: A study of the language of visual perception*. Reading, MA: Addison-Wesley.

Sontag, S. (1979). *Illness as metaphor*. Harmondsworth, England: Allen Lane.

Soucie, R. (1979). Common misconceptions about nonverbal communication: Implications for training. In A. Wolfgang (Ed.), *Nonverbal behavior: Applications and cultural implications*. London: Academic Press.

Sperry, R. W. (1961). Cerebral organization and behavior. *Science, 133*, 1749–57.

Spiegel, J., & Machotka, P. (1974). *Messages of the body*. New York: Free Press.

Stephens, J. (1976). *Loners, losers and lovers: Elderly tenants in a slum hotel*. Seattle: University of Washington Press.

Stephenson, G. M., & Rutter, D. R. (1970). Eye contact, distance, and affiliation: A re-evaluation. *British Journal of Social and Clinical Psychology, 61*, 385–393.

Stone, G. C. (1984). A final word—Editorial. *Health Psychology, 3*, 585–589.

Storms, M. D. (1973). Videotape and the attribution process. *Journal of Personality and Social Psychology, 27*, 165–175.

Strodtbeck, F. L., James, R. M., & Hawkins, C. (1957). Social status in jury deliberations. *American Sociological Review, 22*, 713–719.

Strodtbeck, F. L., & Mann, R. D. (1956). Sex role differentiation in jury deliberations. *Sociometry, 19*, 3–11.

Sunday Correspondent Magazine (1990, July 22nd). "Mistress of the Universe".

Tagg, J. (1988). *The burden of representation: Essays on photographies and histories.* London: Macmillan.

Tajfel, H. (1978). *Differentiation between social groups: Studies in the social psychology of intergroup relations.* London: Academic Press.

Theweleit, K. (1987). *Male fantasies* (Vol. 1). Cambridge: Polity Press.

Theweleit, K. (1989). *Male fantasies* (Vol. 2). Cambridge: Polity Press.

Thomas, L. E. (1973). Clothing and counterculture: An empirical study. *Adolescence, 8*, 93–112.

Thompson, E. P. (1967). Time, work-discipline and industrial capitalism. *Past and Present, 38*, 56–97.

Triplett, N. (1897). The dynamogenic factors in pacemaking and competition. *American Journal of Psychology, 9*, 507–533.

Trower, P., Bryant, B., & Argyle, M. (1978). *Social skills and mental health.* London: Methuen.

Tuan, Y-F. (1982). *Segmented worlds and self: Group life and individual consciousness.* Minneapolis: University of Minnesota Press.

Turner, B. S. (1982). The government of the body: Medical regimens and the rationalization of diet. *British Journal of Sociology, 33*, 254–269.

Turner, B. S. (1984). *The body and society.* Oxford, England: Blackwell.

Turner, B. S. (1987). *Medical power and social knowledge.* London: Sage.

Twain, M. (1953). *Huckleberry Finn.* Harmondsworth, England: Penguin.

Ussher, J. M. (1989). *The psychology of the female body.* London: Routledge.

Van den Berg, J. H. (1952). The human body and the significance of human movement: A phenomenological study. *Philosophical and Phenomenological Research, 13*, 159–183.

Van der Velde, C. D. (1985). Body images of one's self and of others: Developmental and clinical significance. *American Journal of Psychiatry, 142*, 527–537.

Waid, W. M. (Ed.). (1984). *Sociophysiology.* New York: Springer-Verlag.

Walkerdine, V. (1981). Sex, power and pedagogy. *Screen Education, 38*, 14–24.

Walkerdine, V. (1986). Post-structuralist theory and everyday social practices: The family and the school. In S. Wilkinson (Ed.), *Feminist social psychology: Developing theory and practice.* Milton Keynes: Open University Press.

Walster, E., Aronson, E., Abrahams, D., & Rottman, L. (1966). The importance of physical attractiveness in dating behavior. *Journal of Personality and Social Psychology, 4*, 508–516.

Watzlawick, P., Beavin, J. H., & Jackson, D. (1967). *Pragmatics of human communication.* New York: Norton.

Wertz, F. J. (1987). Cognitive psychology and the understanding of perception. *Journal of Phenomenological Psychology, 18*, 103–142.

Whyte, W. F. (1943). *Street corner society.* Chicago: University of Chicago Press.

Wiener, C. L. (1975). The burden of rheumatoid arthritis: Tolerating the uncertainty. *Social Science and Medicine, 9*, 97–104.

Wiener, M., Devoe, S., Rubinow, S., & Geller, J. (1972). Nonverbal behavior and nonverbal communication. *Psychological Review, 79*, 185–214.

Wildeblood, J. (1973). *The polite world: A guide to the deportment of the English in former times*. London: Davis-Poynter.

Wilden, A. (1980). *System and structure: Essays in communication and exchange* (2nd ed.). London: Tavistock.

Wilkinson, S. (Ed.). (1986). *Feminist social psychology*. Milton Keynes: Open University Press.

Willis, P. E. (1975). The expressive style of a motor-bike culture. In J. Benthall & T. Polhemus (Eds.), *The body as a medium of expression*. London: Allen Lane.

Willis, P. E. (1977). *Learning to labour: How working class kids get working class jobs*. Farnborough, England: Saxon House.

Willis, P. E. (1978). *Profane culture*. London: Routledge and Kegan Paul.

Wilson, G., & Nias, D. (1976). *Love's mysteries: The psychology of sexual attraction*. London: Open Books.

Wrong, D. (1963). The oversocialised conception of man in modern society. In N. J. Smelser & W. T. Smelser (Eds.), *Personality and social systems*. New York: Wiley.

Yates, A., Leehay, K., & Shisslak, C. M. (1983). Running—An analogue of anorexia? *New England Journal of Medicine, 308*, 251–255.

Young, A. (1980). The discourse on stress and the reproduction of medical knowledge. *Social Science and Medicine, 14B*, 133–146.

Young, K. (1989). Narrative embodiments: Enclaves of the self in the realm of medicine. In J. Shotter & K. J. Gergen (Eds.), *Texts of identity*. London: Sage.

Young, R. M. (1970). *Mind, brain and adaptation in the nineteenth century: Cerebral localization and its biological context from Gall to Ferrier*. Oxford, England: Oxford University Press.

Zaner, R. M. (1966). The radical reality of the human body. *Humanitas, 2*, 73–87.

Zion, L. C. (1965). Body concept as it relates to self-concept. *Research Quarterly, 36*, 490–495.

Zola, I. K. (1973). Pathways to the doctor—from person to patient. *Social Science and Medicine, 7*, 677–689.

Author Index

Subject Index

Springer Series in Social Psychology
Recent Titles

Springer Series in Social Psychology
Recent Titles